THE JUST PROOF OF GOD

THE JUST PROOF OF GOD

VOLUME 3 : JUST SCIENCE

STEPHEN FOORD

B.SC. PHYSICS, PH.D.

First edition published by Stephen Foord in 2021

Kindle Direct Publishing (KDP) an Amazon self-publishing service.

Contents
The Just Proof of God Volume 3 : Just Science

Contents of the First Volume

The Just Proof of God Volume I :

THE ORIGIN OF BELIEFS

Contents of the Second Volume

The Just Proof of God Volume 2 :

Faith, Soul and Spirit

Plans for Fourth Volume

The chapters below were drafted before Volume 2 for laying out the flowchart of §1.5 but postponed as Volumes 2 & 3 are more vital as regards establishing the nature of reality. This part of the plan is subject to revision in the light of Volumes 2 & 3.

Chapter 14 : A theory of music by study of improvisation

Chapter 15 : A universal ethical theory

Chapter 16 : Truth and university ethics

Chapter 17 : Unification theory for physics, theology, and psychology

Preface

There seem two kinds of idea on how to seek truth. One is by a progressive science of power over reality, the other is to seek a good tutelary spirit to guide into truth. How those paths inter-relate is a moot point as with this book.

The book has its roots in secondary school or earlier with a wish to seek truth in science. It led to a degree in physics. About the second year of the degree, I saw there was not much more to come in the way of truth. From then on it was a matter of putting faith in progress. After the degree, I looked to do a Ph.D. in medical physics as I objected to death and it gave room to ponder on foundations. Funds for that fell through so I tried for a Ph.D. in biophysics instead. During the degree, I took up hi-fi and classical music. As a Ph.D. student, I came across a piano for choir practice in a lecture hall and began to learn to play. Not having much free time or ability for sight reading, I learnt a few bits off by heart and ran them off whilst thinking on research problems. Apparently, that is how to train to improvise. I began to improvise as an off the cuff bid for stress relief at a difficult time. I brought a machine to record some. This was near the end of my research career before I realised I was incubating on the role of conscious mind in the foundations of science. Analysing the improvisations added a theory of the subjective to a theory of the conscious. From there, it was downhill to this proof for God except no support for this work seems possible in a British university.

Looking at how science is run in Britain today, I suspect Newton would have no career in modern science if he stuck by strategic reason whereby the theory of natural selection is a non-starter and a deity has to exist, see the Introduction. He would likely be frozen out of a post as some kind of a 'fundamentalist'. It seems assumed today that his views on God were naive rather than by theoretical insight that modern scientists have yet to catch up with.

I began to attend church after my formal research career was over as I wished to make recordings on church organs. The music became an excuse to hear God's word in a religious setting. A Christian referred a tape to the R.N.C.M. in 1991 where I was told that in parts they resemble French composers for organ like Messiaen or where spacious and sonorous, American composers like Barber or Copeland. It was an effort to go to church at first due to conflict of feelings. I now see religions as places to become aware of spirits, even familiar spirits previously taken for granted. Religion may make aware of a personal spiritual bubble that affects how each person perceives dogma.

God's Spirit is said to be needed to track God's word. Many claim to bubble in the Spirit but God's word warns of a perennial curse for failing to serve well enough. Now if a just God is not arbitrary, there is only one right reading of His word so the Spirit is with a science to God's word. God's word suggests to look for a legal or contractual type of reading that respects freedom of faith so how we choose to read it makes a pact to serve a spirit of some kind. Spirits may corral people like horses to be broken in, *Psalm 32, 8-11, §10.5*, so a faith gone astray corrals in a love and joy not of God's stable, *Isaiah 30, 10-11, James 4, 6-10.* A progressive science of God's word is to discard theories of a just God that do not fit all data of God's word or other data in the world God made. It need not first label and discard false scripture to an unjust god or reject bad science as they have a place in a true science in a converse relation to God. A faith that does not stand just scrutiny may lean toward a tyrannical spirit opposed to just process, *Isaiah 30, 9-15.* An issue of faith is to discern just from tyrannical spirits by the ideas of justice they corral in. To be let into the secret that spirits exist is a large step toward seeing God exists but it does not mean every spirit is God. It is an invitation to seek the true Spirit to God's word as might refute Death, ritual respect for it, and temples to Death like Auschwitz.

Unless a legal science of God's word fails, a science of evolution to cast all religion as in cultural lies is a non-starter. But the latter has, for some reason, proven easier and now has ground even in religion. It suggests evolution, *the idea that death is a builder of life and truth*, New Scientist, *4 December 2004, p 51*, is an idea with spiritual charisma so can be religious. There was faith life formed spontaneously out of mud from millennia before a theory of evolution gave it a rational make over. If a legal science of God's word is now established and collars the theory of evolution as a delusion prophesied in God's word, the scientific method is to discard the theory. But the truth is then past a religious faith in evolution as explained in the chapter 'The Origin of Beliefs'. It means the theory is written up by its faithful as fact before it is fair to do so, to give them success at 'science'. The terms to the theory allow for that and worse.

A professional faith in natural selection can be rattled by asking it how others of faith in it should act in leading situations? What in the theory stops the faithful trying to prove the theory fit by politics? when to their mind other theories, *including of God*, are established that way. Once they 'know' the theory is true, why not frame the hypothesis of it by a system biassed to employ those who find it 'natural'? They would wish to make careers in research and higher education conditional on acts of faith in the theory. That is what tyrannical religion is indicted of. How might that weed out a young Newton? It is about asking everyone to frame hypotheses. For if the theory is itself a framed hypothesis and urges the fit to fame by framing lesser hypotheses then the faithful are happy to frame hypotheses. It goes against Newton's declared view of science so would stress him. He would have to do more work than asked to avoid framing hypotheses so might seem slow to teachers. If he gave in to rage about it, he could be carted off by security staff as a research failure under a 'fair', *same for all*, competitive system. That looks the unsaid ethos to nurturing research students on short-term ear-marked specialist contracts that ask quick results for a career. It is one of a number of procedural failings by which 'science' may have become a technical propaganda outfit for a theory of evolution. It means those of a more impartial mind are routinely weeded out, rare, seen as a discredited minority in a propaganda coup. Minds that issue the propaganda may say the tyranny is of an enlightenment.

In this age, courts try to administer laws fairly and not pass unjust laws. An issue for them is how much to defer to 'pure' or 'natural' science in defining 'justice'? Likewise for the media where the BBC runs a natural but no supernatural history unit as may be an opinion, *propaganda*, to violate its charter. An opinion for courts to anchor by is easy to see. It is a basic truth that a just God should be defendable in a fair court as a legal person or company: as constitutional fact. A just God is the highest justice a court could aspire to. In consequence, if a just God exists then science, cults or religions that wish to deny God may establish outside courts to seek power, say, by blinding with an unjust science of threats to national security and bribes to national well-being. Threats of 'natural' disasters are how religions have asked support for gods as well as by bribes of power to kill enemies, *inspiration to arms*, as a gunpowder plot to blow up 'justice'. What is to stops cults or religions evolving to a common 'science' on those lines? We might expect a technical cult in 'science' with progressive ways of child and animal sacrifice to gods of ambition. It is thus wise not to take science or religion on trust but to subject to just scrutiny. Failure to do that may hide that a just God is easy to prove, hard to disprove. The opposite may seem true if most wish to reserve funds for false teaching in the tradition of religious persecution of truth. The result is a national cult to grade children under a dishonest system that streams out sacrifices to progress (to evolution) to one day meet the shadowy gods to a 'science' of tyranny.

17th February 2005

Acknowledgements

I thank God for everything especially His mercy.

I thank the biblical scholars and translators for their efforts to faithfully deliver God's word to us. Scripture taken from the Holy Bible New International Version, Copyright © 1973, 1978, 1984 International Bible Society. Used by permission of Zondervan Bible Publishers. Other scripture tagged as from the NRSV bible.

I thank my family and church for support during writing it.

I thank all those who by standing up for God's justice in dark times from the heart have kept the path open for greater knowledge of a just God's word.

This book would likely not have been possible without low cost computers especially of the RISCOS kind, the welfare state and low cost modern publishing techniques.

Conventions used in this book

References to sections.

Where a section referred to is in the same chapter, the chapter prefix is dropped. Thus, §2 refers to the second section of the chapter being read but §5.2 refers to section two of chapter 5.

Use of quotation marks to indicate ambiguous meanings.

With rival theories of reality, the meanings of terms often alters. To put terms in 'quotes' can alert to ambiguous meanings. For instance, some say 'science' has shown life evolved by blind luck. If such 'science' is on flawed foundations, a proper 'science' might show 'God' made us. In the last sentence, 'God' is in quotes as ideas on the nature of 'God' that made us may differ even in a same religion. In principle, people can even take the devil as 'God' but move on to God if sound teaching is allowed. That can also apply in 'science' to any view on 'God' there if terms are used as if in a generally accepted sense but really as propaganda or dogma due to a lack of rigor. The truth may at first seem a foreign language to a society steeped in the propaganda of a 'religion' that passes itself off as 'science'.

Splitting of a text column into 2 columns of fine print, e.g. p7.

First drafts set depth or an aside to the main text in marginal boxes with smaller print. Those boxes are here split and set in the main flow of text so the main column splits into two columns of smaller print for an aside and more depth. Sometimes it is essential to read the small print as part of the flow of the main text, sometimes not. Where there is more than one two column area on a page, they may have a common theme if of a same box.

Volume 3

Just Science

11.1 Life-forces from God and Free-will: Spiritual Bodies

A perfect God is a state of living perfection uniquely able to deny the void, *§2.2.* All else relies on that God for existence so is subject to laws of compatibility with His nature. It makes God a 'just' bound to existence life cannot remove, *Genesis 6, 3*, because it relies on life-forces from God, *Genesis 2, 9, Revelation 22, 1-19*:

"Blessed be your glorious name, and may it be exalted above all blessing and praise. You alone are the Lord. You made the heavens, even the highest heavens, and all their starry host, the earth and all that is on it, the seas and all that is in them.
You give life to everything, and the multitudes of heaven worship you…."
Nehemiah 9, 5-6

A proof for God's existence must trace true laws of compatibility with God's nature, *§1.1.* It then samples a global system of reason rising to the nature of Justice. In *chapter 1*, a proof based on a systematic map of human reason is laid out, *§1.5.* It shows the direct path of proof as to take the hypothesis of God, *say, as source of matter and mind*, then derive other features of this world. If a 'just' God exists, all faiths and theories can be covered by a map under a 'just' view of God, *§6.4.* Chapters 2 and 3 are a path in such a map. Other paths may wind through different areas of the map to look like different kinds of proof. For example, the matter, mind path depends on a definition of good. In *chapter 6*, the definition of good is replaced by a definition of sanity to useful effect. Chapter 6 also has a concise inner proof giving a projection from the map in *§1.5* into a few hundred words, *§6.16.* In practice there can be many lines of reason or paths to prove God's existence. This chapter is another direct path. It develops on the hypothesis of God as the source of all life-forces.

Death is due to loss of life-forces from God. In 'God's word', 'the dead' covers mortals whose life is done but may also imply their doppelgänger twin spirits who stay on as their ghosts, *§10.5.* It may also mean a living dead of mortals interned in sin on course to a final death in hell, *Matthew 10, 28*:

When you were dead in your sins and in the uncircumcision of your sinful nature, God made you alive with Christ.
Colossians 2, 13

'For this son of mine was dead and is alive again; he was lost and is found.' So they began to celebrate.
Luke 15, 24

A minimum level or spark of faith in God is needed to draw life-forces and stay alive. Mortals on the edge may be dead in sin, a 'living dead', dying to die but in denial that they have a death-wish, *Proverbs 8, 36, §6.2.*

Natural science avoids thanking God for life by a hypothesis that life-forces have a natural origin in matter, *§6.5.* It hails death & decay as constructive natural processes, *Proverbs 8, 36, §6.2, Wisdom 1, 12-16, §1.2.* 'Natural' is then 'good' of a sort, *§10.1.*
In theory, for life to deny a God who really gives it life, life needs a global map of reason where Death rules and God's Justice is a flawed concept in creation, *§1.3.* Research into that map is led by a 'devil', *§6.1, a 'God' of Death,* who aims to depose God, *§1.15.* A just God then stands for life and freedom of faith against the devil who stands for Death and tyranny against spread of just truth. Such theory makes it easy to see God's word to mortal life should be about salvation from Death. To know evil is then to know the power of Death, and, to support Death is to support evil, *§1.2.* Thus, to deny God is source of life may accept and spread a curse to affliction and death from the devil, *§1.15, §10.4.*
By this easy concise theory, life may depend on finding its place in relation to God to escape death and decay. It is survival of the fittest by different rules to those of 'natural' selection in a Godless universe. 'Natural' selection may head an attempt to depose God for a new world order, *§9.3.* The differences in alleged laws to theories or tactics for survival may mark kingdoms of heaven and hell, *§9.1.*
If there really are two beings of supernatural power who claim to be 'God', they must differ on the brand of 'justice' offered. It makes the nature of God's justice vital to a just proof for God. The highest direct path of proof for God is to take the hypothesis of God and derive God's justice relative to life. That is attempted here and in *chapters 12 & 13.* The 'justice' derived may be the key to open 'God's word'? *§8.1, §9.7.6.* That makes it a scientific theory to be proved by match to observed data, *§8.2, §10.13.*

In theory, to sin against God's nature too much cuts life-forces as disloyalty that may dice with death:

he is not the god of the dead but of the living.
mark 12, 27

it is not the dead who praise the lord, those who go down to silence;
psalm 115, 17

An urbane murderer might tempt life into lethal sin against laws of compatibility with God, *John 8, 42-45, §13.3, chapter 6.* As sin grows, life may gutter as a robot slave to sin, seeking paths towards the goal of a full death, *Psalm 73, Isaiah 14, 12-21, §8.3.*

If a just God exists, free-will is subject to need for life-forces from God. To hate God becomes a death-wish, *Proverbs 8, 36, §6.2.* To underwrite life's free-will even to death, God may make life-forces in part available from non-living or material grounds as places furthest from God. But if God alone is not subject to decay, life on material grounds decays if it strays too far from God. Death and thermodynamics suggest that is the nature of our world. The purpose of life is to relate to God.

Free-will may be modelled in personal interior bafflers that channel life-forces from God in various directions. Life-forces can be taken via matter or neighbours or spirit-life like the Christ or even Satan who kills for it. Personality is in how personal bafflers are set to God and neighbours defining paths by which life feeds best on life-forces. The naive grasp of free-will is then a personal outlook in ambivalent feelings to God and neighbours. Neighbours feel charismatic if they feed on God's life-forces in related ways as makes houses of friends, *1 Corinthians 3, 9-16, §10.2.* The variations in bafflers builds beasts of earth and sea, *§9.4, §9.7.4.*

A just God's recommended law is to enable flows of life-forces to sustain worthwhile eternal life, *chapter 2.* It is a creed of universal love, *§3.7, §8.3, Romans 13, 8-10.* A society lives best in orderly love of neighbours under God whereby life-forces flow between them. Heaven is a community under God as why God's temple is to build social bodies in God's Spirit. Evil must oppose and subvert by an unjust spirit to sacrifice or curse unloved neighbours, *§6.14* to *§6.15, §9.7,* with inner target of God's leading 'just' servants.

God's word is founded on God as source of life-forces. It is set in a world where evil gods seek to legally master the source of life: a just God. The Old Testament below describes God's Spirit, *Isaiah 11, 6-9, §7.6,* as like streams of living water. Hence, the life-force science to cover God's law may be a divine or just hydrology:

now the earth was formless and
empty, darkness was over the surface
of the deep, and the spirit of god was
hovering over the waters.
genesis 1, 2

on that day living water will flow out
from jerusalem, half to the eastern
sea and half to the western sea, in
summer and winter.
the lord will be king over the whole
earth. on that day there will be one
lord, and his name the only name.
zechariah 14, 8-9

It is said God hopes to restore supplies of waters of life to our world by justly overcoming evil, *Psalm 98.* Waters of life will then flow from Jerusalem by rule of God's King and Son: the Christ. The King or Son is one Lord, *Psalm 2 & 98, 6,* and God another, *Zechariah 3, 2, §10.8,* but they are same in nature, *Isaiah 9, 6,* so there is only one Lord. If God is source of waters of life then by identity so is His Son the King and Christ.

We look to the King's rule as to life itself, *Proverbs 8, 36, §6.2.* His rule is denied by sinners even in Israel. For God's people have a tradition of disloyalty to match that of loyalty, *Romans 11, 11-24.* Many partake of copious but unreliable waters of life that flow round idols or false gods like fertility god Baal, *§10.4*:

"has a nation ever changed its gods?
(yet they are not gods at all.)
but my people have exchanged their glory
for worthless idols.
be appalled at this, o heavens, and shudder with great horror," declares the lord.
my people have committed two sins:
they have forsaken me,
the spring of living water, and have dug their own cisterns,
broken cisterns that cannot hold water.
jeremiah 2, 11-13

therefore their people turn to them
and drink up waters in abundance.
they say, "how can god know?
does the most high have knowledge?"

this is what the wicked are like—always carefree, they increase in wealth.
psalm 73, 10-12

The wicked can slosh in spiritual waters to form a sea under Satan's rule, *§9.4*, great waters, *Job 38, 1-11*:

mightier than the thunder of the great waters,
mightier than the breakers of the sea—
the lord on high is mighty.
psalm 93, 4

Floods of evil waters can drown support for a just God, *Psalm 69, 2-3, §11.2.* They vitalise as spirit to unjust gods or idols that curse, *Isaiah 24, Jeremiah 3, 12-13, Wisdom 14, 27-31, §9.5.* The curse is about leaky reservoirs that fail. For evil gods do not relate with God so fill reservoirs by dehydration of material grounds, *Luke 11, 24-26, §5.4*, taken via life closer to God, *§5.* The gods cannot supply more than stored and their needs come first. By stores, they draw into evil spiritual bodies to tax of waters of life to support the gods' life-style, *§5*, at head of evil spiritual bodies, *Daniel 7, Isaiah 30, 1-15, §9.12, Revelation 3, 7-9 & 12, 15-16 & 17.* If mortals cease to supply well, *§9.7.1*, evil cuts off in drought, *just deserts?*, to die like flies, *Isaiah 51, 5-6, §7.11.* Some take *Jeremiah 2, 11-13* above to mean all gods are artefacts of the human psyche but analysis shows living evil spirits lie behind the term, *§8.2, §8.3.* God's promise of mercy in the Old Testament is to restore waters by the Messiah who is to be King as next.

The duel of good and evil, *§8.2,* is over who lesser life, *given the choice by a just God,* prefers to manage its waters of life, *Isaiah 30, 19-21.* God bids to supply direct but evil gods are subsidiary suppliers to make a restless sea of the wicked on earth, *§8.4.* Satan denies them 'peace', *Isaiah 57, 20-21, §9.4.* Victory for God, *Psalm 98,* saves souls from the roaring of the sea of the wicked, *Luke 21, 12-28, §9.1.* God may one day still the sea and cover it, *Isaiah 11, 6-9, §7.6*:

praise awaits you, o god, in zion;
to you our vows will be fulfilled.
o you who hear prayer,
to you all men will come.
when we were overwhelmed by sins,
you forgave our transgressions.
blessed are those you choose and
bring near to live in your courts!
we are filled with the good things of
your house,
of your holy temple.

you answer us with awesome deeds of
righteousness,
o god our saviour,
the hope of all the ends of the earth
and of the farthest seas,
who formed the mountains by your
power,
having armed yourself with strength,
who stilled the roaring of the seas,
the roaring of their waves,
and the turmoil of the nations.
those living far away fear your
wonders;
where morning dawns and evening
fades
you call forth songs of joy.

you care for the land and water it;
you enrich it abundantly.
the streams of god are filled with
water
to provide the people with grain, for
so you have ordained it.
you drench its furrows
and level its ridges;
you soften it with showers
and bless its crops.
you crown the year with your bounty,
and your carts overflow with
abundance.
the grasslands of the desert overflow;
the hills are clothed with gladness.
the meadows are covered with flocks
and the valleys are mantled with
grain;
they shout for joy and sing.

psalm 65

God's will is Justice in all spheres as 'peace' far beyond an end to military war. The wicked do not understand Justice so support rival unjust gods, *Proverbs 28, 5, §8.1, Acts 26, 9-18, §8.3.* The earth is likened to a farm watered by God, *Hosea 6, 3* below, growing people as on vines, *Isaiah 5, 1-7, §12.12,* many of whom struggle to tell their left from right hand, *Jonah 3* to *4.* If God is hope of the earth, *metaphor for the religious?,* and sea, *the wicked?,* His mercy by Justice is open to all:

the people walking in darkness have
seen a great light;
on those living in the land of the
shadow of death
a light has dawned.
you have enlarged the nation and
increased their joy;
they rejoice before you
as people rejoice at the harvest,
as men rejoice when dividing the
plunder.
for as in the day of midian's defeat,
you have shattered
the yoke that burdens them, the bar
across their shoulders, the rod of
their oppressor.
every warrior's boot used in battle
and every garment rolled in blood
will be destined for burning, will be
fuel for the fire.
for to us a child is born,
to us a son is given,
and the government will be on his
shoulders.
6 and he will be called
wonderful counsellor, mighty god,
everlasting father, prince of peace.
of the increase of his government
and peace
there will be no end.
he will reign on david's throne and
over his kingdom,
establishing and upholding it with
justice and righteousness
from that time on and forever.
the zeal of the lord almighty
will accomplish this.

isaiah 9, 2-7

God is to save souls who can accept spiritual knowledge of God, *Isaiah 11, 6-9, §7.6,* from spiritual darkness and humiliation in the shadow of death, *Psalm 23.*

he will swallow up death forever.
the sovereign lord will wipe away the
tears from all faces;
he will remove the disgrace of his
people from all the earth.

isaiah 25, 8

Above, *Isaiah 9* says God's victory will break the rod of a punishing oppressor whose *modus operandi* spiritually yokes to live by war and injustice. The farming metaphor of a harvest covers a dividing of good from evil at Judgement Day, *§9.1.* God's victory reallocates plunder, *Isaiah 17, 14*: *people and property currently held in the land of the shadow of Death.* The means of God's victory is a child born to be King, *an heir to David's throne,* whose status is uniquely one with God, whose reign is to bring true peace, end war and oppression, and end Death forever, *Isaiah 25, 8* above, *Revelation 21, 4* below. The modus operandi of this child to be King is described above and below:

"... as surely as the sun rises he will
appear,
he will come to us like the winter
rains,
like the spring rains that water the
earth."

... ...

therefore I cut you in pieces with my prophets,
I killed you with the words of my mouth;
my judgements flashed like lightening upon you.
For I desire mercy, not sacrifice,
and acknowledgement of God rather than burnt offerings.

Hosea 6, 3, 5-6

A shoot will come up from the stump of Jesse;
from his roots a Branch will bear fruit.
The Spirit of the Lord will rest on him—
the Spirit of wisdom and understanding,
the Spirit of counsel and of power,
the Spirit of knowledge and of the fear of the Lord—
and he will delight in the fear of the Lord.
He will not judge by what he sees with his eyes,
or decide by what he hears with his ears;
but with righteousness he will judge the needy,
with justice he will give decisions for the poor of the earth.
He will strike the earth with the rod of his mouth;
with the breath of his lips he will slay the wicked.
Righteousness will be his belt
and faithfulness the sash around his waist.

… … …

10 In that day the Root of Jesse will stand as a banner for the peoples; the nations will rally to him, and his place of rest will be glorious.

Isaiah 11, 1-5, 10

Jesse is David's father so the King is of David's line. The King is God's will and judgement as at *Deuteronomy 18, 17-22, §5.* He breaks the rod of the oppressor by rod of His mouth, *breath of His lips, 2 Thessalonians 2, 8-12, §9.3,* as suggests by peaceful tuition in righteousness and justice, *Micah 4, 1-5, §12.8.* However, if foes refuse instruction an angry or violent curse may strike them, *Psalms 97* or *2, §9.1.* Now the above does not say God directly strikes at or curses foes for refusing peaceful instruction. It may be oppressors whom God is to defeat that in fact curse their own followers, *people disloyal to God,* for failing to keep God out in a duel of good and evil, *§8.2.* For at *Isaiah 14, 12-21, §8.3,* we see the oppressor Satan, *who is pretender to the King's throne,* is to slay all his own people: *folk who love Death.* The path to avoid the disgrace of *Isaiah 25, 8* above, and be saved from the oppressor's curse is to uphold the King's teaching on Justice, *Isaiah 28, 18, §7.4 & 1, 15-20, §8.6.* A just God will not make servants of enemies by tyrannical force, *Zechariah 4, 6, §12.8,* if God's enemy is tyrannical or unjust force:

the Lord will have compassion on
Jacob;
once again he will choose Israel and
will settle them in their own land.
aliens will join them
and unite with the house of Jacob.
nations will take them
and bring them to their own place.
and the house of Israel will possess the
nations
as menservants and maidservants in
the Lord's land.
they will make captives of their
captors
and rule over their oppressors.

on the day the Lord gives you relief
from suffering and turmoil and cruel
bondage, you will take up this taunt
against the king of Babylon:

how the oppressor has come to an
end!
how his fury has ended!
the Lord has broken the rod of the
wicked,
the scepter of the rulers,
which in anger struck down the
peoples
with unceasing blows,
and in fury subdued nations
with relentless aggression.
all the lands are at rest and at peace;
they break into singing.

Isaiah 14, 1-7

The foregoing is an interpretation of God's word that stems from heraldic scripture, *priority passages.* It can explain hydrological, farming and other metaphors, see *§2.* Jesus made a claim to be the King of David's line by genealogy records destroyed with the Jerusalem temple by Israel's oppressor, *Matthew 1 & 21, 9.* His teaching might show the just path to escape the oppressor's curse and gain God's blessing, see *§5.* He loves to teach 'Christianity' as for the bringing of ample supplies of waters of life *after Hosea 6, 3* above, or *Isaiah 12* below.

in that day you will say:

"I will praise you. O Lord.
although you were angry with me,
your anger has turned away and you
have comforted me.
surely God is my salvation;
I will trust and not be afraid.
the Lord, the Lord, is my strength and
my song;
he has become my salvation.
with joy you will draw water from the
wells of salvation.
in that day you will say:

"give thanks to the Lord, call on his
name;
make known among the nations what
he has done,
and proclaim that his name is exalted.
sing to the Lord, for he has done
glorious things;
let this be known to all the world.
shout aloud and sing for joy, people of
Zion,
for great is the Holy One of Israel
among you."

Isaiah 12

Thus, at the last cut, 'Israel' is to know 'the Holy One' and reject the oppressor, *Isaiah 30, 1-15, §9.12.*

God has promised to establish spiritual bodies led by His King and Son, the Christ, *Isaiah 11, 1-10 & 9, 2-7* above, *Joel 2, 28-32, Psalm 2, Daniel 7, 9-14*. Against that, God's enemy, *the devil*, establishes evil spiritual bodies or empires, *Daniel 7*, as beasts of earth and sea, *§9.7.4*. The just Christ vies by offer of waters of life to baptise into the Spirit of truth. Jesus saw that role in relation to Jacob's house to great depth, *John 14, 1-11*:

Jacob's well was there, and Jesus, tired as he was from the journey, sat down by the well. It was about the sixth hour.
When a Samaritan woman came to draw water, Jesus said to her, "Will you give me a drink?"
(His disciples had gone into the town to buy food.)
The Samaritan woman said to him, "You are a Jew and I am a Samaritan woman. How can you ask me for a drink?" (For Jews do not associate with Samaritans)
Jesus answered her, "If you knew the gift of God and who it is who asks you for a drink, you would have asked him and he would have given you living water."
"Sir," the woman said, "you have nothing to draw with and the well is deep. Where can you get this living water? Are you greater than our father Jacob, who gave us the well and drank from it himself as did also his sons and his flocks and herds?"
Jesus answered, "Everyone who drinks this water will be thirsty again, but whoever drinks the water I give him will never thirst. Indeed, the water I give him will become in him a spring of water welling up to eternal life."
... ...
You Samaritans worship what you do not know; we worship what we do know, for salvation is from the Jews.
Yet a time is coming and has now come when the true worshippers will worship the Father in spirit and truth, for they are the kind of worshippers the Father seeks.
God is spirit, and his worshippers must worship in spirit and in truth."
The woman said, "I know that the Messiah" (called Christ) "is coming. When he comes he will explain everything to us."
Then Jesus declared, "I who speak to you am he."

John 4, 6-14 & 22-26

On the last and greatest day of the Feast, Jesus stood and said in a loud voice, "If anyone is thirsty let him come to me and drink. Whoever believes in me as the Scripture has said, streams of living water will flow from within him." By this he meant the Spirit, whom those who believed in him were later to receive.

John 7, 37-39

'Christianity' runs inns, *social bodies*, to drink in the just Spirit, *§10.3*, and witness to folk tipsy on unjust spirits. Jesus moved Paul to teach about spiritual inns:

the body is a unit, though it is made up of many parts; and though all its parts are many, they form one body. so it is with christ. for we were all baptised by one spirit into one body—whether jews or greeks, slave or free—and we were all given the one spirit to drink.
1 corinthians 12, 12-13

just as each of us has one body with many members, and these members do not all have the same function, so in christ we who are many form one body and each member belongs to the others. we have different gifts according to the grace given us.
romans 12, 4-6

God invites into just spiritual bodies that restore waters of life by baptism into His Spirit via the Christ. Now Christian bodies are anathema to evil yet also a rich source of waters of life that evil must own, *trap in unjust faith*, to depose God. Evil must turn baffles of apathy, anger or hate to God's truth to feed parasitically on life it distances from God in unjust doctrines, *§10.5*. A prophesied rise of false teaching, *§8.6, §10.6*, draws waters from Christian bodies as its target. Evil is at its strongest, *vitalised*, in parasitic relation to good, *§10.5*. That also lets good witness to evil to try to save it.

The imagery of waters of life is taken to its limits by Jesus who, *as God's Son and King of creation*, should be the joint source of waters of life as at *Zechariah 14, 8-9* above or *Revelation 21* below. Jesus is either the Christ or a potent antichrist. Why else would divine law allow anyone to give scripture in a title-contest such as below? It witnesses to Jesus' promise to end a curse to drought in life-forces on life. But Jesus teaches that His name and word will be usurped by the antichrist in unjust readings, *Isaiah 24, Matthew 24, 4-5*:

then the angel showed me the river of the water of life, as clear as crystal, flowing from the throne of god and of the lamb down the middle of the great street of the city. on each side of the river stood the tree of life, bearing twelve crops of fruit, yielding its fruit every month. and the leaves of the tree are for the healing of the nations.

no longer will there be any curse.
revelation 22, 1-3

then i saw a new heaven and a new earth, for the first heaven and the first earth had passed away, and there was no longer any sea.
revelation 21, 1

"he will wipe every tear from their eyes.
there will be no more death or mourning or crying or pain, for the old order of things has passed away."
revelation 21, 4

God's foes are said to love death, *Proverbs 8, 36, §6.2*, so love Satan as pretender to the King's throne, *§10.9, Isaiah 28, 18, §7.4.* Satan stores waters of life to give vitality and 'light' to servants, *2 Corinthians 11, 14-15, §3.9.* True doctrine is like a life-raft to those in peril on the sea: *the deluging spirituality of antichrist that preys by a curse on unjust teaching, §10.3, John 16, 13, §9.4.* Satan poses not just as the Christ but also as the 'God' whose word calls the Christ to test, *§9.7.5.* Hand for hand law, *§8.1, §9.7,* lets Satan call in all scripture to seek victory over God, *to establish as 'holy one of Israel' at Psalm 98,* writing God and the Christ out of creation, *Isaiah 14, 12-21, §8.3.* Satan hopes to govern all waters of life by mastery of God in just law, *§9.7.6*:

"come, all you who are thirsty,
come to the waters;
and you who have no money, come,
buy and eat!
come, buy wine and milk without
money and without cost.
why spend money on what is not
bread,
and your labour on what does not
satisfy?
listen, listen to me, and eat what is
good,
and your soul will delight in the
richest of fare.
give ear and come to me;
hear me, that your soul may live.
i will make an everlasting covenant
with you,
my faithful love promised to david.
see, i have made him a witness to the
peoples,
a leader and commander of the
peoples.
surely you will summon nations you
know not,
and nations that do not know you will
hasten to you, because of the lord
your god, the holy one of israel,
for he has endowed you with
splendor."
seek the lord while he may be found;
call on him while he is near.
let the wicked forsake his way
and the evil man his thoughts.
let him turn to the lord, and he will
have mercy on him,
and to our god for he will freely
pardon.

"for my thoughts are not your
thoughts,
neither are your ways my ways,"
declares the lord.
"as the heavens are higher than the
earth,
so are my ways higher than your ways

and my thoughts than your thoughts.
as the rain and the snow come down
from heaven, and do not return to it
without watering the earth and
making it bud and flourish,
so that it yields seed for the sower
and bread for the eater,
so is my word that goes out from my
mouth:
it will not return to me empty, but will
accomplish what i desire and achieve
the purpose for which i sent it

isaiah 55, 1-11

In one reading this is God's word but in another is Satan's call and word. Satan promises free waters yet not to end Death and curse on all, *Isaiah 65, 17-20.* His offer may be to depose the Christ by King David, *§10.10*, if the Christ sins against God under test, *Isaiah 53*, so a just salvation fails. A title-contest is to settle whose servant David is? *§11.5.* If the Christ triumphs, the section on David reverts to enthrone the Messiah of David's line for God. It ties in with Satan offering a new heaven, earth and hell within his kingdom of hell, *§9.7.5, Isaiah 65, 17-20*, where a curse never ends unlike at *Isaiah 28, 5 & Revelation 22, 1-3* above. If waters of life are really free on 'God's' new earth, why would folk still die? It is not their will unless they love death, *Proverbs 8, 36, §6.2.* If it is natural causes, it is not paradise. If it is will of 'God', is 'God' a murderer? *§10.8, John 8, 44-47, §13.3, Isaiah 25, 8* above.

In its reading for a just God, this scripture says a poor supply of waters from the gods sets mortals to work for a living to the death, never able to satisfy a thirst for waters of life in their work. God offers to remove need to work. People currently work as part of fighting gods of Death, *Psalm 82, §8.3, Micah 4, 5.* To fight, we also look to a covenant with God promised to David by which to prove loyalty to a Lord or King of David's line who seeks to end evil rule, *Psalm 2, §9.4, Proverbs 24, 21-22, Luke 4, 5-6, §1.15.* God's mercy is to pardon not punish. For that, we look to the Lord and King under God who is merciful. The situation implies that sin, *disloyalty to God*, is a contractual act by which gods of evil take jurisdiction of souls, *Proverbs 5, 21-23.* Hence, the covenant promised to David is a system of atonement for sin against God to unyoke from a pact in sin to Death with the gods, *Isaiah 28, 18, §7.4, Romans 6, 23.* Under that covenant, God is to release direct flows of life-forces or Spirit to His people, *Joel 2, 28-32.*

The scripture also says the Lord or King subject to God is a leader and commander of folk. That need not imply a military commander. Jesus claims to be that Lord who wields God's authority, *Isaiah 9, 6*, over spiritual forces, angels and demons. He aims to spiritually lead a people to justly contest the gods as rival spiritual forces in folk, *Micah 4, 5, Ephesians 6, 10-18, 1 Peter 3, 22.*

The divine hydrology to life-forces should tally with farming metaphors in God's word in a same picture or theory. The following may show the overall picture.

11.2 The Farming of Mortals for Waters of Life: Spiritual Food Chains and Hell's Hydrology

All take life-forces from God often by unseen umbilical cords dispersed in creation to respect life's freedom of faith, *chapter 9.* It lets good and evil head to alternative social spaces or feeding grounds, *§5.9.* Good loves God so can feed most directly in heaven. Evil hates God, *the light,* so, *like Dracula,* prefers to feed on life-forces in the shadow of things closer to God like other life. Evil gods farm weaker evil between themselves and God, *in front of God, Luke 19, 26-27, §10.10,* to harvest waters in return for direction on what evil stands for: a plan of rebellion to depose God, *§9.1.* In that context, a baby is a gift from God corded to parents whom evil casts as trainee evil gods. The pull of strong evil makes weaker evil ambivalent to God. If it fails to break free, it may relax towards evil gods but, *being distanced from God,* be less able to feed the gods. The gods lose respect for life they cut off from God in sin as its waters from God dry up. Wages of sin are then death, *Romans 6, 23, §7.10,* from evil gods as parasites who move on to farm new servants of their plan. Hell's order? *Micah 4. 5.*

Hell is ruled by strong evil gods and lower ranks mine waters from God, *e.g. via matter.* The ranks fully reject their right to escape evil gods and plans. They are farm stock to supply waters taken from God's King who then oversees evil's chosen law in hell, *Revelation 14, 9-11, §9.7.4.* Life there loves Death and the ranks are routinely slaughtered in front of God for food, *Luke 19, 26-27, §10.10, Isaiah 14, 12-21, §8.3, Matthew 10, 28.* That order vies on earth, *e.g. in religions for an occult that extols paths for adept souls to depart the ranks and join the gods.* Now if the gods ruin less fit souls, *Matthew 10, 28,* the ranks may erode so, *in time,* the gods fall to them seeking food, *Psalm 82, §8.3.* Once hell is sealed, it may be a one way path in decay and death. Hell is by ways evil draws life-forces to a frustration of its life, *Genesis 3, 22-24, Luke 19, 26-27, §10.9.*

On earth, the gods' feeding strategy traps souls in social bodies of evil spirituality, *Daniel 7, Revelation 13 & 17.* Satan is thereby a god of this world directing a many faceted evil social body, *Luke 4, 5-6, §1.15, Isaiah 14, 12-17, Revelation 12, 9 to 13, 10, Daniel 7 & 12.* He rules Death, *§7.4, §9.4,* and ample sources of stored waters drawn from idolaters, *§1, Revelation 12, 15-16, Psalm 144, 7-8 & 69, 1-3 & 124, 1-5.* But a flood of satanic waters cannot quench thirst of the Godly:

o god, you are my god, earnestly i
seek you;
my soul thirsts for you, my body longs
for you,
in a dry and weary land where
there is no water.
psalm 63, 1

i have come into deep waters; the
floods engulf me. i am worn out calling
for help;
my throat is parched.
psalm 69, 2-3

Now if God offers a just salvation from evil then evil is a passing unjust but legal power: *Isaiah 61, 1 & 9, 2-7; 1 Corinthians 15, 22-28, §7.10; John 15, Galatians 4, 1-9, §5.10.* It claims jurisdiction of weak evil, *sinners,* in a just God's courts to test loyalties, *Job 1 & 2, Galatians 4, 1-9, §5.10.* Sinners are held in the dark from God, *§1.17, §10.5,* by unjust doctrine in a pact to sacrifice life to forces of darkness, *§9.3, Isaiah 24 & 28, 18-20.*

Evil sucks its vitality from social or material fabric as a God-denying power, *Luke 11, 24-26, §5.4, Luke 8, 26-39.* Its downfall is a defining wish to cut links to God, *the source of life.* It then wishes to morally debase life relative to God, *make sinners of life in its power,* to take waters of life. Hence, mortal business, politics, religion or 'science' show forces of moral degradation to separate life from God. If a society degrades too far, life-forces drawn by the gods dwindle so evil may cut off its guiding waters. It is why evil empires fall in decay struck by 'God's wrath', *2 Peter 2, 17.* God's word uses physical drought to characterise 'God's wrath' as metaphor for such curse-law, *Jeremiah 50, 38 & 51, 36-37, Isaiah 19, 3-7, Nahum 1, 4.* When an evil social body has failed Satan in his title-contest with God, Satan de-invests evil waters to it as basic curse-law: its just deserts, *Wisdom 14, 27-31, §9.5, Isaiah 24.*

If evil gods cannot 'evolve' a society balanced in sin, they must instead regiment an horrific crime. For the ruling class loses vitality by ruining weaker life in its care so new blood is needed, *Leviticus 17, 14.* As horror films tell fans, the gods suck the life from weaker evil then move on, leaving it to die as a husk cut off from God in sin, *Romans 6, 23.* They need new life to continue harvesting waters of life. The plan of evil gods must be to yoke and farm 'lesser life' by a 'science' to master God's life-forces: *secure the tree of life to depose God, §9.2.* That is why knowing strong evil makes mortal, *Genesis 3, §7.4, Isaiah 28, 18-20.* Today, the gods farm mortals by forms of consent to cycles of birth and death, *§10.5, e.g. extolling 'natural' selection, §10.1.*

God's word casts Death as an enemy spirit allied to Satan, *§1.2, §9.4,* fought using weapons of God, *Isaiah 28, 18, §7.4; 1 Corinthians 15, 22-28, §7.10, Matthew 16, 28.* Idolaters may greet witness to a just God like drunks who fear being denied drink, *§10.2.* They may be addicted to idols that curse, *§9.5.* Many live in a red mist ready to sacrifice life to evil rather than sober up, see *chapter 6, Proverbs 8, 36, §6.2.*

Under spiritual duress, mortals may be blind and deaf to God's word that casts mortals as die-hard idolaters feeding on lesser life in a realm of 'natural forces' out of full sight of God, *Exodus 33, 20-23; Matthew 7, 11-12, §10.2.* Mortals are top of material food chains but in between Satan and God in spiritual food chains, *§10.3, Genesis 3, 22-24.* They are farmed by evil gods for food, *§10.5, §10.13; I Chronicles 16, 25-27, Zechariah 10, 2.* The gods offer to free them from God, and, dying for the gods is freedom of a kind. The many gods and idols in religion confirm God's word is to mortals farmed in spiritual food chains, *Luke 20, 9-16, §7.10.* Evil spirits inspire mortal leaders to consent to the farm on behalf of less advanced mortals, *§10.5.* Horror films offer the imagery of supernatural beings feeding on mortals to prefigure a more formal theology to it, *§10.5.* The concepts to understand what God's word says of our place in creation and of the different feeding modes of life in hell and heaven are in popular circulation.

All spiritual experience may sup waters of life from God but often via stores redirected by the gods to feed social bodies opposed to God, *§1.* Life in dark bodies sees distorted spiritual images not true to God where twisted flows of waters focus locally. People feed at idols by lies related to strong spiritual feelings, *Acts 17, 22-32, §8.7.* Deep 'sincere' feelings, *§9.5,* compel to accursed idols even to tribute them to a just God, *§10.4.* Now the flow-power of waters in idolatry is likely in proportion to neighbours slaved. That is why oppression or tyranny is the way of idolaters, *Isaiah 30, 1-15, §9.12.* The most compelling or ultimate idol is the antichrist to honour all spiritual experience, every religion, idol or god, except for the just God and Christ, *§9.7.4.* He feeds by unjust readings of God's word, *Isaiah 24,* in fields initially watered by floods of Satan's stored waters to spiritually baptise into lie and murder, *§1, §9.7.5.* It farms mortals in a 'flooded desert' made to test and ruin more sober seekers of God, see *Psalm 69, 2-3 above, Psalm 74, 12-15, Isaiah 35, 4-6, §8.1.*

To swear by unjust doctrine may gain an inebriating source of inner vitality that blocks God's saving truth and law. Thus, the unrepentant sinner draws life-forces by a tortuous path compared to the penitent, *2 Peter 2, 12-18.* The flows feed our hereditary sinful nature: a personal evil spirit doppelgänger who is a subject of the gods, *§10.5.* Its influence is seen in religious hate and violence. Good and evil are thus in principle vitalised by different objects and complexes of feelings though in practice most may be double-minded, *§10.5, Galatians 5, 17-21, §7.11, Genesis 2, 25* to *3, 10.* The feelings we take for granted as natural, fixed, may reflect a spiritual space, *or depth under a sea of evil,* that our soul is at rest in, *Isaiah 11, 6-9, §7.6, Ephesians 2, 1-3, §7.11.*

Life hostile to God draws waters from other life and matter, *Matthew 5, 43-45, 1 Corinthians 6, 12.* God's enemies feel spiritual by stores of God's waters taken from sinful social bodies on paths to seize the tree of life and cut all links to God. Such flows turn to sustain lies like that a just God is disposable. People feel or taste the flows as spiritual forces of darkness. That is the occult source to superstitious terror or joy at idols such as unjust doctrine about God, *Isaiah 24.*

God's word may imply few in God's temple are fully saved before Judgement Day, *Psalm 24, 3-5 & 50, 16-21 & 73, 9-10; Matthew 7, 21-23, §10.2.* Mortals must show faith in God as the love to cover a multitude of their sins on the paths to truth. Meanwhile, God's temple is where idolaters love to help sequester waters of life for the gods, *§8.3, §8.4.* The blind approach God's temple as a table set to demons by unjust doctrine, *§10.3.* But souls are to have chance to repent as a conflict of interest between God and demons becomes clearer down the ages, *§10.4; 1 Corinthians 10.* The Godly must tolerate false teaching in a twilight zone prior to turnings to God, *§10.6.*

God's word suggests many wish to cure world-ills by idols that cause world-ills. Idolatry curses to poverty and injustice, to every evil on earth: illness, crime, death, global warming, *Wisdom 14, 27-31, §9.5, Isaiah 24.* Salvation is from an enchantment of idols, *§9.5.* Spiritual forces of darkness turn the bafflers in a sinners' heart, *§1,* to cause discomfort or suspicion at God's truth. Truth may even feel demonic, *Matthew 12, 24-29 & 11, 18 & 10, 25 & 9, 34.* We next show how evil's legal case to possess sinners arises in more depth.

11.3 The Contest of Laws for Title to Creation: Power bids to divert life-forces to evolution in sin

A perfect God is the essential source of life-forces so no one can make an eternal world of which a perfect God is not the true God. To cut relations to God cuts life-forces from God which defines sin. God's perfect nature may lead to boundaries that life cannot cross and truly be alive. God cannot alter His nature, so laws by which sin or crime cut life-forces are ultimately inescapable. Severe sin then leads to a loss of vitality or death, *Proverbs 8, 36, §6.2, Romans 6, 23, §7.10.*

God can, *in principle*, pad out bounds for life by warning signs in lost vitality as effects of sin, say, by illness or losses due to crime, even by suspension in a state of rest or pseudo-death, *Isaiah 57, 1-2, §7.5, Isaiah 14, 9-11.* Such padding would set minimum standards for life to stop it straying to sudden death. The bounds form a hard-core to God's justice or law met as cause and effect laws relative to conduct that is suicidal or criminal. The bounds may give life a chance to learn to repent of sin that cuts life-forces. If life chooses to work to strip God's life-forces or Spirit from itself and others, that is anti-social behaviour. Life stripped 'naked', *Isaiah 11, 6-9, §7.6*, may one day indict it as crime, *1 Corinthians 4, 4-5 & 6, 2-3*:

> then the eyes of both of them were opened,
> and they realised they were naked; so they sewed fig leaves together and made coverings for themselves.
> then the man and his wife heard the sound of the lord god as he was walking in the garden in the cool of the day, and they hid from the lord god among the trees of the garden.
> But the lord god called to the man, "where are you?"
>
> Genesis 3, 7-9

God's enemies identify with 'crime' to perceive God's bounds for life-forces as tyranny, *oppression.* Now if God is not a tyrant, evil leaders have right to god-like ability to conjecture a science of rebellion against God. The god-fathers of evil suspect barriers of loss of vitality and death around crime hide that what God defines as 'crime' is a path to depose God in creation? It then conjectures that 'crime' is a force for good to liberate life, *overthrow God's standards for life.* In summary, if God is perfect, His foes are criminals with a death-wish led by evil god-fathers, *chapter 6.* The criminality of mortals might be derivative of an evil god-father serpent as in *Genesis 3, §7.4.*

God's enemies refuse to accept God cannot give life-forces without death or loss of vitality round crime or suicidal ways. To liberate life, they must prove God lies in saying His perfect nature is sole source of life-forces. If God is indomitable, *Psalm 50, 3; 1 Kings 19, 11-13, §10.2*, rebel gods have option to seek a new source of life-forces from resources in distant relationship to God, *e.g. from 'lesser evil life' as guinea pigs.* Hence, the defining wish of a just God's foes is to direct material and social evolution in a world separate from God: to build life of infinite vitality to depose God. 'Civilised' evil runs theories of evolutionary rise of a master race to the unholy grail of proof that God is evil, *§9.2.*

"when he comes, he will convict the world of guilt in regard to sin and righteousness and judgement:"
John 16, 8

If God respects evil, He may let it trial evolutionary science in its own world. Hell may begin as a kingdom of willing life for whom aspects of God's law are suspended as next best thing to deposing God. But without its own source of life-forces, hell is still ruled by God under an arm of God's law for life disloyal to God: evil's law. Evil's law is a curse on life because evil elects to live and work near the barriers of death. Hell's laws may let life try states that seem healthy but are close to an automaton, *spirit of brute instinct, Psalm 73; 2 Peter 2, 10-12.* To evil gods, such life is a servant, hell bent on crime that leads to death even by paths deemed high culture. It is a state people can escape to God's salvation from, *Psalm 73, 1-4 & 21-26.*

Hell is for frustrated life that may feel cheated by God. If life outside is healthier, *Genesis 3, 22,* it motivates hell to seek power outside where life-forces look easier to tap. For that, hell seeks a just case to make God disestablish His law outside hell. The case may be that evil's faith that God is imperfect, *like evil,* implies evil's law could prove just for all life. A just God is then obliged to let evil's curse-law trial for jurisdiction of all life. If curse-law triumphs, it is proof that God is evil, imperfect. Since definitions of crime and punishment hinge on whether God is perfect, God cannot justly stop evil enacting laws to test His perfection by 'crime'. Rebel gods may defend sin against God by a theory of alternative laws on crime and punishment to contradict God's. If the gods opt for an evolutionary system, any sin or 'crime' may be given a trial, *1 John 3, 4, §9.1.*

Curse-law is of a plan to farm life for evolution in sin, *rebellion*, that recasts victims and criminals by God's law as criminals and 'freedom-fighters'. Revolutionary mortals use the same game-plan, *follow the gods in basic criminal philosophy?*, when seeking power on earth:

The theory above suggests that to a perfect God, idolatrous or Godless theories of evolution are the heart of organised crime: the seat of a higher system of evil laws, see *chapter 6*. How do folk who wish to teach such theories in schools defend it? They may say that it is scientific truth, *enlightenment*, by reasonable good scientists. But suppose it is criminal philosophy then in fact they are people less able to distinguish right from wrong. Now God's word implies all mortals are morally weak including priests in 'God's temple'. But are supporters of the theory of natural selection more blind to serious sin than most? To test that, we look for oversight or presumption by which the theory is gross fantasy, say, to support sex and blood lusts in the world, *§9.3; §10.13; 2 Peter 2, 12-19*. But failings need to be enough to offend the moral sensibility of mundane sinners to show them it is criminal philosophy, *Wisdom 2, 11-12, §9.2, chapter 6*, e.g. might it violate basic criminal law? *§1.4, §12.1.*
Now the aim of evolutionary science is to engulf every fact in the universe. However, God's word and this theory may be in the way. Scripture prophesies a delusion on origins, *2 Peter 3, 3-6, §9.3*, and there are technical problems to make evolutionary theories a gamble, *§10.13*. More openly religious scientists can take the facts to carbon dating science, fossil dinosaurs, finch beaks, DNA evidence, etc., and turn them to theories where the universe is just a few tens of thousands of years old.
Naturally, dealers in fossil history on scales of billions of years deny systematic funds and careers to such 'unscientific' ideas. However, if they push natural selection as a framed hypothesis for political purposes, that might be criminal by standards of some courts on earth? The truth can be that natural selection fits as a satanic faith or cult, *§10.4*. If such 'science' is demonic fantasy, it may rank beside religion that ignores salvation via the just Christ from God. There is freedom of faith under God, *chapter 9, Micah 4, 5*, for religious authorities to oppose a just God as may imply criminal deception whether in the name of 'good' science or religion? A secular society in the name of human evolution may empower a religious cult, *§10.4, §6.*

Rebellion law claims jurisdiction of life in its rebellion, *e.g. for sin against authority*. It punishes for not sinning well enough to overturn authority, *Luke 1, 74; 1 John 4, 16-18; Jeremiah 31, 34*. It punishes those who fail the rebellion, *Proverbs 25, 21-22, Romans 12, 20-2, Acts 18, 17*. For example, Satan's curse-law is set by a plan to depose God, *so is relative to God*. If he fails, his enacted curse-law is left a predictable arm of God's law, see *Exodus 20, 4-6, §7.9*, that asks God to oversee eternal punishment of evil for crimes of failing to rebel against God well enough, *Isaiah 14, 20-21*.

Satan's curse-law is of a bid to end the 'tyranny' of God's law in barriers of death round crime. For within evil's faith that God is evil, *the dominant evil god*, the barriers suggest God is a murderous tyrant who sets walls of death round 'crime' to subdue enemies, and fool weak life into loyalty. For curse-law encourages evil to vie with God to be a better tyrant, *Matthew 10, 28*:

> Jesus said to them, "The kings of the Gentiles lord it over them; and those who exercise authority over them call themselves Benefactors. But you are not to be like that. Instead, the greatest among you should be like the youngest, and the one who rules like the one who serves...."
>
> Luke 22, 25-26

Evil imagines God is an evil deity in its own image as the basis of idolatry. It may suspect God is a virulent form of evil who evolved in a previous universe by defeating and consuming all other life, now hiding it by claiming to be perfect. Evil can then indict God as an evil that evil gods wish to save weak evil from.

By its bid to prove God imperfect, evil is asking proof that God is perfect. Life harassed by evil's suspicions about God, *its advocacy of crime*, may also wish a reassuring proof that God is perfect. A perfect God who respects life's wishes must give such a proof in a form acceptable to the blinkered ways of life, *i.e. dictated in life's disputes with God.* Evil may demand proof by a contest of laws in heaven and hell because it holds out promise of unending licence to ignore God, '*freedom*'. It may even threaten a program of crime to force God to give that proof else to rule as an evil dictator against evil, as would prove evil right about God.

In summary, evil puts God to the deepest level of proof for His perfection: that He can rigorously defend a principle of respect for life's free-will wishes over how it feeds on God's life-force in creation, *subject to the ineluctable laws around bounds for life.* A perfect God cannot then be found a dictator, *a violator of life's legally interpreted wishes*, at any time in creation because evil may cite it as a trespass on life's free-will by which God unjustly holds power. Thus, a perfect God is a just God who stands by respect for life's wishes throughout eternity. Proof that God is perfect is to come by a duel of antagonistic legal systems over life, both set relative to God's nature. We next sketch God's path to proof.

If God is perfect, Death is the only fulfilment to plans to evolve in sin to cut links to God. If such plans are implemented, a social and material fabric may rise only to decay and enter apocalypse. However, a perfect God must be able to save penitent life from slavery to sin and death under rebellion authority. That task is in reality the test of God's perfection, *§8.1*:

When you were slaves to sin, you were free from from the control of righteousness. What benefit did you reap at that time from the things you are now ashamed of? Those things result in death!
But now that you have been set free from sin and have become slaves to God, the benefit you reap leads to holiness, and the result is eternal life. For the wages of sin is death, but the gift of God is eternal life in Christ Jesus our Lord.
Romans 6, 20-23

Scriptures like this imply a rescue plan of God's in which sinners fight death by subscribing to sacrifice of the Christ, *Psalm 50, Isaiah 53, 5 & 10-12*. We can go on to deduce, *§4*, how a legal evil forces a God's salvation to rest on such a sacrifice, see also *§7.8*.

The gods of evil bid to farm life as slaves to evolution in sin hoping to find a life-source by which to depose God. They invent Death for a death or glory bid, *Wisdom 12-16, §1.2*. If they will not repent, God can take proof He is perfect by designing creation so evil's cause leads it on a path to formally agree it has a death-wish, *Proverbs 8, 36, §6.2*. That consents to death-sentence in hell. To extract that consent is the proof that God is essential to all life, *perfect*. Even if God warns evil of its fate, *Psalm 82, 6-7*, it finds it counter-intuitive so calls God's 'bluff'. Evil's path is a wager that God is fallible leading to bigger wagers that draw it to fulfil prophecy. Evil is to be hoist on the petard or war-machine that it builds to depose a just God in creation, *e.g. held to its chosen curse-laws for farming life in hell.*

Evil claims authority above God on what evil wishes or stands for. It sees its wish as for power not, *as God says*, death, *Proverbs 8, 36, §6.2*. To see who is right, evil must legally ask for the future of law and order to be settled in a contest of laws. It will not accept proof of God's perfection other than by that path. God cannot offer that kind of proof before evil fairly defines itself by enacting its choice of curse-laws on willing citizens of hell to contest God's law and title outside hell.

To appear sane, *chapter 6*, a ruling class of evil must avoid acts to suggest it has a death-wish. It may argue curse-law would not be competitive if its legislators had to sacrifice their lives working in 'crime' near the barriers of death. Thus, to realise a contest of laws, evil gods ask for a servant class of evil willing to sacrifice their lives working for evil gods. It invents mortals as proteges or children of pre-existing guardian evil life. The mortals need a new world set to stage the duel of 'good' and 'evil' as explained next.

Evil's evidence that God is imperfect is firstly its own rebellious discontent that it seeks to spread outside hell to gain power. If God is evil, that discontent can spread to give evil all power. What if it fails to spread? It might imply God was a dictator to violate life's wishes at the start of creation so life is brainwashed by God's design into loyalty to God? Evil's law can only test that by a new world where angels are freed from their 'brainwashing'. Test by 'crime' or torture: *Job 1, 9-12, Zechariah 3, 1, Revelation 12, 10*, might 'free' angels to love a 'God' of inquisition or trial by ordeal? *§6.4.*

By evil's conjecture that creation was flawed from its beginning, a contest of laws in existing creation cannot prove God is perfect to evil. God must agree to the contest being staged in a new world where it can be established mortals are 'free'. Their 'free-world' is then overseen by occult spiritual guardians, *e.g. angels and demons, §10.1, Job 38, 1-7, §13.1.* In *Genesis*, we see first people agreeing to submit their world to know and work for evil in putting God's title or perfection to the test. The test is whether God's law can save the souls of all angels He should be able to save, *Psalm 98*.

The gods of evil only accept proof of God's title as the outcome of God making a world of mortals who 'agree' to work to try to remove barriers of death round crime. But even if God says it is impossible, He cannot justly allow any life to truly die in the contest before evil has formally admitted its death-wish. Nor can God justly make any life that wishes to die from birth. Evil thereby hopes to trap God into showing the solution to the paradoxical problem of how life can commit any 'crime' against God's law without loss of vitality? to escape God's discipline around life-forces. A perfect God then gave this world out of respect for pre-existing life's wishes for proof of His title to creation and to justly establish the future of law and order in creation.

The contest of laws is partly to see if existing life loyal to God, *e.g. angels*, are brainwashed by God? New life is then to relate in character and intellect to old, *Genesis 1, 26-27, Psalm 8, 4-5*, but be 'free' to choose its future in company of 'good' or 'evil' spirits. The intellect of evil gods may let them argue a greater good is met in a murderous scheme to farm 'lesser' evil life. Evil's defence is that acknowledged mortal 'leaders' 'agree' to be farmed by making sacrifice of 'lesser' life to evil. Mortal proteges of the gods side with them in spirit, *e.g. put faith in natural selection or child sacrifice to idols.* Mortals are not 'innocent' by ancestry or sacrificial sin as why God must clear them of sin to save from evil.

A just God cannot let anyone die in a contest of laws before evil legally admits its death-wish. For sake of Justice, the bounds for life of mortals are padded out with a false or pseudo-death before true death. People then suffer greater loss of vitality for crimes against a perfect God's nature than the gods who inspire to it do. That is just because the gods plan to guide mortals to remove all God's discipline. The level of discipline at which they start should prove immaterial. The curse-discipline that mortals suffer is then to be reduced to near that at which the gods live. People may then face full death. God's design must enable rebel gods to be defeated, *admit their death-wish*, before the full death is met, *1 John 5, 16-17.*

Evil sets God a moral minefield in life and death issues to do with creating new life to prove barriers of death round crime cannot be escaped. Any false step would prove God is evil. Evil may 'justify' its tests by arguing that a perfect God should be able to save good from them by a just case. It then indicts God as responsible for every 'crime' or evil that evil can enact under just law to test God's design, *for all evil.* Evil is thereby evil to evil but is a just God or evil to blame? *Micah 4, 5.*

If evil is an evolutionary cause, *§9.1*, gods of evil plan to sacrifice 'the unfit' to poverty, war, science etc., even to deny 'good' birth as Pharaoh tried, *§7.9*, and evil 'science' tries, *§9.2.* If life is to have a fair choice between good and evil, *Genesis 3, 2-5, §7.4*, then God may be for democratic principles, *§12.1*, but evil for one-sided tyrannies that curses its world to decay or apocalypse, *Matthew 24, 15-42.* The contest is then in part cultural: about political and religious authorities in end times as governments of choice:

one night the lord spoke to paul in a vision: "do not be afraid; keep on speaking, do not be silent. for i am with you, and no one is going to attack and harm you, because i have many people in this city."so paul stayed for a year and a half teaching them the word of god.
while gallio was proconsul of achaia, the jews made a united attack on paul and brought him into court. "this man," they charged, "is persuading the people to worship god in ways contrary to the law."
just as paul was about to speak, gallio said to the jews, "if you jews were making a complaint about some misdemeanour or serious crime, it would be responsible for me to listen to you. but since it involves questions about words and names and your own law—settle the matter yourselves. i will not be a judge of such things. so he had them ejected from the court. then they all turned on sosthenes the synagogue ruler and beat him in front of the court. but gallio showed no concern whatever.
acts 18, 9-17

This shows a war of spirits above Jews for and against Jesus. Which Jews, if any, were in a pact to Death? *Isaiah 28.* Roman authority here sided with the new 'Christians' yet elsewhere persecuted as may reflect divine judgements, *§9.11.* Why would any Jews try to stop Paul, *a brother Jew,* in Roman courts if their spirit guardians knew it was futile? Was it to test Paul's faith by bluff? The consul defended Paul by rationalisation of what higher spiritual authorities ruled: that if many in that place would heed Paul, earthly authority had no right in divine law to stop his preaching there. Jesus knew to avoid witness in places where judgements might set death on 'unjust' witness, *Mark 6, 1-6, §9.8.*

In summary, life's wish for proof of a just God sets creation in stages. First, god-fathers of evil arise in a power bid demanding that God proves He is perfect. The agreed form of proof relates to God respecting life's free-will in a contest of laws. It invokes a new world of mortals where bias towards good or evil is demonstrably erased. It is new life related to old, *to old spirit societies?*, to be tested in a fair choice between spiritual guidance of good or evil. It runs under God's plan of prophecy to proof of God's title to creation, *Psalm 98.* Mortals are thus life on test overseen by related spirits: personal guardian angels and demons, *§13.4.* Evil gods set people to live under evil spiritual forces that drive many like lemmings to the walls of death seeking a new life source. The next section deduces the course of the new world and the legal significance of human sacrifice.

11.4 Mortal Beginning: Education in the knowing of good and evil: sacrifices

God-fathers of rebellion may ask a just God who respects life's wishes to allow new life, *'their' children*, to serve in a contest of laws to test if God is perfect or not? *§3, Job 38, 1-7, §13.1.* To 'protect' life from God, they might table a veto on any more old life. Mortals are to have better options to rebel and work for the gods to depose God, *Galatians 4, 1-9, §5.10.* They may begin in guileless accord with God so immortal, *§13.1.*

The new life is to know something of a just God in its beginnings but be free to join rebel gods who asked for the new life be made, *Deuteronomy 32, 17-18, §7.8.* It has right to know evil, rebel gods. The gods' faith is in evolutionary philosophy, *§3*, so they can table it as in the interests of new life, *'their' children*, to be guided by evil from the earliest. The instant new life rebels against God, the gods may demand custody to direct and sustain its rebellion against God, *i.e. farm mortals for food, §3, Genesis 6, 1-4, §8.3.* If all life must rebel against God to validate its free-will, see *§13.1*, how can a just God stop rebel gods moving in as guardians of new life? God may intervene later, *if the children ask*, to steer their rebellion to a just divide into heaven and hell, *Romans 5, 14 & 8, 20-22.*

The new life is to be born to a world with two areas to respect its choice of guardians. It may start near God's truth with an adjacent educating habitat for rebellion with the gods. The rebellion area may be virtual and entered by accepting a lie from 'a serpent' who lies to life to play 'God' with it. At *Genesis 2, 15-17*, it is a forbidden area called the tree of knowledge of good and evil, *§1.2.* 'God' warns Adam and Eve not to eat from the tree as it leads to death. Thus, Death is part of the education that god-fathers of evil deem vital to guide folk to alignment with their higher rebellion against God, *Hebrews 2, 14-15.* By eating from the tree of knowledge of good and evil, people chose a path to get to know the being, law or ethos of good and evil spirits, *1 Corinthians 4, 4-5 & 6, 2-3.* It offers the future to Death and lie yet, *at that stage*, as a matter of opinion:

> And the LORD God said, "The man has now become like one of us, knowing good and evil. He must not be allowed to reach out his hand and take also from the tree of life and eat, and live forever."
>
> Genesis 3, 22

Evil stands for directing evolution in a world separated from God, *§9.3*, for building life forms of unlimited vitality to depose God, *§3*. That aim is justly licensed in a contest of laws to prove God imperfect in which evil seeks jurisdiction of all life to direct its growth in sin against God. It slaves mortals to work at the barriers of death around 'crime', seeking to find out how to evolve to commit any crime against God and stay alive, *Galatians 4, 1-9, §5.10*:

remember not the sins of my youth
and my rebellious ways;

according to your love remember me,
for you are good, o lord;

psalm 25, 7

Mortal access to the tree of life is justly withheld if it betokens direct relationship to God which evil denies is vital to life. The gods are licensed to drill for a source of life-forces independent of God and so save the 'fit' from 'heaven'. Now *Genesis 3, 22* above implies some people could be immortals in the gods' 'heaven', *§9.7.5*, by taking the tree of life by force. But that does not imply God can eternally sustain life in 'crime', *§12.4*. The gods may stay immortal by not directly committing grave crimes against God's nature but driving people to it as slaves, *Genesis 6, 3, §8.3*. Evil gods thereby sacrifice mortals, *Matthew 10, 28*, yet could promote mortal evil leaders to their own station. In that context, to withhold the tree of life is part of Justice for the 'weak'. It may save them from sacrifice to the gods by enabling the gods to be convicted of crimes against people, *§9.7.5*, after a legal failure of their plan to depose God using blind mortals. To save 'the weak', God must prove evil gods cannot side-step death by using people as proxies in crime. A process of law must translate their bid into a legally binding death-wish or sentence on confirmed evil, *Psalm 82, 6-7, Isaiah 14, 12-21, §8.3*. That is then a just God's plan to defeat the rebellion and eternally secure law and order.

If the earth now stages a contest of laws where mortals are tested in choice between good and evil spirits then it is vain to think mortals are masters of their destiny. Rather they answer calls of destiny from good and evil spirits, *§7.3*. This world is directed by people but only as children with choice of guardians, *Galatians 4, 1-9, §5.10*. People are slaves to their choice of spiritual powers by faiths they hold, *§10.5*. People are slaves but with a choice of masters:

I know, O LORD, that a man's life is not
his own;
it is not for man to direct his steps.
Correct me, LORD, but only with
justice—
not in your anger,
lest you reduce me to nothing.
Jeremiah 10, 23-24

the LORD sets prisoners free,
the LORD gives sight to the blind,
the LORD lifts up those who are bowed
down,
the LORD loves the righteous.
Psalm 146, 8

They promise them freedom while
they themselves are slaves of
depravity—for a man is a slave to
whatever has mastered him.
2 Peter 2, 19

The 'freedom' of evil is not to be a slave to God's just truth, e.g. not to see it, *Daniel 12, 9-10, Romans 6, 20- 23, §3, Luke 18, 18-19.* The 'good' evil life is as proud slaves of the gods yet if God is just truth, *Psalm 31, 5, Isaiah 1, 15-20, §8.6,* the gods are unjust lies that kill, *i.e. murder.* They work to lower moral standards for life by slaving to Death in a bid to depose God. It pens outside God's Spirit, *Isaiah 11, 6-9, §7.6,* stripped of knowledge of God, *Genesis 3, 7-9, §3,* to receive offers of evil and good spirit dress, *§9.1.* Many shrink from righteous dress, *Jonah 3 to 4, §9.1, §10.5, §10.10*:

Very rarely will anyone die for a
righteous man,
though for a good man someone might
possibly dare to die.
Romans 5, 7

"I tell you, among those born of
women there is no one greater than
John; yet the one who is least in the
kingdom of God is greater than he."
Luke 7, 28

On hearing this, Jesus said to them, "It
is not the healthy who need a doctor,
but the sick.
I have not come to call the righteous
but sinners."
Mark 2, 17

The contest sets life 'free', *unbiased,* to see if states exist from which all life matures to join evil and reject God? Spiritual guardians are at first occult prompters of thoughts so as not to bias life's decisions, *§7.3.* Mortals can follow spirits on many paths, *§10.1.* What realistic prospect have mortals? Evil claims their sin is of a pact to sacrifice life to rebellion against God led by evil gods, *§7.4.* But if God is perfect, life can never sustain an eternal world separate from God. Mortals face extinction in an impossible mission for the gods unless individually or culturally they work to break a pact to evil gods for a covenant to salvation with God.

Only if some people wish may a just God offer a covenant to salvation, *Psalm 111, 9.* The gods cause mortals to suffer under test, *Psalm 32, 8-11, §10.5*, so some ask God's mercy, *Genesis 4, 25-26, §7.4.* God's salvation plan is implied at *Genesis 3, 13-15.* He must see that the world allows a fair choice of good and evil to reach understanding of salvation from evil's curse. People may then fairly choose between Death under evolution in sin or salvation with a just God, *§9.7.5.*

Now mortals may be slaves in sin to evil gods but the gods are slaves to a legal expression of their chosen plan to depose God. That is why an infallible God may seal a plan of prophecy to defeat evil in the contest even without seeing evil's chosen plan, *Genesis 15, 13-14, §7.8, Isaiah 7, 7-16, 1 Corinthians 15, 22-28, §7.10.* God's plan is to give sinners choice of good and evil law on all levels of validity. Any choice-gap would enable the gods to object the world did not offer every possible path to evolve in sin to abandon God, *to join evil.* God may rank all tests in cultural levels for one world on a journey from low level to high level tests in end times. In later tests, people may fully commit to evil and death in hell, *Revelation 14, 9-11, §9.7.4.* This world is then led by people as slaves to prompts from spirits to a fulfilment of God's plan. To defeat God, evil must break prophecies to God's plan: abolish or change set times, *Revelation 5, 1-5, §7.10, Daniel 12, 4.*

For tests of faith to be valid, God must prove people are not biassed against evil by occult knowledge of God. The pattern to the tests is then for God to withdraw and let sin increase to full tyranny in a test area. It may bring society to verge of degeneration as is said to have occurred under evil before the flood, *§7.7.* Evil gods then hold minds of people at start of a test, *Matthew 7, 11-12, §10.2*, by which it is easier to stand by evil than move on to God. God's influence is by servants who walk as if with God in steps to salvation, *§8.6.* Strongholds of evil are tested by a servant's messages and the servants are tested by the stronghold. If the message falls on deaf ears to be lost forever, evil wins its contest of laws. Total victory for evil may only be possible up to a critical stage in history after which a division into heaven and hell is inevitable. After each test, the world travels on to the next stage. God's plan then comprises many situations where mortals in the dark await advance on the paths to God, *§8.5.*

Mortal consent is a key issue in a contest of laws. Mortals must pact to good or evil paths before fully understanding the social architecture they lead to, *§3.* How is consent to heaven or hell taken from people as children? It is partly resolved by giving mortals their own children. People are children relative to a deity, so can mime consent to good or evil in how they treat their children and neighbours.

People raise children as subject to parental authority till mature enough to go their own way, *Deuteronomy 5, 16, Ephesians 6, 1-4, Galatians 4, 1-9, §5.10.* If some parents are unfit, courts may gather evidence to dispute custody and take children into care. By analogy, to recover custody of people, God first has to establish the full nature of good and evil law in creation, then ensure people who wish for it know how to make an effective complaint against evil, *1 Corinthians 4, 4-5 & 6, 2-6*, as a legally binding wish for salvation, *Galatians 4, 1-9, §5.10.* Does that lead to trials on 'Judgement Day' where good and evil dispute souls in open review of past lives? *§9.11, §13.12, Job 16, 19-22, Matthew 5; James 3; 1 John 2, 1-2; Ephesians 6, 10-18*:

"when the son of man comes in his glory, and all the angels with him, he will sit on his throne in heavenly glory. all the nations will be gathered before him, and he will separate the people one from another as a shepherd separates the sheep from the goats. he will put the sheep on his right and the goats on his left.
"then the king will say to those on his right, 'come, you who are blessed by my father; take your inheritance, the kingdom prepared for you since the creation of the world.
for i was hungry and you gave me something to eat, i was thirsty and you gave me something to drink, i was a stranger and you invited me in, i needed clothes and you clothed me, i was sick and you looked after me, i was in prison and you came to visit me.'
"then the righteous will answer him, 'lord, when did we see you hungry and feed you, or thirsty and give you something to drink? when did we see you a stranger and invite you in, or needing clothes and clothe you? when did we see you sick or in prison and go to visit you?'
"the king will reply, 'i tell you the truth, whatever you did for one of the least of these brothers of mine, you did for me.'
"then he will say to those on his left, 'depart from me, you who are cursed, into the eternal fire prepared for the devil and his angels. . . "

matthew 25, 31-41

Sacrifice of life to deities is predestined to legal significance because rebel gods need servants who will routinely sacrifice life disloyal to their rebellion *(who try to turn to God)*. To rebellion gods, human sacrifice can begin as a primitive act and evolve to sophisticated ways of sacrifice to be institutionalised, *§9.5.* Servants of evil learn to sublimate their death-wish in drives for power to eliminate God's support. The gods dress sinners to feel a need to sacrifice God's servants to the gods, *§9.1.* They inspire to high level theories of life in a Godless social universe *that tacitly take Satan as 'God'.* Before such theories are well developed, the unrefined instinct of evil may be to eliminate anyone, *servant of evil or good,* in way of their power bids.

The start of a culture of sacrifice, *§7.8,* is described in *Genesis.* Adam and Eve's first act of rebellion was taken as their wish to leave God's guardianship to get to know gods of sacrifice. At that stage, people could in principle ask a return to God's care by making the right offerings, *as a matter set in rebellion law.* Thus, Adam and Eve's children, *Cain and Abel,* made offerings to 'the Lord' out of their work in livestock and arable farming. The Lord indicated livestock has higher value for securing a deities' guardianship. It implies curse-law regards animals as higher life, worth more than fruit in offerings to deities. That left Cain downcast and 'the Lord' asked Cain to do better:

"If you do what is right, will you not be accepted? But if you do not do what is right, sin is crouching at your door; it desires to have you, but you must master it."

Genesis 4, 7

All the ways of the Lord are loving and faithful
for those who keep the demands of his covenant.

Psalm 25, 10

To this day, right gestures of consent to God's rule are asked to escape curse-law, *Psalm 25, 10* above, *Isaiah 24.* The default position is consent to the rebellion by which the gods drive deeper into sin. For example, 'the Lord's' reproof led to Cain murdering Abel in rage. If his rage was spiritual direction of the gods, *§10.5,* Cain in effect sacrificed Abel to evil. That offering is higher than livestock to make Cain a leader to bind all under curse-law, *§10.5, Genesis 4, 10-12.* A counter sacrifice is then needed to God. Jesus taught that it obliges to the sacrifice of God's willing Son to God, *§9.7.5, Isaiah 53, Genesis 3, 13-15, Psalm 50, 2-23* below.

With complicity of mortals, the gods set up sacrifices of life to idols as a pact to evolve in sin to full knowledge of what evil stands for, to know evil, *§9.1.* Idols are toys from the gods to drill in their aims. The peak consent is sacrifice of youth to idols in schools offering the future to evil, *§7.8, §9.4; 2 Kings 23, 10-13, Jeremiah 32, 34-35, Psalm 106, 36-38.* It trains in 'Godless' unjust theory: *carved images or doctrines to tacitly set Satan as 'God', §9.5.* Sacrifice of life is a currency of curse-law sealing a pact to die for with rebel gods. Sacrifice is offered either for power or as a plea for relief in a cursed world, *§7.8.* Ceremonial and other murders pledge to the gods' farm and their curse drives stock to work in a slimy pit of *evolution in sin* to try to depose God, *§9.2:*

I waited patiently for the Lord;
he turned to me and heard my cry.
He lifted me out of the slimy pit,
out of the mud and mire; he set my
feet on a rock and gave me a firm
place to stand.
He put a new song in my mouth,
a hymn of praise to our God.

Psalm 40, 1-3

To escape a sacrificial pact to death in curse-law needs a counter-pact with God to salvation, *Isaiah 28, 16-18.* It is some law that if taken in a just spirit sets 'free', *Joel 2, 28-32, §7.11, Jeremiah 31-33 & Romans 2, 29, §8.3.*

The Lord confides in those who fear him;
he makes his covenant known to them.

Psalm 25, 14

God's word may collate good and evil law as one body of law under God, *§3.* His word may allow freedom of faith in God or Satan, *§9.7,* by unjust and just readings of God's law to good or evil spirits for a contest of laws, *§10.13, Isaiah 24.* God's judicial system, *§10.8,* can then be seen as led by Satan or God in rival faiths. It gives mortals the highest level choice of good and evil. Until just discrimination rises, God's word remains a sealed book, *§8.1, Psalm 13.* But mortals are entitled to training in Justice which may begin with laws of covenant, *e.g. commandments,* that forbid human sacrifice as murder, *Exodus 20, 13.* Life is judged by the spirit in which it reads God's law, *Psalm 51, 1-12, 10.10.* The plan of evil gods is to train mortals to be religiously unjust on God's law, *§9.7.1, §9.7.6, Isaiah 28.* God's plan is to raise standards of 'justice'.

Training in Justice is a cultural process taking place under a spiritual war, *§7.3*. It leads to the Spirit poured out in end times, *Joel 2, 28-32, §7.11*. To try to leave the gods yet still sin against God draws a curse driving back to evil paths. Degeneration may follow as to the flood, *§7.7*, when it is said God saved Noah as root of a chosen people, 'Israel', *§9.7.3*. 'Israel' is then a root for God's word to guide the world on in tests. Prophecies of apocalypse show a curse on failure to serve the gods or God well, *Matthew 24, 37-41*. It may become severe as evil approaches defeat in open creation. It is a defeat of religious and 'scientific' faiths whose 'justice' is overruled as unfit for power under some just case, *e.g. in God's court, Daniel 7, §1.4, §6.4, §9.11, §12.3*:

Rebellion against God is by faith in a perfect crime to prove God's Justice fallible in creation. The gods inspire to seek that crime as seen in the 1924 trial of two students in the USA, *Leopold and Loeb*, who wished to prove they were superior people by *their* reading of Nietsche's theories, *by evolutionary ideology*. They planned to prove themselves fit by a perfect crime of murder on Loeb's cousin whom they deemed inferior for lacking their free-will for crime. It was not a perfect crime because they were caught, *tried and imprisoned for life*, spared a death sentence on account of young age and concern over their mental states.
They were spared as rich people with an inspired defence lawyer, Clarence Darrow, to whom Leopold confided the killing was an experiment, as easy to justify as killing a beetle in entomology. Darrow decided to make their case part of his crusade against capital punishment, arguing for charity, love and understanding. It sounds a service to a God of love and mercy? Yet Darrow went on to defend free of charge teaching of evolution in schools alongside teaching that a perfect God made a perfect creation. He defended teaching to children of a realm of theory that led Leopold and Loeb to murder and incites to break laws for selfish gain, *§9.7.6*, so against universal love, mercy, charity. Did Darrow serve God by supporting freedom of faith for the age? or the gods by exploiting a law of freedom of faith to pervert justice in an earthly court as part of a quest for the perfect crime?
If the gods of auto-evolution run a belief system parallel to Loeb and Leopold, it is on a higher level. Were the two inspired in their beliefs by feelings of pride and freedom as reward from the gods? To the gods, they may be our leaders in evolutionary rebellion: proof mortals can evolve to love the full implications of evolutionary rebellion? *§12.2*. Could the trial have been staged as part of the gods' case for industrial murders of 'inferior life'? *§9.2*. Such cause and effect may abound in supernatural history, *§9.11*.
A difference between Leopold and the devil is that the devil is his own legal counsel. If Satan incites crimes against life relative to God's law, it is by cover of a legal defence to suspend God's justice in creation, seeking to commit the perfect crime. Scripture tells us it in coded form, *§7.4*, showing a serpent who represents Satan, tempting Adam and Eve into a wish to join the rebellion. It makes Satan the leader in all creation for raising of a god of auto-evolution, and fittest in creation to be that god, *§13.1*.

The worst sin against rebel gods is turning to God so curse-law sets a death-penalty on it, *§9.7.1.* The gods' law is to spiritually shepherd or pen souls in accursed sin against God, *§7.3.* Now if sinners by rights live under jurisdiction of curse-law, God's just atonement must be valid inside curse-law. God frees by a just system to annul sins, *Luke 20, 9-16, §7.10.* It may be a loophole in the gods' own systems for atoning for sin against the gods based on sacrifice of life. What higher loyalty is there than to offer life to a deity? Human sacrifice may set a pact to a deity as how to ask forgiveness for 'sins' against rebel gods, *Micah 4, 5.* That may oblige a just God who forbids murder but respects life's wishes to design for a cardinal human sacrifice to God, *higher than animals or thank-offerings, §7.8, Psalm 50, 2-23,* to annul evil's farm-rights. But how can any sacrifice of life be to a just God if He stands for giving and not taking life? *§9.7.5*:

from zion, perfect in beauty, god shines forth.
our god comes and will not be silent;
a fire devours before him and around him a tempest rages.
he summons the heavens above, and the earth that he may judge his people:
"gather to me my consecrated ones, who made a covenant with me by sacrifice."
and the heavens proclaim his righteousness for god himself is judge.

"hear, o, my people, and i will speak, o israel, and i will testify against you:
i am god, your god.
i do not rebuke you for your sacrifices or your burnt offerings, which are ever before me.
i have no need of a bull from your stall
or of goats from your pens,
for every animal of the forest is mine,
and the cattle on a thousand hills.

i know every bird in the mountains,
and the creatures of the field are mine.
if i were hungry i would not tell you,
for all the world is mine, and all that is in it.
do i eat the flesh of bulls or drink the blood of goats?
sacrifice thank offerings to god, fulfil your vows to the most high,
and call upon me in the day of trouble;
i will deliver you, and you will honor me."

but to the wicked, god says:
"what right have you to recite my laws
or take my covenant on your lips?
you hate my instruction and cast my words behind you." … … …
"he who sacrifices thank offerings honors me, and he prepares the way
so that i may show him the salvation of god."

psalm 50, 2-17, 23

In *§3*, we saw the laws to God's blessing and the gods' curse-law may form one body of law under God, *Deuteronomy 30, 17-20, §7.8, Exodus 20, 4-6, §7.9.* The gods' curse-law threatens death on inept loyalty to their rebellion against God, *Micah 4, 5.* Sinners who turn to God then face death even for trivial sin against God unless on path to the sacrificial covenant with God by which God's blessing may protect, *Psalm 50* above. Even if God's servants stop sinning, they still face a curse of association over witness to 'evil' kin, *§9.7.2.* God's design may focus on a redeeming human sacrifice where both priests and sacrifice act justly, *1 Peter 1, 18-21.* A human sacrifice fit for a just God should be of a willing non-sinner and its priests absolved of murder else a just God cannot accept it.

The book of *Genesis* establishes that leading mortals are ready to sacrifice, *offer*, their children to a 'just' God by the faith of Abraham and Isaac, *§7.8, Genesis 22.* Now the offer of Abraham's son, *Isaac*, was not taken perhaps as Isaac, *though willing*, was a sinner so property of the rebellion. If all are sinners, *Ecclesiastes 7, 20*, the gods' atoning currency of human sacrifice then locks God out unless a non-sinner is found. If sin is inherited down the father's side, *Exodus 20, 4-6, §7.9*, God must father the non-sinner, say, by a virgin birth as prophesied for the Christ of *Isaiah 7, 14, §6, God's Son of Psalm 2*, to be born in Bethlehem, *Micah 5, 2, §7.9.* Secondly, if God's law respects life's wishes then to absolve priests who support the sacrifice, *§3, Matthew 5, 23-26 & 7, 11-12, §10.2*, may require the Son and other parties, *Satan*, to forgive or be unable to prosecute it as a murder, *Isaiah 1, 15-20, §8.6, Luke 23, 34, §6.8*:

> "Receive the Holy Spirit, if you forgive anyone his sins, they are forgiven; if you do not forgive them, they are not forgiven."
>
> John 20, 22-23

Not to forgive sins might hold all sides to sentence in the gods' curse-law prison, *§10.11*, but to forgive may not absolve every sin, *1 John 5, 16-18, §9.7.2.* Now murder of a sinless man of God at *Isaiah 53* is not a just God's direct will? *§9.7.5*, so is by sinners driven by the gods trying to goad the non-sinner to sin, *Isaiah 53, Acts 2, 22-24, §10.9.* He must not sin and must forgive the sinners, *Luke 23, 24, §6.8*, yet hold rebel gods to account. Thus, at *John 19, 10-11, §7.10* Jesus indicts Satan as ruler of this cursed world leading the wicked in the sacrifice, *1 John 5, 19, §6.10, Luke 4, 5-6, §1.15.*

For many, faith that God directly curses for sin, *§9.7.6*, is to their own nature and idea of being in God's image, *§9.1*. It might be legally true that 'God' punishes for sin but not of a just God's nature or hand, *§8.1*. Sinners have a just right to be punished for sin and to punish for it even out of unjust fear, spite, or pride in the sinful nature, *§10.5*. To punish or curse sin may be hell's 'holy' eternal institution, *Genesis 3, 2-5, §7.4, Isaiah 28, Matthew 23, 15-28, §10.13*. The vindictive feel 'holy' in crusades to punish 'the wicked'. They may crown Satan as God's judicial will or hand on sin against God's direct will, *Lamentations 3, 33, §8.1*. Satan is a master of just law else a contest of laws is void whilst a better evil is sought, *§13.1*. His proud role as 'Lord' of sinners may exemplify how evil gods are slaves to curse-law they enact to depose God. For that, Satan is spirit of antichrist in 'God's temple', *§10.3*, and enacts a sacrificial test of His rival: God's Son the Christ and King elect, *§9.7.5, §10.8*. A just judge in that system is to see no one is unjustly punished.

A just God's word and sacrificial atonement system can only be established by (*blind?*) wish of mortals, *Luke 23, 34, §6.8*. For freedom of faith, God's servants may receive death-threat warnings for sin in terms to let the unjust think God's will is 'murder', *§9.7.6, §10.8*. Many are driven to 'God' as a harsh disciplinarian of capital punishment on sin. If that is sin, it can be covered by God's blessing whilst on path to higher just truth, *Isaiah 1, 15-20, §8.6*. But when God's people refuse to move on at a stage, *§8.3*, they lose God's blessing to live as hostages to Satan's curse against God entering their world, *Psalm 50, 2-17* above. They become Satan's servants in a pact to Death as forecast for both 'Israel', *Isaiah 28, 18-20* and Gentiles, *§9.7.4*.

Jesus saw Satan as god of sinners testing Jesus' path to the cross, *§9.7.5, Luke 4, 5-6, §1.15*. It makes Satan the one above guilty of a greater sin at *John 19, 10-11, §7.10*. Jesus' test-punishment was legislated for by the devil, *§10.9*, to stop the King taking authority above him in a spiritual war, *1 Peter 3, 22 & Colossians 2, 13-18, §8.3*. Satan tests the Messiah, *as he did Job*, even intervening as God's hand to let the Christ through if a test is passed. For both walk paths under God's plan, *§10.9*, and God's might may disqualify either for unjust moves. If the non-sinning Christ is the sacrifice to God in *Psalm 50* above, evil may execute it by law of curse of association with sinners to be saved, *§9.7.2, §9.7.5*.

Satan's curse-law is his best shot at a just case to torture and topple God's King elect in creation: to make the King abandon subjects to Satan, *John 9, 11-18.* To bait the trap, Satan establishes, *for a while*, as acting deity to 'Israel', perhaps using prophets who call the Christ to test, *§8.6.* They then live on similar terms to the Christ when He comes. If He plays His part without fault, new terms to life on earth may begin where His sacrifice is gateway to a path to God, *§12.7, Psalm 50.* Jesus claims to be the Christ, *God's Son*, enough to resist temptation and punishment, *sin*, and be a cardinal sacrifice for sinners to God, *§7.10, §7.11.* His sacrifice or punishment was executed by sinners in the dark to parallel other sacrifices made in the dark to idols that anchor the rule of evil gods, *§7.8, §7.10, Luke 23, 34.*

Sinners aside, who is to blame for suffering on earth? Rebel gods say it is God's will to curse life because God is the prime mover for creation. They may deny evil has free-will unless it can break God's prophecies. God's reply is that His plan to prove title to creation, *Psalm 98*, is a just process to jail evil in hell by its own wish for curse-law. It will set life that loves God free from curse-law. To justly deliver that prize, mortal servants related to the Christ are preordained from before the world, *Jeremiah 1, 5; 1 Peter 1, 18-21*, to pass tests of evil, *§7.5*, by a 'fear of God' appropriate to the age. Rebel gods oppose by servants of spiritual tyranny in 'the Lord's' name, even unscrupulous liars who veil the face of a just God, *Isaiah 35, 4-6, §8.1*:

> Yes, this is what the Lord Almighty, the God of Israel says: "Do not let the prophets and diviners among you deceive you.
> Do not listen to the dreams you encourage them to have. They are prophesying lies to you in my name. I have not sent them," declares the Lord.
>
> Jeremiah 29, 8-9

> And we know that in all things God works for the good of those who love him, who have been called according to his purpose.
> For those God foreknew he also predestined to be conformed to the likeness of his Son, that he might be the firstborn among many brothers.
> And those he predestined he also called; those he called, he also justified; those he justified, he also glorified.
>
> Romans 8, 28-30

If a just God hates 'violence', *Psalm 98 & 11, §9.1, Isaiah 30, 1-15, §9.12*, mortals best seek Him in 'just' ways, *Isaiah 1, 15-20, §8.6, Proverbs 28, 5, §8.1.*

11.5 **Jesus' Discipline for Leaving the Rebellion against God,** *see also §9.7.5, §9.7.6, §10.8.*

Jesus is either the Christ or an antichrist, *§1*: a king against or for rebellion against God, *1 Samuel 8* below, *John 6, 14-15.* God's word may serve either view for freedom of faith, *§9.7.* Unjust views of 'Jesus' serve rebels, *§9.7.4.* Jesus' teaching is a pole in a duel of good against evil. His enemies set rival poles to make Jesus a star-guide to alternative camps in the 'truth'.

The proof that 'our' world is in rebellion against a just God is injustice to death, *§12.4.* Mortals need to depart rebellious alliances with Death. God's word says do it by covenant to God's peace led by the just Christ, *§9.7.5, Isaiah 9, 1-7 & 11 & 1, 15-20, §8.6.* God's peace is a form of 'justice' that is not oppressive, *Psalm 146, 7; Isaiah 30, 1-15, §9.12.* The covenant is a legal construct for forgiveness of sins of rebellion against God. It invokes God's Spirit, *§9.1, §10.13,* to seal loyalty to God against aggressive claims of a rebellion to own souls as slaves to sin and death. Thus, the guidance of the just Christ is a life and death issue as perspective on any 'humiliations' or self-control that Jesus asks of God's servants. Jesus asks to serve God firstly by not rebelling and keeping an orderly society:

Nevertheless, each one should retain the place in life that the Lord assigned to him and to which the Lord called him. This is the rule I lay down in all churches. Was a man already circumcised when he was called? He should not become uncircumcised. Was a man uncircumcised when he was called? He should not be circumcised. Circumcision is nothing and uncircumcision is nothing. Keeping God's commands is what counts. Each one should remain in the situation which he was in when God called him. Were you a slave when you were called? Don't let it trouble you—although if you can gain your freedom, do so. For he who was a slave when he was called is the Lord's freedman; similarly, he who was a free man when he was called is Christ's slave. You were brought at a price; do not become slaves of men.

1 Corinthians 7, 17-23

Slaves submit yourselves to your masters with all respect, not only to those who are good and considerate, but also to those who are harsh.

… … … …

Wives in the same way be submissive to your husbands so that if any of them do not believe the word, they may be won over without words by the behaviour of their wives, when they see the purity and reverence of your lives.

1 Peter 2, 18 & 3, 1-2

Jesus' 'Christians' maintain an orderly society in face of evil provocation until 'God's wrath' breaks enemy powers. His instruction sits most directly with the Old Testament in places such as *Lamentations 3, 25-33, §12.8*, or *Proverbs 25, 21-22* quoted by Paul below:

Bless those who persecute you; bless and do not curse. Rejoice with those who rejoice; mourn with those who mourn. Live in harmony with one another. Do not be proud, but be willing to associate with people of low position. Do not be conceited.
Do not repay anyone evil for evil. Be careful to do what is right in the eyes of everybody. If it is possible, as far as it depends on you, live at peace with everyone. Do not take revenge, my friends, but leave room for God's wrath, for it is written: "It is mine to avenge; I will repay," says the Lord. On the contrary:

"If your enemy is hungry, feed him;
if he is thirsty, give him something to drink.
In doing this, you will heap burning coals on his head."

Do not be overcome by evil, but overcome evil with good.
Romans 12, 14-21

Jesus' 'Christians' not in authority are to preach God's word submissive even to harsh authority, and to bless enemies, *not curse*, yet not serve causes of evil:

Do not be yoked together with unbelievers. For what do righteousness and wickedness have in common? Or what fellowships can light have with darkness? What harmony is there between Christ and Belial? What does a believer have in common with an unbeliever? What agreement is there between the temple of God and idols?
2 Corinthians 6, 14-16

But since we belong to the day, let us be self-controlled, putting on faith and love as a breastplate, and the hope of salvation as a helmet.
1 Thessalonians 5, 8

Jesus' 'Christians' are to wage a war that is not military but spiritual, *2 Corinthians 10, 3-5, §8.2*, led by Jesus from heaven, *1 Peter 3, 22, §8.3*, to crash houses of demons, *§7.15, Matthew 7, 24-27.* The goal is to untie souls from delusions, *§9.3, Matthew 12, 26-32, §9.8, 1 Corinthians 1, 18-21, §10.13*, from unjust ideals of the antichrist, *§10.3, Isaiah 24; 2 Corinthians 11, 3-4, §10.7.* The weaponry is the sword of truth, *God's word, §9.7.2*, and spiritual armour, *1 Thessalonians 5, 8* above, *§10.10, Romans 13, 14.* If 'Christians' gain authority, do they then wield the military sword for peace?:

everyone must submit himself to the
governing authorities. for there is no
authority except that which god has
established.
the authorities that exist have been
established by god. consequently, he
who rebels against the authority is
rebelling against what god has
instituted, and those who do so will
bring judgement on themselves. for
rulers hold no terror for those who
do right, but for those who do wrong.
do you want to be free from fear of
the one in authority? then do what is
right and he will commend you.
for he is god's servant to do you good.
but if you do wrong, be afraid, for he
does not bear the sword for nothing.
he is god's servant, and agent of
wrath to bring punishment on the
wrong-doer. therefore, it is necessary
to submit to the authorities, not only
because of possible punishment but
also because of conscience.
this is also why you pay taxes, for the
authorities are god's servants, who
give their full time to governing. give
everyone what you owe him: if you
owe taxes, pay taxes; if revenue, then
revenue; if respect, then respect; if
honor then honor.
romans 13, 1-7

A simple reading is that Jesus' 'Christians' wage military war for whoever they are under. That reading fails if they are not to fight one another over any cause, *e.g. whether a master race is to be Nazi or 'free', §9.2, §12.2.* One way out is to see God's word as a bilateral contractual form: ambidextrous for freedom of faith in the Christ or antichrist, *§8.1, §9.7.* It has double-meanings for freedom of faith making it a sealed book to the one-track wicked, *Daniel 12, 9-10*, or their prey, *Isaiah 35, 4-6, §8.1, Psalm 24, 3-5, Matthew 7, 12-14.* There is then freedom of unjust faith for an antichrist or 'Christ' who asks faith, total obedience, to a tyrannical 'peace'. Jesus' 'Christians' seek the just reading whereby those who fear God are not slaves to rulers who do not fear God yet ask total obedience.

The Old Testament agrees God legally endorses, *as his hand on evil*, even genocidal leaders who test His people's faith, like Pharaoh, *Psalm 66, 10-12, §7.9.* But that also reads as a condensed legal truth that unfolds to show evil authority is set up by rebel gods, *§7.9, §8.1, §9.7.6, Micah 4, 5, §12.8.* God cannot justly stop the gods raising leaders of evil so just law deems them as approved by God as His hand or wrath on evil, *sin.* In fact, they are God's enemies acting against God's direct will in a bid to depose God, *§8.1.* They obey 'the Lord' of rebellion, *Satan*, as 'God's wrath' on sin, *§10.8.*

Now 'justice' deems that God's authority backs evil rulers, *Micah 4, 5, §12.8*, so how can God free a people from them? People must first give God a just case by a stand of 'faith', *Psalm 66, 8-12, §7.9.* When God has that case, His gentle might obliges Satan who, *as God's left hand sets up rulers like Pharaoh or Hitler*, to be 'God's wrath' on them for failing him, *Zechariah 4, 6, §12.8.* For rebellion law curses evil for failing to end faith in a just God, *§3, §9.7.1.* Satan's way is violence, *e.g. war*, that gives credit to evil for ending evil. Satan sets up evil leaders to test faith in God but punishes them for failure, *§9.7.6.* The stages to God's plan betoken Satan as 'God's wrath' erasing one set of failures to send the next, *Genesis 15, 13-14, §7.8.* If a just God is not a direct curse on life, *§9.7.6, §10.8*, He cannot ask servants to be 'God's wrath' in war anymore than He can ask genocidal rulers to test His people. In both cases, the simple reading lacks in 'just' sense.

Divine law lets folk be 'God's wrath' on sinners even when they do not know God and spite His direct will, *§8.1.* Moses and David are not proof 'good' leaders ply the sword as 'God's wrath' on sin. They may be 'good' in the sense that they will repent of it and opened the path to God for sinners. Their lives ended under a curse to show all they did was not God's direct will even if to His legal will, *§10.8, §10.10.* For God is to forgive some scarlet sins at *Isaiah 1, 15-20, §8.6.* Did Satan lead Moses to kill 'kin' at *Exodus 32, 27-29, §10.8*? Two or more faces to 'the Lord' in Moses' age, *§10.8*, continue below where 'the Lord' is rejected as king of Israel, see also *§8.1* on Ezekiel. Whichever 'Lord' was rejected, to militarise Israel under kings is cast as poor witness to a just God, *Exodus 19, 5-6, §7.9*:

But when they said, "Give us a king to lead us, "this displeased Samuel; so he prayed to the Lord.
And the Lord told him: "Listen to all that the people are saying to you; it is not you they have rejected, but they have rejected me as their king. As they have done from the day I brought them out of Egypt until this day, forsaking me and serving other gods, so they are doing to you. Now listen to them; but warn them solemnly and let them know what the king who will reign over them will do."... ... ...
But the people refused to listen to Samuel. "No!" they said. "We want a king over us. Then we will be like all other nations, with a king to lead us and to go out before us and fight our battles."

1 Samuel 8, 6-9 & 19-20

God may save 'Israel', David, Moses, *if they so wish*, but by *1 Samuel 8* above, the just King of Israel might not be military? Military kings take credit for security, but, is it a trade of God's blessing for a curse-discount from Satan with popular support? Below, Paul quotes *Psalm 44* where the sword is proving no sure defence of 'Israel' from murdering foes, no sure blessing, *Psalm 44, 3-22*:

If God is for us, who can be against us? He who did not spare his own Son, but gave him up for us all— how will he not also, along with him, graciously give us all things? Who will bring any charge against those whom God has chosen? It is God who justifies. Who is he that condemns? Christ Jesus who died—more than that, who was raised to life—is at the right hand of God and is also interceding for us. Who shall separate us from the love of Christ? Shall trouble or hardship or persecution or famine or nakedness or danger or sword? As it is written:

"For your sake we face death all day long;
we are considered as sheep to be slaughtered."

Romans 8, 31-36

Why does the sword defend 'the Godly' fitfully in war? Perhaps a military Israel takes Satan as 'the Lord' who only acts as 'God's wrath' in ways to obfuscate the covenant path to the just King? *Psalm 44, 17-18.* Are God's people to grow out of military options to be a holy priesthood to a just God? *Exodus 19, 5-6, §7.9.* Whatever the path, it is by the just Christ, *Isaiah 1, 15-20, §8.6*, against an antichrist who is a menacing power of Death, *§1.2*, likely military in sympathy, *Isaiah 30, 1-15, §9.12.* To 'defenceless' sinners, the choice is hail the power of Death or die. Hell now, repent later?

To review on *Romans 13, 1-7* so far, just law obliges Satan to cull rulers who oppress, *do not defend*, God's people from persecution if their just faith holds. To oppress 'faith' draws a curse to injustice and death, e.g. apocalypse if by unjust doctrine, *Isaiah 24 & 30, 1-15, §9.12.* If 'the faithful' under test are patient, *Revelation 13, 10*, Satan acts as 'God's wrath' on foes for failing to end 'faith'. Love for foes is then a virtue in witness to save them from Death, yet, will heap coals on them if they refuse to be saved, *Romans 12, 14-21* above. 'God's wrath' may be act of evil on evil, never good on evil.

Evil will slay the wicked;
the foes of the righteous will be condemned.

Psalm 34, 21

If a military sword is not wielded in just faith, it is a curse-discount system of Satan's, *§9.8*, so wars to end war end at the antichrist who had Jesus murdered, *§10.13, Luke 21, 12-28, §9.1, Revelation 13.* The just read R*omans 13, 1-7* for a path to defy the antichrist, *Isaiah 1, 15-20, §8.6; 1 Corinthians 6, 1-9, §10.7.*

Now *Romans 13, 1-7* says all earthly authority is *endorsed by God* to be 'the sword' and agent of 'God's wrath' on 'wrongdoers'. But Jesus allows for a conflict of loyalties with authorities in reply to the Pharisees who tried to trap Him into rebellion against Rome:

then the pharisees went out and laid plans to trap him in his words.

... ...

"is it right to pay taxes to caesar or not?"
but jesus knowing their evil intent, said, "you hypocrites, why are you trying to trap me? show me the coin used for paying the tax." they brought him a denarius and he asked them.
"whose portrait is this? and whose inscription?"
"caesar's," they replied.
then he said to them, "give to caesar what is caesar's, and to god what is god's."
when they heard this, they were amazed. so they left him and went away.

matthew 22, 15 & 17-22

How is this consistent with *Romans 13*? Suppose to disobey earthly rulers makes a 'wrongdoer' but in rebellion curse-law as a lethal sin against Satan, *§9.7.1.* Now God is a higher ruler still who forgives sins by covenant, *Psalm 32.* It leaves a loophole to defy rulers for God by reading a 'wrongdoer' as one whose sin is not forgiven by God, *Psalm 32.* For example, the midwives below defied Pharaoh's order to kill firstborn Hebrew baby boys yet were blessed as it put fear of God above fear of Pharaoh, *above fear of Satan even*?:

the midwives, however, feared god and did not do what the king of egypt had told them to do; they let the boys live. then the king of egypt summoned the midwives and asked them, "why have you done this? why have you let the boys live?"
the midwives answered pharaoh, "hebrew women are not like egyptian women; they are vigorous and give birth before the midwives arrive."
so god was kind to the midwives and the people increased and became even more numerous.
and because the midwives feared god, he gave them families of their own.
then pharaoh gave the order to all his people: "every boy that is born you must throw in the nile, but let every girl live."

exodus 1, 17-22

Pharaoh later took up the sword as God's wrath against Israel so *Romans 13, 1-7* is strictly correct. It bids fear 'the one in authority'. We can read that as Pharaoh, or Satan, or a just God, *Matthew 10, 28, John 19, 11; Revelation 13, 15-17, §9.7.4.* To fear a just God empowers God to forgive sins against unjust rulers and may check Satan in his role as 'God's wrath' on 'wrongdoers'. It is clearer where Shadrach, Meshach, Abednego, *Daniel 1, 3-7,* were thrown into a furnace as 'wrongdoers' for loyalty to God in disobeying King Nebuchadnezzar's order to worship Satan's false gods and idols. The fire did not harm because God's blessing overrode 'God's wrath'. It elaborates *Genesis 12, 3*:

> Shadrach, Meshach and Abednego replied to the king, "O Nebuchadnezzar, we do not need to defend ourselves before you in this matter. If we are thrown into the blazing furnace, the God we serve is able to save us from it, and he will rescue us from your hand, O king. But even if he does not, we want you to know, O king, that we will not serve your gods or worship the image of gold you have set up."
>
> Daniel 3, 16-18

> "… … I will bless those who bless you, and whoever curses you I will curse; and all peoples on earth will be blessed through you."
>
> Genesis 12, 3

God's forgiveness of sins can at times takes precedence over curse-law, *§10.13.* To 'do what is right', we seek the just Spirit to God's law and to endure, *Revelation 13, 10.* To obey rulers who ask sin against God is cursed, even if the ruler is David:

> Satan rose up against Israel and incited David to take a census of Israel.
>
> … … … …
>
> Joab reported the number of fighting men to David: In all Israel there were one million one hundred thousand men who could handle a sword, including four hundred and seventy thousand in Judah.
>
> But Joab did not include Levi and Benjamin in the numbering, because the king's command was repulsive to him. This command was also evil in the sight of God; so he punished Israel.
>
> 1 Chronicles 21, 1 & 5-7

David was tempted to faith in military might. It tells us of a military antichrist else why a dire curse for it? See end of *§8.1* on God's and Satan's nature. David thereby feared Satan as 'one in authority' so 'God's wrath' shaped punishments to fully take David from God:

so gad went to david and said to him, "this is what the lord says: 'take your choice: three years of famine, three months of being swept away before your enemies, with their swords overtaking you, or three days of the sword of the lord—days of plague in the land, with the angel of the lord ravaging every part of israel.' now then, decide how i should answer the one who sent me."
david said to gad, "i am in deep distress. let me fall into the hands of the lord, for his mercy is very great; but do not let me fall into the hands of men."
so the lord sent a plague on israel, and seventy thousand men of israel fell dead. and god sent an angel to destroy jerusalem. but as the angel was doing so, the lord saw it and was grieved because of the calamity and said to the angel who was destroying the people, "enough! withdraw your hand." the angel of the lord was then standing at the threshing floor of araunah the jebusite.
david looked up and saw the angel of the lord standing between heaven and earth, with a drawn sword in his hand extended over jerusalem. then david and the elders, clothed in sackcloth, fell facedown.
david said to god, "was it not i who ordered the fighting men to be counted? i am the one who has sinned and done wrong. these are but sheep. what have they done? o lord my god, let your hand fall upon me and my family, but do not let this plague remain on your people.
1 chronicles 21, 11-17

The Lord who sent Gad gave David a terrifying choice of punishments yet David chose 'the Lord' of mercy not in that offer, *§10.8*. If curse by sword is not a just God's direct will, *§9.7.2*, Satan was 'the one who sent' Gad. It goes on to says God sent an angel of 'the Lord' to kill but 'the Lord' overrode in mercy. Now if God's angels kill, God's people can surely kill by the sword? But if God never directly takes life, *§1.2*, was 'the angel' a demon from Lord Satan, a hell's angel, *Matthew 25, 41, §11.4*, or 'son of God' in *§8.3*. For if Satan wins a title-contest, demons are God's true sons and angels. Thus, where it says God orders angels to kill, it may exemplify God accepting legal responsibility for what enemy rulers do in hand for hand law, *§8.1*, as Jesus may also do at *Revelation 6, 1-10* below. Now demons do not willingly obey God, so was it Lord Satan who countermanded 'the angel' to offer a curse-discount termed 'God's mercy' in law? The above is then of a bilateral contract like *Romans 13, 1-7* where faith that 'God' and 'angels' kill is hell's 'truth', *§9.7.6, §9.1, Isaiah 24*. Either faith fits under *Genesis 12, 3* above.

We thus see *Romans 13, 1-7* allows 'the sword' double-meaning as military force or God's word, *§9.7.2*, so it is part of a bilateral contract to Christ or antichrist. To summarise, *Romans 13, 1-7* asks to obey 'authority' in a way that respects personal choice of deity and bears the relevant sword (*God's word or/and the sword?*) as agent of 'God's wrath'. The trap, *pact to Death*, is to disobey or obey leaders in a spirit of antichrist as rebellion against God, *§10.13*. To fight the devil is not as easy as the unjust think but God's atonement for sin may cover scarlet sin till repentance dawns, *Isaiah 1, 15-20, §8.6*. To murder God's servants is not a fair way to end just faith but befalls some as a test of faith to oblige Satan to be 'God's wrath' on their murderers. To escape death and hell is by a just God's truth and repentance, else by showing mercy to bearers of God's truth, *§9.7.2*.

To hear and be intolerant of just faith risks a curse to harsh punishment in rebellion law as Satan's system. Those who reject the Christ in person may especially draw 'God's wrath', *Luke 10, 8-16, Matthew 26, 23-25*:

"If I had not come and spoken to them, they would not be guilty of sin. Now, however, they have no excuse for their sin.
He who hates me hates my Father as well. If I had not done among them what no one else did, they would not be guilty of sin. But now they have seen these miracles, and yet they have hated me and my Father.
But this is to fulfil what is written in their Law: 'They hated me without reason.' "
John 15, 22-25

"And blessed is anyone who takes no offence at me."
Matthew 11, 6 (NRSV)

Hate without reason flags to an unjust spirit of duty, *Psalm 38, 19*. It builds up houses of prejudice with a taboo against the offers of a just salvation that threaten their downfall, *Matthew 7, 24-27*. Such houses can be attentive to preachers of an unjust salvation who join or oppose, *chapter 5*, helping them rally for death and injustice in beasts of earth and sea, *§2*. The plague on such houses drives work on paths to end faith in a just God, *§1.3*, in denial of a tacit sacrifice of life to evil. Hence, 'science' on dogma that 'God's wrath', *the curse on life*, is 'natural' is a tragedy by its curse to a precarious 'natural' life, *§1.15, §10.4*. Is that house safe or built on an unjust edit of facts? *§9.3*. It plants all in fields struggling towards just truth past a supernaturally directed curse of disasters on sin, *§9.1, §10.1*:

now there were some present at that time who told Jesus about the Galileans whose blood Pilate had mixed with their sacrifices. Jesus answered, "do you think that these Galileans were worse sinners than all the other Galileans because they suffered this way? I tell you, no! But unless you repent, you too will all perish. Or those eighteen who died when the tower in Siloam fell on them—do you think they were more guilty than all the others living in Jerusalem? I tell you no! But unless you repent, you too will all perish."

then he told this parable: "a man had a fig tree, planted in his vineyard, and he went to look for fruit on it, but did not find any. So he said to the man who looked after the vineyard, 'For three years now I've been coming to look for fruit on this fig tree and haven't found any. Cut it down! Why should it use up the soil?'
" 'Sir,' the man replied, 'leave it alone for one more year, and I'll dig around it and fertilise it. If it bears fruit next year, fine! If not, then cut it down.' "
Luke 13, 1-9

Jesus teaches that if evil chokes faith in a field, Satan can summarily reap it as harvest for hell. Unjust doctrine is then a curse like on the Jews of *Isaiah 28.* A precarious life is allowed only whilst progress in quality of 'Christian' witness is not dead, *John 15, 1-2, Matthew 7, 19.* Hence, punishment for sin under curse-law is rated relative to potential for growth of truth, *John 15, 22-25* above. Thus, body circumcision was once truth enough to be blessed by 'God' but may not suffice now, *§8.3.* Today, teachings of the antichrist might not be a deadly sin since they can be progressed from to faith in the just Christ. But at times' end when rival faiths are fully fledged, *e.g. when Christ and antichrist openly vie*, it may be a deadly sin, *§9.7.4, §10.11.* Meanwhile, faith in an antichrist may enjoy a precarious life, *Isaiah 42, 16-25, §1.16*, cursed yet not damned if a just path forward is tolerated, *Matthew 11, 6 above, §9.7.2.*

Prophecies imply faith in the antichrist rises prior to the Christ's coming to suspend destruction of this world due to a curse on faith in the antichrist, *§8.6, §10.6.* The prejudiced are ready to sacrifice life for love of the antichrist. If martyred as 'saints', *Isaiah 14, 12-21, §8.3*, they only invoke 'God's wrath' if Satan sees it right to spread faith in the antichrist. The unjust choke open debate by prejudice. Such 'violence' defends a general curse on sin to establish a god who plays 'God's wrath' or hand against unjust doctrine, *Isaiah 24*:

see the Lord is going to lay waste the
earth
and devastate it;
he will ruin its face and scatter its
inhabitants—
it will be the same
for priest as for people,
for master as for servant,
for mistress as for maid,
for seller as for buyer,
for borrower as for lender,
for debtor as for creditor.
the earth will be completely laid
waste
and totally plundered.
the Lord has spoken this word.

the earth dries up and withers,
the world languishes and withers,
the exalted of the earth languish.
the earth is defiled by its people;
they have disobeyed the laws,
violated the statutes
and broken the everlasting covenant.
therefore a curse consumes the earth;
its people must bear their guilt.
therefore earth's inhabitants are
burned up,
and very few are left.

Isaiah 24, 1-6

Like *Luke 13, 1-9* above, this shows Satan's rebellion law knows no innocent victims, not children, *Psalm 51, 1-12, §10.10,* nor saints taken by association where a global curse culls sinners, *§9.7.2.* Just teaching on the curse is a true way to oppose evil, *§1.13.* The 'just' need to ask forgiveness for sin in a covenant to God via the just Christ. Outrage at 'innocent' lives lost to a curse is hollow unless it moves for just witness to the Christ, *Matthew 5, 43-48.* He may be the only path to truly oppose such outrages, *Luke 21, 12-28, §9.1.*

Sinners whose atonement for sin is flawed may turn to Satan for a curse-discount, e.g. by war. But wars to defend sin tee-up future disasters. If the enemy is at the door in disaster or war, it is by a curse on sin from long before. If at war's end, liberated 'innocents' are not on path to the Christ, they have a stay of execution, a curse-discount. But if the just Christ is not for military war, 'just' wars lead step by step to rule of an antichrist, *Isaiah 11, 4* above. '*Out of the frying pan into the fire*'. But scarlet sins may be covered if progress to the Christ follows, *Isaiah 1, 15-20, §8.6.* The Christ's rod on the path to 'freedom' is vital, *Proverbs 8, 26, §8.1, Isaiah 24 above & 30, 1-15, §9.12; 2 Peter 2, 19-22, §7.11*:

he will strike the earth with the rod
of his mouth; with the breath of his lips
he will slay the wicked.

Isaiah 11, 4

he who spares the rod hates his son,
but he who loves him is careful to
discipline him.

Proverbs 13, 24

Jesus claimed to act as God in human form, *i.e. the only human non-sinner, Isaiah 9, 6, Deuteronomy 18, 17-22* below. That implies the gospels are where God's nature is least veiled in 'God's word', *Job 28, 20-22, Daniel 12, 9-10, 2 Peter 3, 15-16, §10.5*:

Jesus answered, "I am the way and the truth and the life. No one comes to the Father except through me. If you really knew me, you would know my Father as well. From now on, you do know him and have seen him."
Philip said, "Lord show us the Father and that will be enough for us."
Jesus answered: "Don't you know me, Philip, even after I have been among you such a long time? Anyone who has seen me has seen the Father. How can you say 'Show us the Father'? Don't you believe that I am in the Father, and that the Father is in me? The words I say to you are not just my own.

John 14, 6-10

If other scripture seems to cavil with the gospels, Jesus' sheep hold to the gospels pending a proposal of divine law to reconcile all scripture, *Isaiah 1, 15-20, §8.6.* The gospels should fulfil prophecies on the Christ, *§8.1*:

The Lord said to me: "What they say is good. I will raise up for them a prophet like you from among their brothers; I will put my words in his mouth, and he will tell them everything I command him. If anyone does not listen to my words that the prophet speaks in my name, I myself will call him to account. But a prophet who presumes to speak in my name anything I have not commanded him to say, or a prophet who speaks in the name of other gods, must be put to death."
You may say to yourselves, "How can we know when a message has not been spoken by the Lord?"
If what a prophet proclaims in the name of the Lord does not take place or come true, that is a message the Lord has not spoken.

Deuteronomy 18, 17-22

In this, 'the Lord' of Israel calls God's King to test, see *§10.8.* He says wait and see if a prophet's word is true as may mean leaving it to 'God' to kill. But for freedom of faith, the violent may hear it as their 'God's' call to put prophets that offend to death, *Matthew 23, 33-39.* Does it say prophets from God cannot be killed? The unjust assess 'truth' by trial by ordeal, *§6.4, e.g. inquisition, Isaiah 53, §9.7.5; 1 Corinthians 1, 18-21, §10.13.* The ability to kill and torture is 'justice' to many a mind. Does faith in a military messiah abbreviate 'justice' for murder? *§9.7.6, Wisdom 2, 11, §9.2.*

If the gospels show a supernatural investment, is it divine or satanic? *§1.* Such investment obliges all 'Christians' to a stand on how the gospels bear on earlier and later scripture? *Isaiah 1, 15-20, §8.6.* Spiritual prejudice is not a safe guide if evil spirits lead to violate the eternal covenant, *Isaiah 24.* Do the gospels or God's word sanction military witness to God? If they do, God may spiritually lead in just wars to establish 'peace'. If not, is war always led by the antichrist as the company of Death? *Wisdom 1, 12-16, §1.2.* Should the world look to the Christ to seal 'peace' by force? or is it a platform of the antichrist? Outside the gospels, God's word may be more legally folded for freedom of faith, *a sealed book*, to respect even faith in a 'God' of murder, *§9.7.6.* That may apply to scripture before and after the gospels as below. Where is gentle Jesus in this extract from the book of Revelation or in *Daniel 7*?:

I saw heaven standing open and there before me was a white horse, whose rider is called Faithful and True. With justice he judges and makes war. His eyes are like blazing fire, and on his head are many crowns. He has a name written on him, that no one knows but himself. He is dressed in a robe dipped in blood, and his name is the Word of God. The armies of heaven were following him, riding on white horses and dressed in fine linen, white and clean. Out of his mouth comes a sharp sword with which to strike down the nations. "He will rule them with an iron scepter." He treads the winepress of the fury of the wrath of God Almighty. On his robe and on his thigh he has this name written:

KING OF KINGS AND LORD OF LORDS.

And I saw an angel standing in the sun, who cried in a loud voice to all the birds flying in midair, "Come, gather together for the great supper of God, so that you may eat the flesh of kings, generals, and mighty men, of horses and their riders, and the flesh of all people, free and slave, small and great."

Then I saw the beast and the kings of the earth and their armies gathered together to make war against the rider on the horse and his army. But the beast was captured, and with him the false prophet who had performed miraculous signs on his behalf. With these signs he had deluded those who had received the mark of the beast and worshipped his image. The two of them were thrown alive into the fiery lake of burning sulfur. The rest of them were killed with the sword that came out of the mouth of the rider on the horse, and all the birds gorged themselves on their flesh.

Revelation 19, 11-21

Is this about the Christ waging spiritual or/and military war? It is sin to tribute unjust acts to God or the Christ, *Job 1, 22*, but especially murder, *§9.7.6*. God's word is a sealed book, *Daniel 12, 9*, to the unjust, *§9.7.5, §9.7.6*. For freedom of faith, it can be read to honour an antichrist who takes the Christ's name as Jesus warns, *Matthew 24, 5; 2 Corinthians 11, 1-4*. Should we read into *Revelation* a just God who curses and kills for sin? *Proverbs 8, 36, §6.2*. The casework above shows all scripture can meet *Isaiah 11, 4* for a non-violent King who witnesses faithful and true on God's word to force Satan as 'God's wrath' to curse evil to death, *Psalm 34, 21* above.

The Christ as God's King leads in God's justice so has divine ability to discern and act by just truth. He would see safe paths under God's blessing to avoid Satan's curse-law traps, *as to walk on water*. He would discern Satan's being and skill in just law holding 'Israel' hostage, even putting Him to a humiliating test to save, *§10.9, Hosea 13, 9-14, Isaiah 53*. After the test, the King's full victory may be by gathering an elect about whom Satan's frightening anger trashes evil servants for failing to break just faith, *§10.11*. Evil servants blame the curse on their life not on Satan but on supporters of the just Christ they hate, *Psalm 2, §9.4*, even at world's end, *§10.11*. At that time, Satan may spiritually craze them as a house divided, *§9.8*, so they destroy one another over their failure to depose God. They may be bundled off like tin soldiers in Satan's power.

A 'God' of Death, *§1.2*, is not so easily read into the gospels, *Deuteronomy 18, 17-22* above. Jesus refused to lead armed rebellion, *Matthew 26, 52-56, §8.7, Romans 13, 1-7* above, and submitted to Pilate's authority at the cross, *1 Corinthians 1, 18-21, §10.13*. Pilate was set-up by Satan to test Jesus' faith, *John 19, 10-11, §7.10*, later killed for failing Satan in some way. Refusal to use military force suggests war is not in Jesus' sphere of witness to God, *§9.7.2*. Moses seemed of that spirit for a time in leading Israel out of Egypt. He awaited Pharaoh's consent to leave Egypt though Pharaoh turned genocidal. At length, Satan as God's wrath began to devastate Egypt for failure to end Israel's faith in 'God', *§7.9*. Moses was made Israel's leader then led to take up a military sword to kill brothers and quell a rebellion, *§10.8*. Did that put Israel under Satan as 'God's wrath' on sinners? If so, when did Israel turn back? *Isaiah 28, 11-22*.

Jesus now claims authority as overall ruler of this world to Satan's defeat, *1 Corinthians 15, 22-28, §7.10.* 'The lamb's' rule is from courts over this world, *§9.11*:

I watched as the Lamb opened the first of the seven seals. Then I heard one of the four living creatures say in a voice like thunder, "Come!"
I looked and there before me was a white horse!
Its rider held a bow, and he was given a crown, and he rode out as a conqueror bent on conquest.
When the Lamb opened the second seal, I heard the second living creature say, "Come!" Then another horse came out, a fiery red one. Its rider was given power to take peace from the earth and to make men slay each other. To him was given a large sword.
When the Lamb opened the third seal, I heard the third living creature say "Come!"
I looked and there before me was a black horse!
Its rider was holding a pair of scales in his hand. Then I heard what sounded like a voice among the four living creatures, saying, "A quart of wheat for a day's wages, and three quarts of barley for a day's wages, and do not damage the oil and the wine!"
When the Lamb opened the fourth seal, I heard the voice of the fourth living creature say, "Come!" I looked and there before me was a pale horse! Its rider was named Death, and Hades was following close behind him. They were given power over a fourth of the earth to kill by sword, famine and plague, and by the wild beasts of the earth.
When he opened the fifth seal, I saw under the alter the souls of those who had been slain because of the word of God and the testimony they had maintained. They called out in a loud voice, "How long, Sovereign Lord, holy and true, until you judge the inhabitants of the earth and avenge our blood?"

Revelation 6, 1-10

Now the King from a just God, *§3*, never quells evil by an unjust use of miraculous power. Why read the above to think 'the lamb' directly orders horsemen of the apocalypse to kill enemies? Are the horsemen not violent cursing spirits allied to the antichrist? enemies of Jesus? *Revelation 22, 1-3, §1.* For the pale horse, Death, *§9.4*, is Jesus' enemy to be destroyed at *1 Corinthians 15, 22-28, §7.10.* The white horse above, *cf.. the white horse in Revelation 19 above*, might betoken the 'justice' of the antichrist? Satan then sends out horsemen to justly meet the wishes or faith of leading sinners to drive their world to evolve in sin to depose God, and seal it under Satan, *§4, Isaiah 24.* The above seals are described in ambidextrous terms, *§8.1*, to respect freedom of faith about what 'justice' is.

The fifth seal shows a company of souls killed for one of the two kinds of 'saintly' witness to God's word, *Isaiah 14, 12-21, §8.3.* They demand 'God's' vengeance on evil at Judgement Day as seals evil into hell. 'The lamb' may meet that wish indirectly by upholding all God's law whereby Satan justly takes unforgiven and unforgiving to eternal punishment in hell, *§1, §9.1.* Their fate is hell whether mediated as God's direct or judicial will, *2 Peter 3, 9, §2.3, Luke 15, 7, §7.10.* The sins God cannot forgive, *1 John 5, 16-18, §9.7.2,* reject His Spirit of mercy, *Matthew 12, 26-32, §9.8.* Hell is shelter under a tyrannical curse from the just Spirit of mercy, *§1, §2, Isaiah 11, 6-9, §7.6 & 8, 19-22, §10.11.*

Sinners who want a military Christ to their gospels may envisage a 'justice' that swaps 'Jesus' for the antichrist whom Jesus fights. The antichrist asks to see it as God's direct will to punish the Christ to save sinners, *§9.7.5,* since that is 'God's' or Satan's direct will. Jesus asks to be seen as the good shepherd who willingly sacrifices His life to save subjects, *§9.7.2,* and is now justly resurrected as a spiritual authority who freed Paul from the antichrist to give *Romans 12* above:

"I am the good shepherd; I know my sheep and my sheep know me—just as the Father knows me and I know the Father—and I lay down my life for the sheep. I have other sheep that are not of this sheep pen. I must bring them also. They too will listen to my voice, and there will be one flock and one shepherd. The reason my Father loves me is that I lay down my life—only to take it up again. No one takes it from me, but I lay it down of my own accord. I have authority to lay it down and authority to take it up again. This command I received from my Father."

John 10, 14-18

Where 'God's wrath' murders loved ones, a war to defend may feel 'just'. Where folk are being shot, to shoot the gunman saves life short-term. People may rebel if rulers do not war, *1 Samuel 8, 6-20* above. God gives evil a just right to slay evil, *Psalm 34, 21* above, *as in hell, §9.1,* but it does not make evil 'just'. If war is sin against God, war adds to the sin that brings 'God's wrath' in first place. Wars give curse-discounts to some but on the road to apocalypse, *Luke 13, 1-9, Isaiah 24* above. To wage war 'the Christian way' may not stop Death fast but has any other strategy a prayer? *Isaiah 42, 16-25, §1.16.* Satan is a veil on 'the Christian way' in 'free' minds, *§10.5, Isaiah 6, 9-13; 2 Corinthians 3.*

11.6 Faiths and Theories: Just mercy

This theory of a just God, *§6.4*, as source of life-forces shows foreseeable stages to life under God. It explains religion by predicting mortals as farm stock in spiritual food chains between evil gods and God. It explains the observed course of 'science' by predicting the theory of original evolution as a delusive totemic cult, *§10.1, §9.5, §9.6, §10.4*, of unjust genius, *§9.2, §9.3, §9.11*. Thus, if that theory proves partial, *§1.4, §9.2, §9.3, §9.11*, this theory of God succeeds it. It sees original evolution a cult in the old drive to sacrifice youth to evil spirits via carved images of nature, *§4, §7.8, §10.2*. Now cults avoid just reason, *e.g. as an 'unnatural' abomination, §10.13*, which blinds to a just basis to 'God's word' but opens to a tyrannical 'God', *§8.1, §9.7.6*. They beg the question of whether mortals, *children to their gods*, *§4*, think children need, *§9.5*, *or have?*, rights in criminal law against teachers who would select them for unjust governments? *§1.4*. Such teachers ape the gods. Is to save from child-labour so cults can brainwash, *lie to kids on industrial scales*, 'civilised'? *§9.2, §10.4*:

The theory of soul and guardian spirits in *§10.5* says people live with spirits from birth. A mortal is seasoned to life with afflicting evil spirits, angels, or the Spirit even if unaware of it, *§7.3*. Mortals can be blind to being in a spiritual room till changes in spiritual station, say, on joining a cult or religion. They may then experience a degree of spiritual baptism into a doppelgänger god or God, and even suffer severe inner spiritual conflict between them as Paul describes, *§10.10, §8.5*. To become aware of spirits can be traumatic but religions provide backup teaching so spiritual birds of a feather can flock together. Spirits thereby pen and shepherd flocks.

If people are blind to spirits, are they spiritually static? perhaps for a just reason, *§1.5, §4.10*. There is much evidence for spiritual forces in religions of the world. For some, the first step to freedom may be to see that mortals may live at the mercy of spirits, *Luke 13, 1-9, §5*. The evidence for spirit forces obliges a material science of reality to a theory of spiritual reality to validate its research, *§10.1*, else is it one more cult putting authority above just reason? The 'Secret World of Cults' by Sarah Moran classifies cults as follows. There are ones searching for ancient wisdom. There are esoteric and Christian offshoot cults, UFO cults, doomsday cults, sinister sects in magic and murder, modern militant cults that fight for beliefs in terrorism. Viewing pictures of cult-groups, it is easy to think some kind of mind-control science or spirit is behind it. Are they spiritually penned in behaviour and beliefs others find dubious?

Now cults, being unjust, would be paths to meet the devil. He is thought to be a megalomaniac murderer, *§9.7.5*. who lies to life in order to play 'God' with it: *i.e. to lead its evolution in sin, Genesis 3, 2-5, §7.4, chapter 9, §3*. He sells life a pact to Death, *§10.8*. In that light, why would teachers not warn that 'natural' science might be a cult? *§10.4, §6.2*, and secular society a lie to empower it (*their cult?*) *§1.4*.

'God's word' is allegedly to educate in God's justice, *§5*. It focuses on mortal need to atone for sin by pledge to a sacrifice related to the Messiah, *§4, Isaiah 1, 15-20, §8.6 & 7, 9-14* below. Justice may require fair teaching on what faith in the just Christ is? *Psalm 104, 8, §10.3*. It may decry simple slavery to religious or 'scientific' rules, *§10.13, Isaiah 28*, or rulers, *§5*, by tracking God as the just Spirit, *Isaiah 11, 6-9, §7.6, 1 Corinthians 1, 17 & 2, §7.15, Romans 10, 9-10, §10.3*. 'The just' show sympathy with a spirit of just process, *Isaiah 1, 15-20, §8.6, Matthew 17, 20, Luke 7, 35*, as might lead to know the just Christ, *2 Corinthians 10, 3-5, §8.2.*

Justice may only rule on earth if evil gods lose ground in a contest of laws over the 'justice' mortals wish to believe in, *§3*. Freedom of faith implies right to unjust faiths, *§9.7.1*, which may constrain just witness to God, *Isaiah 53, 7-9, Matthew 27, 11-26*. Hell's unjust 'justice' may be 'good' enough to many. The unjust love evil gods, *§10.5, §10.10*, and rule by 'magic' arts, *Psalm 35, 19-20*, to a destructive end, *Isaiah 24, 1-6, §5, Matthew 7, 24-29 & 12, 26-32, §9.8*. If folk are entitled to know evil, *§10.6*, they are entitled to intimidating and slippery shows of evil to help prove 'faith' in evil:

> help, lord, for the godly are no more; the faithful have vanished from among men. everyone lies to his neighbour; their flattering lips speak with deception.
>
> psalm 12, 1-2

Those who raise injustice as their 'God' may raise hell as their 'heaven', *§9.1, §9.7.5*. Faith in idols, *e.g. unjust ideas of God*, is in evil gods or spirits. Such 'faith' is not in God, *§10.3*, but may still presume on God's mercy to save from evil, *Isaiah 10, 20-22, §8.6, Romans 2, 17-24, §8.5*. The pitfall is to fully deny God's mercy in a spirit of antichrist, *Isaiah 24, 1-6, §5*. Thus, *Isaiah 24* suggests strongholds of faith in the antichrist that the true Christ witnesses to, and against, *John 10, 14-18, §5, Matthew 12, 26-32, §9.8*. His coming may be amidst fear and mourning, *Matthew 24, 7-22 & 23-30, §10.11*, for God confronts rebellion against God to save souls from injustice: an accursed 'peace', *Isaiah 24, 1-6, §5*. The just may put faith in the mercy of God's King and Son: the just Christ, *§10.3*. But their right to it is disputed and tested by evil. Is such loyalty to be confirmed at Judgement Day? *Isaiah 35, 4-6, §8.1, Matthew 25, 31-41, §4, John 10, 14-16, §6*. The saved accept enough 'justice' to enable God's mercy, *§10.3*.

'Faith' is more than lip-service, *§10.3, Psalm 12, 1-2* above as why people of 'faith' may be scoffed at:

therefore, since we have been justified through faith, we have peace with god through our lord jesus christ, through whom we have gained access by faith into this grace in which we stand.
romans 5, 1-2

What defines good 'faith'? The 'Sea of Faith' sect scoffs at God's existence yet sets its 'faith' by meditations in 'Christian' ritual dogma. The 'International Raelian Movement' decries God's reality for aliens 25,000 years ahead of us called 'the Elohim': *a biblical Hebrew term linked to God.* The Elohim made us in their image by DNA modification giving the prophets and God's word to guide a 'faithful' in the way of the Elohim: *liars who play god with 'lesser' life*? Their Jesus' resurrection was a cloning by the Elohim to join many prophets in their grand evolutionary plan, *§9.7.4.* But Jesus saw lying to play god with life as satanic? *§9.2, §10.8.* Where do such faiths stand if an antichrist taking Jesus' name shows up? or at Judgement Day? Now if such cults are not real 'faith', what of sects to totem-science? *§10.4*, or to the Virgin and saints? *§10.11.* Any saint can be an idol by lies about them. Even 'the Christ' who loves works of the devil is an idol: *the antichrist §10.11.* The just Christ confronts unjust 'faith' to save from sins by which evil claims souls. Just 'faith' then orbits a just atonement for sin in its bid to be loyal to God, *Wisdom 14, 27-31, §9.5.* If heaven is faith in Justice, *§9.7.5*, injustice is to respect lack of faith in a just God:

then jesus told his disciples a parable to show them that they should always pray and not give up. he said: "in a certain town there was a judge who neither feared god nor cared about men.
and there was a widow in that town who kept coming to him with the plea, 'grant me justice against my adversary.'
"for some time he refused. but finally he said to himself, 'even though i don't fear god or care about men, yet because this widow keeps bothering me, i will see that she gets justice, so that she won't eventually wear me out with her complaining!' "
and the lord said, "listen to what the unjust judge says. and will not god bring about justice for his chosen ones, who cry out to him day and night?
i tell you, he will see that they get justice, and quickly. however, when the son of man comes, will he find faith on the earth?"
luke 18, 1-8

The woman represents faith in justice fighting a curse of association with souls whose lack of faith invokes unjust judges, *§9.7.2.* Now 'peace' ends injustice. If mortals cannot abide just efforts to tell Christ from antichrist, do they defend injustice till God's holy arm is seen at the King's coming? *Psalm 98*, to gather up souls who reject death and curse for the blessings of Justice, *Deuteronomy 30, 17-20, §7.8, Isaiah 9, 2-7 & 11, 4 & 35, 4-6, §8.1, Proverbs 8, 36, §6.2.* But under spiritual duress, it is said folk flee in panic or shame from God's mercy into the dark, *§7.3.* A just education, *if feasible*, upholds children's rights to faith in Justice:

a truthful witness saves lives,
but a false witness is deceitful.
he who fears the lord has a secure fortress,
and for his children it will be a refuge.
the fear of the lord is a fountain of life,
turning a man from the snares of death.
a large population is a king's glory, but without subjects a prince is ruined.
a patient man has great understanding,
but a quick-tempered man displays folly.
a heart at peace gives life to the body,
but envy rots the bones.
he who oppresses the poor shows contempt for their maker,
but whoever is kind to the needy honours god.
when calamity comes, the wicked are brought down,
but even in death the righteous have refuge.
wisdom reposes in the heart of the discerning
and even among fools she lets herself be known.
righteousness exalts a nation,
but sin is a disgrace to any people.
a king delights in a wise servant,
but a shameful servant incurs his wrath.

proverbs 14, 25-35

The above looks at first sight like folksy art. To analyse it may bring out its science or wisdom on the terms to mortal life. It talks about rules of curse and blessing on people and nations. It flags to the Prince of Peace to be crowned King of subjects He delivers by just witness. They are saved from a shadow kingdom of lies holding subjects to Death. It may be run by a shadow to the Prince of Peace: *the Prince of Darkness.* That dark noble kills life in the jurisdiction of curse-laws that uphold his playing 'God', *§10.8*, to worlds of sin, evil. His curse is on folk loyal to evil, *Micah 4, 5, e.g. any to sin against God*, shaped to dash life off paths to a just God, *§9.1, §3, Isaiah 14, 12-21, §8.3.* God's mercy is to save all Justice can, even souls of weak of faith who barely know God's word, *Isaiah 35, 4-6, §8.1,§10.3*, as below.

Mortals are invited to sup life-forces from God directly, *§1*, by reading God 'justly', *§9.7.6.* 'God's word' is then like spiritual bread to feed faith in God, *Deuteronomy 8, 2-3, Psalm 1, 1-3, Matthew 4, 4 above & 6, 11.*

> Jesus answered, "It is written: 'Man does not live on bread alone, but on every word that comes from the mouth of God.' "
>
> Matthew 4, 4

But 'faith' may be tested for being within just limits set between Satan and God for knowing a just God, *§7.3.* Satan is a master to sees lies spiritually fed, *Isaiah 24*, so weak faith seeks a just God subject to test, *§8.5, §10.3*:

> Accept him whose faith is weak, without passing judgement on disputable matters. One man's faith allows him to eat everything, but another man, whose faith is weak, eats only vegetables. The man who eats everything must not look down on him who does not, and the man who does not eat everything must not condemn the man who does, for God has accepted him. Who are you to judge someone else's servant? To his own master he stands or falls. And he will stand, for the Lord is able to make him stand.
>
> … … …
>
> For none of us lives to himself alone and none of us dies to himself alone. If we live, we live to the Lord; and if we die, we die to the Lord. So whether we live or die, we belong to the Lord. For this very reason, Christ died and returned to life so that he might be the Lord of both the dead and the living.
>
> You then, why do you judge your brother? Or why do you look down on your brother? For we will all stand before God's judgement seat.
>
> … … …
>
> Therefore let us stop passing judgement on one another. Instead, make up your mind not to put any stumbling block or obstacle in your brother's way. As one who is in the Lord Jesus, I am fully convinced that no food is unclean in itself. But if anyone regards something as unclean, then it is for him unclean. If your brother is distressed because of what you eat, you are no longer acting in love. Do not by your eating destroy your brother for whom Christ died. Do not allow what you consider good to be spoken of as evil. For the kingdom of God is not a matter of eating and drinking, but of righteousness, peace and joy in the Holy Spirit,
>
> Romans 14, 1-4 & 7-10 & 13-17

Weak faith is double-minded, *James 4, 6-10, §10.5*, due to Satan disputing 'the faithful' for his subjects. The weak are stained by 'faith' in the spirit of the world as slaves to sin in areas, *§10.10.*

Paul instructs to preach the gospel and conduct oneself sensitive to social situations and times, *§7.15*:

> though I am free and belong to no man, I make myself a slave to everyone, to win as many as possible. to the Jews I became like a Jew, to win the Jews. to those under the law I became like one under the law (though I myself am not under the law), so as to win those under the law. to those not having the law I became like one not having the law (though I am not free from God's law but am under Christ's law), so as to win those not having the law. to the weak I became weak, to win the weak. I have become all things to all men so that by all possible means I might save some. I do all this for sake of the gospel, that I may share in its blessings.
>
> 1 Corinthians 9, 19-23

Paul claimed just faith by sight of the risen Jesus as an authority few can claim yet many lack faith in Paul's word, *§10.4.* How are the weak of faith to tell just from unjust faith amongst teachers for more than one 'Jesus'? *2 Corinthians 11, 4, §10.7.* It seems everyone's right, *Isaiah 24*, to take in God's word and pass out unjust teaching to please the sinful nature, *§10.5.* The test is to be fair on God's word according to what the age allows and to make atonement for sin over what is left dark in the age, *§8.1, §10.6*:

> "don't you see that nothing that enters a man from the outside can make him 'unclean'? for it does not go into his heart but his stomach, and then out of his body." (in saying this, Jesus declared all foods clean.") he went on: "what comes out of a man is what makes him 'unclean.' for from within men's hearts, come evil thoughts, sexual immorality, theft, murder, adultery, greed, malice, deceit, lewdness, envy, slander, arrogance and folly. all these evils come from inside and make a man 'unclean.' "
>
> Mark 7, 18-23

Jesus may see the human heart as a complex of soul with good and evil spirit, *§7.11, §10.5.* Mortals may be homes to personal inherited ancestral evil spirit(s) that feed in their lives in spiritual food-chains, *§2, §9.1, §10.5, 1 Corinthians 2, 11-14, §10.5; Galatians 5, 17-21, §7.11.* The Spirit is God's offer of a spiritual circumcision of that sinful nature, *§10.5, §8.3*, by a just case to cut personal possessive evil spirits from souls.

Our right to know good and evil, *Genesis, 3, 2-5, §7.4,* leads to a duel of just and unjust in God's temple, *Isaiah 7, 9-14* below, *Romans 14* above. Even signs as acute as below lead to rival camps in 'just' faith, *§9.7.4, §10.7*:

" 'If you do not stand firm in your faith, you will not stand at all.' "

..."Therefore the Lord himself will give you a sign: the virgin will be with child and will give birth to a son,..."

Isaiah 7, 9 & 14

Just faith is aptly tolerant in witness to a just God. That may seem weak to the unjust seeking to serve 'God' in tyrannical ways. The world is franchised to let unjust faiths develop for freedom of faith. If such faith is slow to establish, 'weak' faith may inherit the bulk of religion to 'God' so the world can labour deep into sin. Put another way, Satan may restrict 'the just' in God's temples by mortal right to 'freedom' of unjust faith outside it, *Acts 17, 22-32, §8.7,* and aim to shame the temples when his unjust teaching is exposed, *§8.6.* But the true cause of vague witness is the outer world rejecting witness to a just God: *its just deserts.*

By *Romans 14* above, just faith is tolerant in disputable matters and accepts indisputable facts in relation to God's word. The just then wage war on unjust 'faith', *§5,* by indisputable facts of God's word according to what is justly clarified in an age, *Isaiah 1, 15-20, §8.6.* The indisputable facts to God's word may advance as disputable matters recede to fetter the world, *Psalm 2, §9.4, Proverbs 8, 1-9, §8.1.* Will the world stand by Justice? or injustice? *Proverbs 28, 5, §8.1.* If God is perfect, *§1,* He is the Spirit of Justice to defend life from Death, *§10.13.* The devil as God's enemy, *§13.1,* is then source of Death as spirit of injustice. The choice may be life with Justice else the pure tyranny of Death.

As standards of 'justice' progress, theories or faiths that pact to Death may be stranded in just courts. If a just god exists, society best shape laws with Justice to survive, *Isaiah 28,* but may struggle on under a curse whilst enacting laws to the devil's tyranny, *Isaiah 30, 1-15, §9.12, Micah 4, 5.* Injustice exists to satisfy souls who wish to see neighbours cursed. God's word implies conflict on the nature of freedom or 'justice', *Isaiah 5, 20,* even inside 'God's' temples. People are free to define 'justice' as their way to support God or Satan: to know good and evil, life or Death.

If a just God exists, there is a case for His nature that courts on earth cannot uphold an objection as reasonable against, *Isaiah 11, 4, §11.5; 2 Thessalonians 2, 9-12, §3.9; Psalm 2, §9.4; Luke 21, 12-28, §9.1.* How else may God justly save from Death? *Isaiah 35, 4-6, §8.1, Psalm 98,* if evil gods hold sinners in a pact to death, *Isaiah 13, 9-14, §8.1, Micah 4, 5.* By Judgement Day, a just God has proven title to loyal souls in courts against objections of evil gods that He is not their true God, *Isaiah 14, 12-21, §8.3.* Now God's word can seem to say 'God' kills, wars, does as He likes. That gives freedom of faith for a tyrannical 'God' or a just God who wishes to give mortals Justice, *§9.7*:

"... declare to my people their rebellion
and to the house of Jacob their sins.
For day after day they seek me out;
they seem eager to know my ways,
as if they were a nation that does what is right
and has not forsaken the commands of its God.
They ask me for just decisions
and seem eager for God to come near them.
'Why have we fasted', they say, and you have not seen it?... ... "
"Is not this the kind of fasting I have chosen:
to loose the chains of injustice
and untie the cords of the yoke,
to set the oppressed free
and break every yoke?
... ...
"...If you do away with the yoke of oppression,
with the pointing finger and malicious talk,
and if you spend yourselves in behalf of the hungry
and satisfy the needs of the oppressed,
then your light will rise in the darkness, ..."
"... If you call the Sabbath a delight
and the Lord's holy day honourable,
and if you honour it by not going your way
and not doing as you please or speaking idle words,
then you will find your joy in the Lord,
and I will cause you to ride on the heights of the land and to feast on the inheritance of your father Jacob."
The mouth of the Lord has spoken.
Isaiah 58, 1-3, 6, 9-10, 13-14

As for *Isaiah 55, 1-11, §1,* this may be Satan's mocking word to his 'faithful', '*declare to my people their rebellion*', urging to temper dark ritual by 'justice', *§9.7.5, §9.7.6, §10.11.* It calls to establish a just Sabbath and an end to malicious talk, *§10.7, §10.12,* meeting *Isaiah 1, 13-20 & 30, 1-15, §9.12.* Does it steel against Jesus' teaching on a 'just' Sabbath? *Matthew 24, 7-22, §10.10.* It needs a heart to tell Justice from tyranny, *chapter 12.*

12.1 Freedom and Oppression are matters of Justice

The rule of law draws a line between truth related to evidence for legal disputes and rights of folk to any faith they wish, *e.g. faith in 'crime'*. Some would set the line by selfish political bargain, others by a just science on the terms to mortal life. It is a bread-line for scholars, *§1.4, §1.5*, as why teachers of unjust sciences have to crook the line, *§9.2, §9.11.*

In theory, order among ants or scholars shows an agreed rule of law. Ants seem slaves to chemical laws but folk slaves to 'spirits', *§11.4*, where materialists conjecture that spirits are chemical forces but the religious think real spiritual beings exist, *§2, §6.5, §8.3, §7.12, §9.11, §10.1.* Either way, folk are bridled as if by 'spiritual forces' that guide or possess, *§7.1 to §7.6, §8.3, §10.5*, so all fields on earth, *§9.1*, raise 'gods' and 'devils' in antagonistic spirits of duty, *§11.4*:

Chapter 6 models this world as a god-devil cosmos where a 'god' is a faith credited to defend life and a 'devil' is a faith credited to curse to death. One soul's 'god' is another's 'devil'. As sustainable life is stronger than death, the true 'god' is the almighty. That a 'devil' can contest rule of the Almighty suggests the justice of 'god' respects life's wishes, *§11.3*, or freedom of faith, *chapter 9*.

A catholic curse to death drives mortals to seek shelter by personal 'gods' against personal 'devils' as faiths on sustainable and unsustainable life, *§10.1.* The many ways to die suggest the 'devil' is a murderer whose native language is lies, *John 8, 42-44, §13.3.* If the 'devil' is Lord of Death, he can threaten use of deadly force to deceive, *1 Kings 19, 11-13, §10.2.* Mortals may take his power of Death as vital to plans to sacrifice life to him. Sacrifices are asked by wrath or mind-control sciences, propaganda. To think a 'devil' is vital to life is to think he can overcome a 'god' to cheat death. The 'devil' preaches to folk as death in denial.

Now a just 'god' may only rule life that agrees to his law. Others may put faith in an unjust 'god' or tyrant for a home land, *Isaiah 14, 18-21, Micah 4, 5, §8.* War may arise as in *§11.3*, when unjust 'gods' lead bids for global power. A just 'god' may triumph over an unjust 'devil' by helping subjects to a binding just pledge to His rule, *Psalm 98.* A 'devil' is then a tyrant seeking to rule by interpreting life's wishes as for tyranny before a 'just' god's rule, *§9.1, Isaiah 14, 12-21, §8.3.* His devilish 'justice' is in deceit led oppression, forces of darkness, that a just God lightens by offer of life with 'justice'. If mortals fail to fully reject 'tyranny', tests of faith may follow as stressful accelerators of tendencies, *§7.5.* It is a dispute about what 'justice' is? *Proverbs 28, 5, §8.1*, in rival definitions of 'oppression' and 'freedom', *Isaiah 9, 2-7; Psalm 2, §9.4; 2 Peter 2, 19, §11.4.* Regard for freedom of faith may oblige a real God to finesse a real devil into openly admitting defeat. The devil may then retreat into hell with all souls he can justly take using a power of vindictive injustice to destroy the earth. To summarise, the battle of good and evil is about beliefs to sustain life long-term, *§2.3*, expressed in ideas of 'justice'.

A religion enshrines a spirit of duty in work and ritual, *§10.5*, so all work may be basic to some religion. An evil spirit of duty leads life into a desert of lie and death, *John 1, 19-23, §10.5, e.g. a wilderness of sin, §10.8.* Political history is then about bids of the spiritually biassed or franchised to order society. Some parties, *e.g. for a secular society led by 'science'*, push dogma that lying spirits of duty form religion but not 'science', *§1.5, Introduction to Volume 1.* Power bids are by religious and scientific leaders, tyrants and judicial bodies who, *like devil and God*, claim to respect 'wish of the people'. Governments educate in their 'justice': *conflict management for state life or border disputes.* They try to be 'just' by their own scales of 'justice'.

Both a 'just' God and 'just' devil invite to marry into *their* 'justice' as the highest science. Hence, education is shaped by whether local courts accept doubts on 'God' as reasonable? *§9.7.6, Psalm 2, §9.4.* Does 'justice' exist as keeper of a promised land? *§6.4, Jeremiah 32, 22-23*:

> follow justice and justice alone, so that you may live and possess the land the lord your god is giving you.
> deuteronomy 16, 20

A just God stands by just reason. Hence, a failure to prove God suggests lack in just reason, *e.g. conspiracy to pervert justice by unjust science or religion, §1.3.* Such a conspiracy needs to unhitch 'reason' from just law, say, to float a 'pure' science above 'justice', *chapter 1*, or ask an inapt respect for cultural diversity. For *their* academic freedom, unjust scholars spin lies for power, *'freedom' from 'oppression'*, for schools. But if just reason fairly relates truth to evidence, only just scholars want a society less oppressive of truth. To the unjust, the just 'oppress' by exposing lies fielded for jobs in education, *§9.2*, as 'cause' of violence. However, if an evil curse to apocalypse exists, it is on the unjust, *§10.1, Isaiah 24.*

The just definition of an inflammatory theory is one to back injustice, *forms of violence.* To prove a just theory of God is never a cause of violence but to oppose a just God, the unjust equate God to *their* violence, *§1.3.* Suppose 'peace' is to establish a just theory of life then can 'peace', *truth*, be had with no talk of a just split of just from unjust? *Matthew 24, 35-41.* Scholars may never truly comprehend religious conflict in the middle east or at Jesus' crucifixion, *§9.7.5, Matthew 26, 11-44*, except as a war of just or unjust ideas of 'God'.

A just proof of God may confirm people are spiritually biassed. For God is Spirit, the devil is spirit, so reality may be spirited, *§9.1.* Do scholars then run spiritual traps as any religion? *§4* to *§11.* By unjust spirits, they are vain or overconfident, *chapter 6*, of a genius for new dogmas that lie. Folk may only tell 'good' philosophy, science or religion as issues of truth or lie in relation to 'justice', *1 Kings 22, 16, §13.12, John 8, 47, §8.4 & 16, 13, §9.4.* It raises the Spirit of Justice. Can there be a just division of 'science' from religion by denying spirits bear on 'scientific' minds? *§10.2*, The prize is evidently privilege as public servants in politics or education in what might be arcane religious fraud? *§9.2, §10.13.* Is it science or religion? *§9.3, §10.1.*

Education respects people's wishes but subject to a rule of law. Without law and order there is no society to pay scholars. Scholars either accept they are paid to avoid illicit theories in education else run a closet tyranny to select others of a spirit to weed out threats to 'freedom' under 'the system' (*tyranny*). Now an inflammatory theory must divorce 'reason' from just law. Suppose an unjust 'science' takes schools over then it may fruit in law and order problems, *§9.2.* That entitles courts to regulate theories in education. A good theory satisfies a court as truth related to evidence, *§6.4.* Any theory to disestablish 'justice' (*theories from hell?*), *i.e. to conjecture an origin where 'justice' has no jurisdiction or place*, should be justly examined, *§1.4, §1.17, §6.4, §9.2, §9.11.*

A scholar's ethics index to their theory of reality. If few theories are viable, even fence-sitting scholars may be ascribed ethics consistent with theories they tacitly work for. It brings out a gulf in ethics between a natural or supernatural 'peace'. A natural 'peace' rests on the hypothesis of material causes, *§10.1*, as may lead to impatient power-bids for resources, *Daniel 7, 15-27.* It may presume folk are, *ask to be treated as?*, highly evolved yet disposable ants. However, a supernatural 'peace' may indict that view as serving world conflict. It may warn of 'nature-scientists' as dealers in carved images, *§9.2*, who ask child-sacrifice to idols in media and education? *§9.6, §10.13.* It may tell of religious crooks in 'science' trying to make life of unlimited vitality in a world kept from God, *§11.3.* It may warn that unjust 'sciences' curse to apocalypse as a rival 'big bang theory', *§1.15.* It then opposes a moral and rational 'elite' striving to 'reform' the law for survival by 'natural science' as an unjust cult, *§1.4, §9.2, §9.11.*

WWII has evidence of oppressive eugenics movements eager to rid of 'God's people' (*the just?*) by satanic prejudice, *§9.2.* Churchill's finest hour speech, *§1.17*, asked 'Christians' to rally against a perverted science, *§9.2, §9.11.* It asked to turn to God even if the bearing of 'Christianity' in regard to war is hazy, *§11.5.* In supernatural reality, his speech may mark a ruling in divine law to respect enduring 'faith' of 'God's people': to end open war for education to dispel ignorance on the issues, *Daniel 12, 9-13.* WWII may now continue by educational programs in which some seek by stealth to take what force failed to win: 'peace' based on a master race of 'gods' allied to an antichrist, *§9.2.*

'Natural' law asserts a cause and effect approximate to supernatural laws of curses and blessings under God, *Deuteronomy 30, 17-20, §7.8.* That approximation can be evil if God exists. It may carry a curse to injustice rising to complicity in crimes like the holocaust, *§1.15, §9.3.* Most understand bad science curses by side-effects like pollution, *§1.13.* If God exists, the pollution to 'natural' science may include even plagues it asks funds to cure. Now the afflicted only know they need help, and faithful suffers with unfaithful by curse of association, *§9.7.2.* The devil's strategy is to afflict the unfaithful but keep them from flight to God by curse-discount systems: *e.g. medical/faith cures.* Good science accepts curse-discount systems in ways to oppose further curse, *§9.8, e.g. giving thanks to God for all mercies granted by evil gods to delay God's open rule, §5.6.*

To index professional ethics to theories may expose scholars on public funds who gamble with public safety, *§10.13.* For ethics rest on faith about what 'good' science is, *i.e. faith on who will win a contest to define 'just' law.* Is it ethical to see people as evolved ants in a bid for power or to seek a rule of just law to dispel ignorance about God? *§1.17.* It is said God's truth feels oppressive to souls trapped by evil spirits, *Proverbs 28, 5, §8.1, §10.5, Psalm 2, §9.4,* so God's foes promise 'freedom' meaning freedom from a just God, *2 Peter 2, 19, §11.4.* Scholars in warring spirits of duty assert their ethics in art, science, religion, *§9.6.* To even discern justice from tyranny may be hard for a harassed people, *§11.4, Proverbs 1, 20-33, §9.7.6.*

the sceptre of the wicked will not remain over the land allotted to the righteous, ...
psalm 125, 3

Tyranny is defined as a science of government to force or deceive into supporting and rewarding it:

> a tyrannical ruler lacks judgement,
> but he who hates ill-gotten gain will
> enjoy a long life.
> Proverbs 28, 16

The definition cannot directly say tyranny is evil. Faith in tyranny hopes to prove it the form of rule most fit to survive. A tyranny might one day be loved for a 'successful' society? Rule by oppression or lie might prove the only 'truth' fit to survive? Such 'idealism' identifies tyranny with evolving sciences seeking to establish their 'justice'. They are dogmatic so religious in spirit. Tyrannies seek to establish their dogma as the definition of 'good', *§2.3.* If a tyranny fails, leaders can keep faith by seeing it as punishment for not being strong or tyrannical enough, and try again. Even tyrannies that fail repeatedly are not necessarily evil though a curse on many. Their leaders can claim failed bids removed weaknesses in society to improve it.

Every tyranny thus hails itself as 'good', *the one true faith,* but some or all are evil. Their propaganda offers unjust objects or gods as 'good', *Luke 22, 25-26, §11.3.* They seek to perfect their mind-control sciences to rule. They may even brainwash a 'democracy'. It requires prejudiced scholars to select for mutual sins or intellectual failings, *§1.7, §9.2.* In that context, the theory of natural selection, *survival of the fittest,* is surely total faith in tyranny? a tyrant's charter, *chapter 6.* Nevertheless, it might justly be proven true by a scientific case relating to evidence, *§6.4.* However, the short-cut to 'proving' it is to back or become the most fit tyranny as in WWII. The enemy tyrannies must fear is a just God yet they can defer to 'God' by presuming an unjust god who is above the law, *§1.1.* Is the god to survival of the fit in a natural universe not a tyrant?

The real proof that a just God exists is that no tyranny is fit to survive under justly enacted laws, *§9.1.* This world fits as part of that proof, *chapter 11.* In principle, a just court may one day limit freedom of all tyrannies, religious or scientific, *e.g. confine to hell.* Are courts the part of the ecology to show a theory of natural selection a lie? *unfit to survive.* To rebel against just process is a bid for tyranny, *e.g. against a just God, Luke 21, 12-28 & 1 John 3, 4-5, §9.1; 2 Thessalonians 2, 9-12, §9.3, Revelation 13, 11-17, §9.7.4.*

'God's word', *Jeremiah 10, 23-24 & 2 Peter 2, 19, §11.4*, suggests all government is a mind-control science of some kind, even God's, *Isaiah 11, 6-9, §7.6.* 'Freedom' is a threshold education for fair choice of government, *e.g. to fit for life in heaven or death in hell, §9.1.* God may allow a place to know good and evil, *Genesis 3, 2-5, §7.4.* If Justice is life and blessing but injustice is Death and curse, *Genesis 12, 3, §11.5, Isaiah 10, 1-3*, scholars who divorce 'freedom' from 'justice' may curse pupils to death. Anarchists who see 'freedom' as the absence of law may find that equates to survival of the fittest in hell, *§9.1*, if that is the rational extension to life by the idea. But would they work to prove it?

Now 'God's word', i*f synonymous with the Christ, §11.1, Deuteronomy 18, 17-22, §11.6 & John 14, 6-10, §11.5*, sees freedom as a life and death issue married to an idea of social justice to which the Christ is party, *Proverbs 8, 36, §6.2 & 28, 5, §8.1.* It calls to argue from indisputable facts of the Christ's word, *Deuteronomy 18, 17-22, §11.5*, for a path towards full Justice, *Isaiah 1, 15-20, §8.6.* The trap is simple faith in lie and Death that for ever balks at reason on just premises, *§1.7, Psalm 35, 19, Proverbs 1, 20-23, §9.7.6.* Death may build vast houses in denial of reason on just foundations, *chapter 5*, penning the confused in twilight zones, *§10.6, 1 Corinthians 3, 9-15, §10.2.* Only just casework may be of a ladder to the 'freedom' of heaven, *Proverbs 28, 5, §8.1.* Rival ladders abound, *§8.5*:

True 'Christianity' may link 'freedom' and social justice. Compare it to that area of Buddhism that sees 'freedom' as to detach from the world by meditation. Some say the highest fulfilment to that ladder is extinction of personal consciousness or Nirodh which few achieve. It could be construed as a ladder to death, *§4.5, chapter 6.* Some Buddhists agree spirits exist and some teach love for neighbours as seemingly fine social justice without mention of God, *perhaps a path to God.* But love is judged by its objects, *1 Timothy 6, 10, §1.14*, and what love upholds devotion to death? *Proverbs 8, 36, §6.2.* To add a faith in reincarnation might seem to refute a death-wish but how is reincarnation run? where does it lead? *§10.1.*

'Christianity' is to meditate on a just God's word to seek the Spirit, *Deuteronomy 18, 17-22, §11.5*, who is source of life and salvation from death. It only achieves its goal of life if God's word is read in a just spirit else it too is a ladder to death in form of the punishing 'justice' of the antichrist, *§10.13.* For freedom of faith, God's word allows for grave error on all cultural paths to be crisscrossed by truth up to end-times. If God is source of life, a government ascribing acts of death, curse, punishment to a just God may be in the dark by a poor view of 'justice'. A simple faith in death or murder may not build a just society but their power is hard to escape, *§9.7.6.*

Jesus made priority claims for the gospels in the disputable matter of God's just nature, *§11.5*, and may have raised Paul's scripture in the disputable matter of how Jesus says to guide Gentiles out of relationship with Satan to God, *Acts 26, 9-18, §8.3*, to show God to Israel, *Isaiah 1, 15-20, §8.6, Acts 9, 15, §10.4.*

"...a bruised reed he will not break, and a smoldering wick he will not snuff out, till he leads justice to victory..."
matthew 12, 20/ isaiah 42, 3

Jesus shows supernatural authority as his/His claim to be God incarnate is ongoing, *§11.1, §9.7.4, Isaiah 9, 6.* Is Jesus the prophesied one talking as God to a world in the dark where 'God's word' is a sealed book? *Isaiah 35, 4-6, §8.1, Daniel 12, 9-10, §3, Deuteronomy 18, 17-22, §11.5.* Paul's authority is by a claim to special sight of Jesus ensuring Paul's word is sound despite hard areas, *1 Corinthians 7, 25, §10.4 & 14, 32-40, §10.4.* To split faith in God from faith in antichrist may rest on acts, *§9.7.2*, and on indisputable matters *for the age, §11.5.*

Now if God's law respects freedom of faith, *chapter 9*, tyrants rule by will or sin of leading groups, *e.g. scholars.* The freedom to sin is subject to amplification in just law by God and gods to test hearts and minds: *see what mortals really want? §8.2.* For that, the unjust appear 'blessed', *Psalm 73*, by 'the secret power of lawlessness', *2 Thessalonians, 2, 7,* helping them establish to test 'faith', *§4.10.* But 'God's word' warns oppression, *rule by unjust law*, will fail so be cursed to ruin, *Isaiah 30, 1-15, §9.12.* If that 'God's' idea of tyranny arises, it is to test faith in 'justice' for souls who wish 'blessings' of tyranny by evil spirits of duty, *§10.5*, as puts 'the just' to test. Thus, to avoid the curse of tyranny, scholars best agree academic 'freedom' is for supporting Justice (*God?*).

Under a just God, a tyrant like the King of Babylon, *Isaiah 14, 13-14, §1.2*, has a mandate based on will of some people, *be it a will for revenge, resources, power by unjust science, or to make a holy land by force, Psalm 50 & 73.* If faith in a just God survives oppression, divine law may call time on a tyranny by further edict. To eyes blind to spiritual courts, *§9.11*, tyrants fall by ill-luck, revolution, economic failure, war, natural disaster. But those things come by a curse on failure to end faith in a just God. An interplay of just faith and tyranny is seen in *Daniel.* Any government may fall by a curse till a just God's blessing, *rule*, is beyond doubt, *Psalm 98, §11.5.*

A classic case of tyranny downed by a curse is Pharaoh's oppression of the Hebrews. Some Hebrew's led in worship of Egyptian idols as a trap of evil gods. They gave the gods a case for Pharaoh, *a trainee evil god,* to test all by tyranny to see if faith in God would buckle? It did not so a curse then struck Egypt for failure, and to make it release the Hebrews, *§7.9.* All trials of 'God's people' may reflect lack of direction at crossroads on the path to a just God, *Deuteronomy 16, 20* above, *Isaiah 42, 16-25, §1.16.* Israel is tempted to sins that invoke tyrannies to test faith. The Gentiles experience the same laws. The world of tyranny, *unjust law*, has no long term future if the author of injustice is obliged to curse the earth to an apocalyptic end at his defeat, *Isaiah 24*, to veil retreat of curse-law into hell, *§11.5.* 'Peace' is true justice and may prove a God-centred science, *Psalm 98*, tested by tyrannies, *Micah 4, 5, §8.*

A democrat may define 'freedom' as a mind-control science to run with the grain of good minds: *'our' innate good qualities.* The religious can agree in principle if their heaven is not oppressive, I*saiah 30, 1-15, §9.12.* It remains to argue over what 'our' good mind is? *§1.7, §10.5, Isaiah 5, 20.* As people are erratic, it suggests that spiritual reinforcement in both good and evil qualities of mind may be usual. Are souls who kill and curse spiritually reinforced in good or evil qualities of 'our' minds? *i.e. dressed for heaven or hell? §9.1.* Conflicting opinion shows rival views of 'justice' to rival spirits, *§9.7.6, Proverbs 28, 5, §8.1.* All democrats may live as slaves to spiritual forces, *§11.4.*

An advantage of democracy can be its aim to respect will of the people. If democratic rulers are cursed to fall by will of the people, legal order can continue. But democracy does not refute a curse to war, plague or crime on weak faith in 'justice' among voters, *Luke 13, 1-9 & Isaiah 24, 1-6, §11.5.* Lack of faith, *say to confuse antichrist for Christ*, may lead outside a just atonement for sin whereby death and curse hit all by curse of association, *§9.7.2.* To take leaders towards 'God' may earn best curse-discount or stability as why loyalty to David or Moses served 'Israel'. 'Christians' wage war by standing up for just law synonymous with the Christ and freedom of faith. They may question seditious or inflammatory theories in education though many see it as oppression of (*their*) 'freedom'. However, being alive is basic to true 'freedom', *§11.1.* What 'justice' truly defends life? *1 Corinthians 1, 18-24, §10.13.*

12.2 The professional ethics or license of 'natural' science

Scholars are obliged to support a rule of law but may lay down what just law is in theories, *§1*. In a just universe, (*who says not? for what crooked aim?*) faith in unjust science or religion defines 'prejudice'. It establishes as a conspiracy to pervert justice, *i.e. to deny some fair rights.* Now scholars in a conspiracy to pervert justice can proclaim 'freedom', (*for funding their interests*), *Proverbs 28, 5, §8.1, Psalm 38, 19.* So, why have 'the free' failed to develop branches of the rational education system relating to a just God? *Taboo? Lack of ability? Duplicity?* Thus, scholars against the proof of God in *§1.5* begin compromised. It is a case to redirect funds to school for researchers on a just God. Now no doubt about God is strictly 'reasonable' till shown to fit in a global map to prove God's justice a flawed concept in reality, *§1.3.* If that map is not up front, are doubters prejudiced? By asking to see such maps, we expose ideas of 'justice'.

To map out theories that scholars presume to work for on public funds reduces chances of deception. Suppose we ask if scholars can close gates, *exit arguments*, leading out of 'secular' labyrinths? *§1.6.* The gates may appear unimportant by authority of scholars in a systematic taboo on work to prove a just God, *chapter 5.* There is a dogma that to prove 'God' is impossible. Certainly, to prove an unjust 'God' is impossible save by tyranny, but a just God is proven by just process else not just, *§6.4.* A taboo about reality does not excuse need for sound foundations, *§1.7*, or giving jobs to specialists who lack in scruples about stoking social prejudices to defend a prevailing idea of 'science', *§1.8, §9.3, Isaiah 29, 13-16, §1.5.* To blind with 'science' can be a religious failing in support of inflammatory theories, *§1.*

A just court is entitled to call any profession to account in relation to theories it expects society to live by. A theory may be formally licensed for public funding given a good case for it as truth related to evidence and *provided* it supports 'justice'. The map of *§1.6* shows no good case, *as yet*, to divorce 'pure' science from 'justice'. How many scholars take public funds for illicit bids to divorce 'reason' from 'justice'? *§9.2.* A formal license system may be needed to end systematic discrimination against lines of reason that respect 'justice', *§11.4*, for 'freedom' to employ scholars interested in working for just truth. It need not imply a licence to 'creationism', 'intelligent design' or 'evolution', *§1.5.* It may confirm the equity of theories on lines of

§7, chapters 11, 13.

If a just God exists, no other theory is legitimate. Even in earthly courts, it need not be hard to prove a just God exists if all rival theories are gross, *e.g. support murder and lie by a faithful, John 8, 42-45, §13.3.* Could education today be run by tacit crooks? teachers of faith in right to bend 'justice' for popular tyrannies? *§9.2.*

their mouths lay claim to heaven, and their tongues take possession of the earth.

therefore their people turn to them and drink up waters in abundance.
psalm 73, 9-10

The rival theories of 'justice' can be classified as to a just God, or, to tyrannical 'gods' but who claim to be 'just', *Proverbs 28, 5, §8.1, Micah 4, 5*, or, tyranny by 'secular' theories but that *might* invoke unjust gods. A first step is to evaluate 'secular' theories of no deity at all. There is one well-developed theory in 'natural' science, *chapter 1.* Now natural science is said to imply an ethic of survival of the fit in regard to reproduction and death in a world ruled by natural forces. The ethic is to obey natural forces that cause 'good' behaviour, *altruism say.* But other natural forces curse to death so the bottom line to natural ethics is what survives wins, *chapter 6.* The professional ethic may temper altruism by ability to turn to crime when the fit judge time right for advantage or survival? But that is an inflammatory theory as defined in *§1.* Leopold and Loeb, *see panel §11.4*, deduced the super-fit are ready to break any law for gain in life. Those for survival as the fit must then say why they are not also for opportunistic murder and theft? How does their theory not tacitly incite to violate Articles 1 & 2 of the Human Rights Act?

The most fit nature-faith scientists would arguably be ones ready to find and serve the most able tyrants, *e.g. ones of ability to get away with murder*? Thus, the core professional ethic seems to endorse tyranny. Tyrannies issue propaganda on their 'altruistic' wish to serve (*tyranny on*) society. By this analysis, for nature-faith 'science' to gain its licence likely hinges on it claiming in court that natural forces exist (*the spirit of 'good' science*?) holding the true fit from crime and tyranny. They then ask all professions to live in harmony with their natural forces or spirit. Their 'justice' is to obey natural science, *e.g. to save the world from punishing disasters due to natural forces.* That casts them as a religion of a spiritual 'feel-good' prejudice to define or term every spiritual force as a natural force.

The 'feel-good' natural forces to natural science would relate to ancient 'gods' who cursed to 'natural' disasters, *§8.3, §10.4, §5.* Priests of those gods threaten disasters unless folk worship their gods' carved images of nature, their totems, for curse-relief, *§7.8.* To be sure of a licence, 'natural science' needs a solid case that the gods are myth: a Grand Unified Theory to replace *every* spirit by natural forces, *§10.1.* The professional ethic is thus to claim to serve 'natural' spirits better than prophets for 'God' who were 'deluded'. It is a path to enshrine 'spirits' as a natural resource by pushing the Spirit of a just God out of the way for survival of the species, *idolaters?*, *§6.16*, guided by violent 'natural' forces invoked, *sent by the gods*, to 'help' them to power, *Isaiah 24.* They are to harness natural spiritual forces both by machines and breeding a spiritual master race to, *of course*, deny a just God, *§9.2, §9.11.* Under this analysis, those for a just God can reasonably call 'natural' science satanic, *§9.2, §9.6, §10.4, §10.13.*

Natural science is of a breed to take fire from heaven by perfecting 'natural' spiritual prejudice, *Revelation 13, 11-18.* The professional ethic is natural 'justice' by harnessing natural power-sources. It enslaves society to natural forces that guide towards sacrifice of 'the unfit', *§9.2.* That ethic or spirit may lead to a prophesied mind-control abomination that curses to desolation, to be set in God's place, *§6.16, §10.11.* Mind-control by spirit of nature allows no valid reason to opt out of 'nature'. Is its professional ethic for a tyranny to end all tyrannies, gambling it will not doom the world by a just curse on unjust sciences, *§10.1.* Safe science?

Now if natural scientists can be inspired to quantum physics, general relativity, 'natural' selection, why not inspired to say where such theories lead in their professional ethics? Is natural science a road to bring tyrants like Hitler to power and dash hopes of just law under a just God? Suppose the fit need to claim in court to be better than their theory? In other words, they deny their ethics are as bad as the theory implies to look 'good' in court. That would prove them either hypocrites in saying they believed it in first place else hypocrites whenever need arises to cheat for power. Is hypocrisy of the professional ethic to natural selection? The whole theory could be a cultish arcane fraud in relation to public funds: a power bid to incarnate evil gods by fuddling ethical standards. Many of its faithful, *schoolchildren*, may be brainwashed cult members.

Scholars for survival as the fit know public funding depends on a respectable front. Is the professional ethic to systematically deny a just God exists until a sympathetic tyrant of faith in natural forces takes them under his wing? Today, natural science is preached as a path for the fit to survive disasters by natural forces and take comforts. Funds are asked to relieve nature's curse. But 'natural' disasters also occur in supernatural science, *Isaiah 24, 19-23 & 51, 5-6, §7.11*, where natural scientists may in fact invoke them as the curse on seeking power by unjust sciences, *§10.1, Wisdom 14, 27-31, §9.5.* The supernatural world is also about survival but of life fit or fortunate by a god's blessing, *§8.3, Job 1, Psalm 22 & 73*, as a theory to cover facts better, New Scientist, *9 February 2002, p28-31.*

Natural science may relieve suffering but also cause it if an unjust science, *§9.3.* With the devil as patron, *§10.4*, it could curse billions to poverty and illness that just science opposes by accepting religion as evidence real afflicting spirits exist, *§9.8* to *§9.11.* Is a natural cosmos not astronomically unlikely? *§10.13*, so more likely a spiritual enchantment to lure into deep space away from seeking Justice. If natural science is a tyranny and blocked, the faithful may go (*remain*?) underground as befits a profession or cult rooted in deceit or oppression. Satan's plan is to send disasters on his world of unjust science or religion to drive the wicked to ruthlessly back tyrannies for survival, *§9.1.*

Under a just God, die-hard natural scientists may be kin to gods of crime hoping to breed life of unlimited vitality to disprove God, *§11.3.* Their call is to tempt to crimes that invoke an incarnation of the devil, *§6.14, §6.16, §13.5.* It does not mean natural scientists like Darwin, *who had a 'Christian' wife, §11*, are damned. But if courts rule an untrustworthy criminal ethic to the theory, it supports the case that the theory in *§11.3* is true. It leaves natural science in the context of *§11.3* for schools as, *possibly*, the one fully legitimate theory. It may be hard to put curse-discounts by unjust science into perspective of a just science of curses and blessings in supernatural reality. It may be for courts to decide if 'justice' is to follow a just God or 'natural' science? Just principles do not oppress 'science' if Justice is the highest science. If natural science weighs light on the scales of justice, what of other unjust theories, *e.g. faith in gods who by basic court standards appear to murder and lie? §9.7.5, §9.7.6.*

12.3 The professional ethics or licence to 'God's word'

Science is a form of progress to the truth based on conjecture and rebuttal. The conjecture-rebuttal model allows science to conjecture anything it likes as long as it is open to rebuttal yet, to respect courts, not lies to empower criminal gangs, *§6.4, §9.2, §9.3.*

Take the conjecture that 'God's word' is an unreliable human construct. It tacitly submits it to a field of human expertise, *§1.4, §13, chapter 6,* making it a power bid that 'God's word' covers as by mortals who are slaves to spirits, *§11.4,* to unjust gods, *§6.* 'God's word' indicts the conjecture as the unreliable construct. It says to read 'God's word' as spiritually determined so no prophesy is solely a prophet's own understanding:

> these are the last words of david:
> "the oracle of david son of jesse,
> the oracle of the man exalted by the most high,
> the man anointed by the god of jacob,
> israel's singer of songs:
> "the spirit of the lord spoke through me;
> his word was on my tongue...."
> 2 samuel 23, 1-2

> above all, you must understand that no prophesy of scripture came about by the prophet's own interpretation. for prophesy never had its origin in the will of man, but men spoke from god as they were carried along by the holy spirit.
> 2 peter 1, 20-21

This allows for many layers of meaning to God-breathed scripture. There may be what a prophet read into it in its day, and, what spirits guide both just and unjust readers to read into it in several later ages. The word may be tightly regulated under divine law in regard to right of mortals to freedom of faith? *chapter 9.*

'God's word' says it is only fully opened in relation to the Just Spirit, *Isaiah 11, 6-9, §7.6, 1 Corinthians 2, 11-16, 1 John 2, 20-29.* But unjust spirits may bend 'faith' into an 'f'-word for swearing love for injustice, *2 Chronicles 18, 18-27, Isaiah 24, 1-6, §11.5 & 5, 20, §8.1, Jeremiah 7, 4-10, §9.10, Micah 4, 5, §8, Luke 13, 23-30.* The trap is spiritual adultery away from the just Spirit, *§8.5, §10.4, §11.* Thus, where a charismatic faithful uphold a conjecture on God's word, it does not imply it is 'just', *Isaiah 24.* Tests of spirit apply such as those to focus on the Christ, *§10.3,* but the root to all tests of spirit is a person's own sense of 'justice'.

'God's word' states clearly, *even to scholars who dismiss it by skill in other fields*, that the art to understanding it is just law. To sum up, *Proverbs 8, 1-9, §8.1*, says 'God's word' is 'just'. That means it is set or coded under just law. And, *Daniel 12, 9-10* below says it is a sealed book to the wicked who, *by Proverbs 28, 5, §8.1*, do not understand 'justice', *2 Peter 3, 15-16, §10.5*. Faith in unjust ideas of 'justice' are a calling to prophets or priests of unjust gods in power bids for God's temple, *Psalm 50 & 73*, to defame a just God. That idea may upset spiritual comfort in some places but offers an opportunity for sinners to move on closer to God by 'just' reason, *§8.5, §8.6*. For theology is faith in Justice. The wicked deface Justice as 'blasphemy' to their spirit:

> He replied, "Go your way, Daniel, because the words are closed up and sealed until the time of the end. Many will be purified, made spotless and refined, but the wicked will continue to be wicked. None of the wicked will understand, but those who are wise will understand.
>
> Daniel 12, 9-10

That 'God's word' is a just construct is implicit to a Day of Judgement to divide by tastes in 'justice'. The house of the unjust may weep and gnash teeth as part of a way of life in hell they chose, *§9.1*. God's word is fully just if it lets spirits attend readers, *§7, Galatians 4, 1-9, §5.10*, for fairly dividing souls by spirit loyalties taken up in a duel of good and evil to open 'God's word'. Therefore, the art by which God's word might be inerrant is a technical field related to covenants or contracts in human law. That may sound easier than 'natural' science but in reality spiritual prejudice, *superstitious fear*, may close eyes and ears to it, *§8.1, §9.4, §10.5*.

In summary, a just court will not licence judgements on 'God's word' from fields low on 'justice' even if known depth of just content to God's word is low. Another basic truth for courts, *see Isaiah 28, 16-19, or, 'Many will come in my name' Matthew 24, 5*, is that 'God's word' has to be a bilateral contract between either a just God (*party of first, second, third parts termed 'the Lord' by followers*) or between a devil (*party of fourth part termed 'the Lord' by followers*) and mortals (*parties of fifth part termed sinners by every Lord*). People are 'free' to vote for 'the Lord' by a type of 'justice' ascribed to God in His word, *Isaiah 28, 18*, or mimed to in daily life, *Romans 2, 14-16*. 'God's word' thus reflects sin in unjust readings though God is not a mirror to sin, *§9.1*.

In a just contractual sense, 'God's word' must be inerrant to fairly divide goats from sheep. But for freedom of faith, it may abound in every type of 'error' that respects 'expert' fields deficient in 'justice'. The 'errors' are not set by a just God but by unjust gods with a just case, *based on freedom of faith*, to guide, curse and feed on mortals who love their unjust ways, *Proverbs 8, 36, §6.2.* God upholds freedom of faith for crooked paths, *Proverbs 8, 1-9, §8.1*, so the wicked can bed with evil spirits in a pact to divide goats from sheep. Mortals are thereby given a fair choice of guardian spirits, *§9.1, Genesis 3, 2-5, §7.4, Micah 4, 5, §8, Daniel 12, 1.*

To belong to God, people do not have to be inerrant at 'God's word' but to show some just conduct represented as sufficient loyalty to God. Do scriptures even have to be fully known for that? *Romans 2, 14-16.* The beatitudes are to show just conduct that fights injustice and death with a just God. Might the first be saying God's servants are not all charismatic, or, not all rich?:

"Blessed are the poor in spirit, for theirs is the kingdom of heaven,
Blessed are those who mourn, for they will be comforted.
Blessed are the meek,
for they will inherit the earth.
Blessed are those who hunger and thirst for righteousness,
for they will be filled.
Blessed are the merciful,
for they will be shown mercy.
Blessed are the pure in heart, for they will see God.
Blessed are the peacemakers, for they will be called sons of God.
Blessed are those who are persecuted because of righteousness, for theirs is the kingdom of heaven.

"Blessed are you when people insult you, persecute you and falsely say all kinds of evil against you because of me. Rejoice and be glad, because great is your reward in heaven, for in the same way they persecuted the prophets who went before you."
Matthew 5, 3-10

To fail to find just content to 'God's word' may activate a pact to injustice, *§4*, whereby we need a Godly lawyer, *the Christ, say*, to undo citizenship of hell at Judgement Day, *Matthew 25, 31-41, §11.4.* Jesus suggested God sees folk as like children refusing to eat their greens in doctrinal areas they are weak, *Romans 14, 1-17, §11.6.* At or by a Day of Judgement, our advocate in heaven is to prove sinners redeemable hypocrites to save from Satan's claim to own. Who has no secret faults or merits? *Psalm 19, 12-13 & 90, 8.*

If God is just, any field built on the conjecture that 'God's word' is an unreliable human construct is not worthy of a license. The unjust may organise it as a democratic brotherhood of love of injustice: *conspiracy to pervert justice, §1, §9.7.4.* If sinners genuinely want to be just, they uphold just principles. A just court may qualify 'God's word' by its expertise in principles of justice on which the court is run. A tyrannical court cannot guide past a tyrannical god. God's experts on 'justice' may not be simple enforcers of laws, *§15.*

Every science asserting 'reality' qualifies 'God's word' from some direction. Thus, every science seeks to be licensed in principles of 'justice' for the task. It is not 'good' science to dogmatically discount need for a just license to 'pure' theory. However, if in reality a just God supports freedom of faith, *chapter 9*, faith in unjust science, *disunion of 'science' from 'just' law*, must be let to develop. That may oblige many of 'God's people' to dwell in twilight zones amongst lies that bar the Spirit to them, *Wisdom 1, 3-5, §10.3*, so they cannot defend 'justice' effectively, *§10.6.* It may not effect right to know their angels? *Daniel 12, 1.* Only after unjust sciences are established, *wide-spread*, may the Spirit sanction increase in just signal to unjust noise ratio in readings of 'God's word' to fulfil prophesy. 'God's word' then rises as a stumbling block to unjust science, clearing the path to God, *Isaiah 1, 15-20, §8.6.*

Just science is to assess scriptures for inerrant Justice though it be a mess of contradiction to rival areas of knowledge. Under God's guarantee of freedom of faith to mortals, a predictable (*to God*) succession in species of theories may occur in a duel of good and evil. The coming of 'just' science is to indict unjust sciences as seditious, *§9.2.* The unjust can vote against a just God by support for injustice, *'violence', Isaiah 53, Luke 20, 9-16, §7.10, §10.2.* In summary, the conjecture that 'God's word' is an unreliable human construct is rebutted by reading it from a field of expertise more advanced in Justice than fields from which it is said to be an unreliable human construct. Just science is then a path to God in education, *Psalm 98.* It may bring out just content to 'God's word' for just courts to license a just God as rightful heir to education and field cases on His just nature: *ideas of Justice.* To clear God of murder against unjust religion or science may be necessary to that licence forming a proof for a just God: *§9.7.5, §9.7.6, §10.8. Q.E.D.?*

12.4 Theory of Justice and God: Crime and Forgiveness

The aim of 'justice' is to value and sustain worthwhile life, *chapter 6*, subject to the hypothesis that upholding truth related to evidence in every dispute can sustain life, *is not a deadly failing.* Without a unique truth not all disputes can be justly settled. Till it is found, freedom of faith is just and for a while after, *Micah 4, 5.*

Crime strips life of just rights, *is a curse to injustice.* To preach that crime, *i.e. existence of evil,* proves an unjust universe is crime, *evil,* in a just universe. Instead, the just put faith, *Habakkuk 2, 4,* in just process to end crime as a just God then says, *Matthew 24, 7-22, §10.11, Romans 8, 19-22, §6.12 & 6, 23, §7.10.* Thus, if crooks cannot repent of cursing neighbours in a just universe, *Psalm 11, §9.1,* they will die out by Justice. They truly die unless there is a just path to repent and lift their death-sentence, *Matthew 5, 44, §9.7.6*:

> the lord is righteous in all his ways
> and loving toward all he has made....
> ...
> the lord watches over all who love
> him, but all the wicked he will destroy.
> psalm 145, 17, 20

Only crooks take life by unjust 'justice', *§11.5,* so that in a just world, crooks only die by a just case, *§11.3, Proverbs 8, 36, §6.2.* But we are mortals, *§1.2,* so are crooks if this is a just universe? *§9.7.2, Matthew 7, 11-12, §10.2.* True Justice then hinges on a path to repent of crime and be saved. A law profession on any other basis may be a tyranny, *a curse to injustice, Luke 18, 1-8, §11.6, Romans 2, 17-24, §8.5.* If this is a just universe, Justice will end both crime and death, *Isaiah 25, 8, §11.1; 1 Corinthians 15, 22-28, §7.10.*

Mortals learn 'justice' as a science of 'just' process that rewards good, punishes crime. To understand Justice more fully may help crooks give up crime, *hell?,* and find just conduct more rewarding, *Isaiah 11, 6-9, §7.6.* Now, *in a just universe,* punishment for crime ends at a realisation of perfect Justice, *heaven.* Punishments exist to guide out of crime else curse to death for it, *Matthew 13, 36-43, §9.1.* Mortals meet death by a process of Justice in relation to their wishes deemed to pact with death, *§1.2.* By Justice, they must repent of a death-wish and pact to life. That two-sentence theory is basis of all 'just' science in a just universe. It should be the basis of a just merciful God's word to life as part of the proof a just God exists, as seen next, *Q.E.D.?*:

The Old Testament says God called a chosen people, 'Israel', to witness to a covenant-path to God that allows criminals to repent, *Exodus 19, 5-6, §7.9*:

praise the lord, o my soul;
all my inmost being, praise his holy name.
praise the lord, o my soul, and forget not all his benefits—
who forgives all your sins
and heals all your diseases,
who redeems your life from the pit
and crowns with love and compassion,
who satisfies your desires with good things
so that your youth is renewed like the eagle's.

the lord works righteousness
and justice for all the oppressed.

he made known his ways to moses,
his deeds to the people of israel:
the lord is compassionate and gracious,
slow to anger, abounding in love.
he will not always accuse, nor will he harbour his anger forever;
he does not treat us as our sins deserve
or repay us according to our iniquities.
for as high as the heavens are above the earth,
so great is his love for those who fear him;
as far as the east is from the west,
so far has he removed our transgressions from us.
as a father has compassion on his children,
so the lord has compassion on those who fear him;
… … …
but from everlasting to everlasting
the lord's love is with those who fear him, and his righteousness with their children's children —
with those who keep his covenant and remember to obey his precepts.
psalm 103, 1-13, 17-18

This God is to pardon penitent crooks, *Micah 7, 16-20* below. But there is prophesy of 'Israel' overcome by crime so failings in faith break a pact to life for a pact to death, *Isaiah 28, 11-19, §15*. God is to annul that death-sentence by just tuition to bring faith on, *Isaiah 1, 15-20, §8.6*. Meanwhile, Jews fight a curse of evil on a holding faith, *Isaiah 28, 11-19, §15*. The holocaust may show a curse on some Jewish grasp of God's law, *Isaiah 42, 16-25, §1.16*, and on some Gentile grasp if *Isaiah 28, 11-19, §15*, indexes Israel's recovery to Gentile tuition, *§8.6, §9.7.3*. Recovery is also indexed to the Messiah or Christ, *Deuteronomy 18, 17-22, §11.5, Isaiah 9, 2-7 & 11, 1-10, §11.1*. Jesus' angle is that God's plan is for Jews to reject the Christ, *Isaiah 53*, so Gentiles are saved in learning to tell 'Israel' what 'Israel' is formed to teach the Gentiles (*Justice*). Jesus agrees failings in faith pledge to death but claims to offer a just God's pardon, *Colossians 2, 13, §11.1*:

is God the God of Jews only? is he not
the God of Gentiles too? yes, of
Gentiles too, since there is only one
God, who will justify the circumcised
by faith and the uncircumcised
through the same faith.
Romans 3, 29-30

The death-sentence on mortals is suspended for a short cursed life subject to possible progress to a just God, *Luke 13, 1-9 & Isaiah 24, 1-6, §11.5,* and for goats to mature in evil as a testing curse on nations like 'Israel' where progress to God is possible, *Genesis 15, 13-14, §7.8, Psalm 66, 10-12, §7.9.* The Christ offers a just forgiveness for sins to depart areas of God's law that rival gods enact to punish or curse sin to death, *§9.7.5, Micah 4, 5.* His is a sobering ministry to crooks, *§10.2*:

nations will see and be ashamed,
deprived of all their power.
they will lay their hands on their
mouths
and their ears will become deaf.
they will lick dust like a snake,
like creatures that crawl on the
ground.
they will come trembling out of their
dens;
they will turn in fear to the Lord our
God
and will be afraid of you.
who is a God like you,
who pardons sin and forgives the
transgression
of the remnant of his inheritance?
you do not stand angry forever
but delight to show mercy.
you will again have compassion on us;
you will tread our sins underfoot and
hurl all our iniquities into the depths
of the sea.
you will be true to Jacob,
and show mercy to Abraham,
as you pledged on oath to our fathers
in days long ago.
micah 7, 16-20

In a just world, crooks meet a just death, *e.g. go to live it up under hell's tyrannical law.* Now 'God's word' is often read as if God is direct agent both of forgiveness for sin and a curse to death on sins that reject God. But is that not tyranny? Rather, a death-sentence on sin is enacted by rival unjust gods with a just case to take jurisdiction of sinners, *Micah 4, 5, §8.* They take power of souls disloyal to God to curse them for not sinning well enough to fully depose God, *§11.3.* That is only strictly fair if sinners consciously agree to sacrifice lives to what God's enemies stand for, *a plan to depose God,* in preference to life with God, *§9.1.* God's word is then to guide towards formal choice of a curse on sin by unjust gods, or, eternal life with God's Spirit or blessing, *Deuteronomy 30, 17-20, §7.8, Isaiah 11, 6-9, §7.6.*

In summary, a just God's word addresses a title-contest for life between good and evil where evil claims evil is legitimate heir to creation, *chapter 8.* The devil claims this is his creation, *Isaiah 14, 12-21 & Acts 26, 9-18, §8.3, Luke 4, 5-6, §1.15,* and leading criminals are his freedom fighters, *§11.3.* But God says it is a just world where just process will confine the gods' law and death-sentence to 'willing' unjust citizens of hell.

The title-contest rides on God's respect for life's freedom of faith: for a way of life or 'God' to be heir to creation, *§8.2, §8.4.* Mortals are to receive a fair choice of a tyrannical or just deity. 'God's word' is thereby a progressive bilateral legal contract, *Isaiah 24, Matthew 24, 5 & 11, 23-25,* between either God (*e.g. Father, Son, Holy Spirit, all called 'the Lord' by a faithful*) or Satan (*called 'the Lord' by a faithful*) and mortals (*called sinners by every Lord*). In that context, Satan is justly termed God's hand or wrath on sinners in 'God's word', *§8.1, Job 1, 11-12 & 2, 4-7.* People can choose their Lord by 'justice', *just or tyrannical,* ascribed to 'God', *§9.7.6.* And, all may get the deity they love, *Psalm 50, 16-23.* Meanwhile, by low knowledge of covenant law, God's word seems paradoxical, *a shifty human construct or sealed book, Daniel 12, 9-10, §3.* Yet it does its work to enable guardian spirits to pen the spiritual in their faiths. Where legal folding of the word is light, a metaphorical or literal reading is good. Where legal folding is high, a simple literal reading is evil, unjust. It lets two camps in sinners live and worship side by side in spiritual prejudice to a just God or to unjust gods, and intermigrate, *§10.3, §10.8.*

The unjust oppose a just God's word as an unholy lie: *a rival unjust bid for power.* To prove it in court they need non-dogmatic expertise on 'God's word' to prove no just reading exists. But God's word implies His foes cannot stand in a just court, *Daniel 12, 9-10, §3,* as in a conspiracy to pervert justice, *Proverbs 28, 5, §8.1.* A just court is where 'God's word' can be proven before or at Judgement Day. To deny a just God is work for the hypothesis that no just reading of 'God's word' exists. Such work requires familiarity and skill on 'God's word'. Good religion or science do not deny Justice, *§2,* anymore than just lawyers will cut Justice to define human rights in a conspiracy to pervert Justice, *§1.4.* But the unjust or tyrannical presume they, *or the deity to guarantee 'justice' to mortals,* are outside or above the law or 'justice' by privilege or might, *Psalms 49 & 50.*

12.5 **'God's word' and a just God's anti-tyranny principle**

Justice rests on relating truth to evidence as implies a basic human right to a reasonable truthful education. The cardinal enemies of just law are Death, *§9.4, Proverbs 8, 36, §6.2, 1 Corinthians 15, 22-28, §7.10,* and lies, *1 Kings 22, 16, §13.12.* Thus, the archenemy of Justice, *the devil,* is a master of lies asking sacrifice of life to him, *§1.2, Psalm 106, 37, §7.8, Isaiah 28, 11-19, §15 & 10, 20-22, §8.6 & 14, 12-21, §8.3, John 8, 42-45, §13.3.* Justice is to check that the spirit to 'science' or religion is not for sacrifice of life to lies. Is academic freedom about defending a just education or to empower scholastic tyrannies? *§1.*

Justice is a science to relate truth to evidence where, if God is not unjust, even 'God's word' is submitted to mortals as evidence, *§3, Isaiah 1, 15-20, §8.6; 2 Corinthians 10, 3-5, §8.2.* A just God puts cases to win over a just court fairly, *John 18, 38.* If a title-contest sets mortal 'justice' to begin in the dark, courts must defend adult freedom of faith for possible paths to just truth, *i.e. sufficient freedom of faith in schools.* As part of that, the licence to faiths in child sacrifice to oppressive idols must be limited, *§9.5.* If 'justice' later proves the real world does not sustain freedom of faith, it may uphold parental right to reserve children for restrictive 'faith' schools, *§7.8, §9.6.* Such parents presume a just case against freedom of faith to children? *Micah 4, 5, §8.* But to school that way might set all in an unjust cursed society, *Isaiah 30, 1-15, §9.12.*

A title-contest fields views on the nature of 'justice'. Now if 'God's word' says God is not a tyrant, His will is for 'just' courts to deny theories or faiths that imply He acts in ways that, *if mortals did it,* would be tyranny. A just God's anti-tyranny principle then asks mortals to show just constraint in how they read 'God's word'. The Almighty may do as He chooses but chooses to guarantee Justice to mortals. Thus, the just do not read 'God's word' to see God in acts of tyranny, *no matter how 'holy', charismatic or tempting it may feel.* Rather, they seek a just reading to show love for a just God that may put aside simple literal views as unjust and cursed, *Proverbs 1, 20-33, §9.7.6, Isaiah 24.* Should courts licence scholars who deny that principle? *§1.* Only satanic religion or science may uphold an unjust basis for 'God's word', *Psalm 38, 19, Isaiah 5, 20, §13.7.* But Jesus claims injustice has jurisdiction of all mortals, *§1.2, Luke 4, 5-6, §1.15; 1 John 5, 19, §6.11.*

Suppose people trial with 'justice' that oppresses truths that just process can lead to. They then pass unjust laws to defend lies and stop just settlement of disputes in areas, building an unjust fence for courts to sit on. If a just God exists, it is partial to sit on the fence over His existence because no just case, *beyond passing ignorance*, can licence the fence. The fence is an unjust concept?:

may the lord cut off all flattering lips and every boastful tongue that says, "we will triumph with our tongues; we own our lips—who is our master?"
psalm 12, 3-4

However, suppose Justice supports freedom of faith for mortals, *Micah 4, 5*. God will not then lead earthly 'justice' to stop illicit scholarship before unjust faiths establish. Courts may later open eyes to unjust scholars and restrict their funding to direct public subscription.

For just schools, the prophesied Christ might be an essential advocate of God's just word and law, *a stumbling stone to unjust theories, Isaiah 8, 11-17 & Romans 9, 30-33, §8.6*. He is expected to lead in just readings of God's word against unjust readings, *Deuteronomy 18, 17-22, §11.5, John 8, 42-45, §13.3, Revelation 2, 26-28*. Many may stand by faith in Satan's side of a bilateral reading to 'God's word' for it is said God's covenant to life is violated to the end, *Isaiah 24*.

The scrutiny of 'God's word' by courts recalls prophesy of 'Christians' in peril from unjust courts, *Luke 21, 12-28, §9.1*. If unjust courts overrule a just God, it may curse society, *§11.5*. Thus, folk for a just God are in peril from unjust courts whose 'God' is a tyrant, *Luke 18, 1-8, §11.6*. A tyrannical court may ban just process past a point, *e.g. wash hands of issues of religious truth*, to leave tyrannies above the law. Nevertheless, just courts have to limit power or licence to some scholars of faiths who deny 'justice' in education. Scholars would ideally not serve a conspiracy of unjust faiths to defraud the public. Should they seek a just analysis of 'God's word' to indict sacrificial faiths that imply an unjust world? Every court counters some such faiths, *e.g. faith in murder*, led in lies with a suicidal or homicidal leaning, *§1, Isaiah 30, 1-15, §9.12 & 28, 11-19, §15, Psalm 38, 19, chapter 6*. Is to seek a just God by 'justice' 'heresy' or anathema to a just God? or an unjust 'God'? But since an unjust 'God' poses as just, both may ask it but one by a mockery of 'justice', *Proverbs 28, 5, §8.1*.

woe to those who make unjust laws to
those who issue oppressive decrees, to
deprive the poor of their rights and
withhold justice from the oppressed of
my people,

Isaiah 10, 1-2

To kill for 'blasphemy' against 'holy' grounds of a deity, *§10.7, §10.8*, looks a special case of child-sacrifice to appease gods who curse. The anti-tyranny principle suggests to forget 'holy' grounds, *Jeremiah 3, 9-17, §11*. If a just God is not for child-sacrifice, *§7.8*, why is He for 'blasphemy' killings? Now once God's covenant to life is on offer, *§4*, child sacrifice may 'civilise' by schooling in contempt of the offer, *§9.5*. To cut out bloody child-sacrifice or harsh blasphemy laws is not so 'civilised' if God's just pardon to crooks is censored.

Material wealth may be given as a 'civilising' curse-discount to rulers, priests, generals, sorcerers, scientists, traders who work to perfect human sacrifice to evil. Wealth may trap in the dark, *Isaiah 24, 2 Kings 17, 34-41*, so empires rise and fall by their 'civilising' gods' curse for not ending 'just' faith, *§7.9, Revelation 22*:

lowborn men are but a breath,
the highborn are but a lie;
if weighed on a balance, they are
nothing;
together they are only a breath.
do not trust in extortion
or take pride in stolen goods;
though your riches increase, do not
set your heart on them.
one thing god has spoken,
two things have i heard:
that you, o god, are strong,
and that you, o lord, are loving.
surely you will reward each person
according to what he has done.

psalm 62, 9-12

The hopeless prospects to denying God's pardon may be seen at the Passover, *Exodus 12, 2-29, §7.9*. Unjust gods set Egypt to slave and break Hebrew faith off paths to a just God. Egypt failed so a harsh curse, *slaughter of firstborn from livestock and prisoners to Pharaoh*, made it let the Hebrews go. That uniform arbitrary death-sentence marked all in Egypt as criminal, *Luke 13, 1-9, §11.5, even babies.* To preach such a merciless curse is of a just God's nature, *Job 1, 22*, blind to readings that ascribe it to God's enemy, *the supreme god of ancient Egypt, §7.9*, may be unjust 'faith'. If God delights to justly pardon criminals, why kill any unread folk for not taking His pardon? *Micah 4, 5, §8, §9.7.6.*

Many are made angry at blasphemy against their faith so demand a 'justice' to sacrifice offenders. Two camps of 'infidels' may war over 'blasphemy'. War is only ever a victory for 'just' faith if Justice supports trial by ordeal where war really vindicates a winner, *§6.4.* But after millennia of wars, there is no clear victory for faith in war so, *though war goes on,* military strategy may not be of a just or sane path? If faith in might is unjust and cursed, *§11.5,* war may still take short-range prosperity or peace but subject to a curse climaxing in fall of the empire or apocalypse. Do wars give just witness to God or are they an oppression to deny chance to turn to God? It is true that 'God's people' at times seem to gain by sacrifice of life in war but it does not allow a general conclusion that God backs military war, *§11.5.*

The defining weapon of the unjust is 'injustice'. Good is tested by 'injustice', *trial by ordeal,* in evil's plan to depose a just God, *§7.5; Lamentations 3, 25-32, §8; 1 Peter 2, 19-25, §10.* Jesus underwent trial by ordeal of a kind later advocated as a 'Christian' inquisition. God's word suggests mortals only ever triumph over enemies by a supernatural ruling, *§9.11.* Thus, Jewish leaders for a 'just' God laid a blasphemy charge of claiming to be 'the Son of God' against Jesus, *John 19, 7,* expecting Jesus to die by divine will, *§9.* They asked gentiles to crucify for it but gentiles preferred to crucify for being 'the king of the Jews'. Was that a test of injustice giving God a prophesied key victory over the unjust? *Isaiah 53.* Yet the unjust may suppose it their 'just' victory by trappings of law used, *§9, Proverbs 28, 5, §8.1.*

The Christ is to teach about Justice which may respect right of the unjust to the 'justice' they wish, *Micah 4, 5, Proverbs 1, 20-33, §9.7.6.* When 'Israel' is led by the unjust, testing injustice may follow to reinforce unjust leaders. Persecution can reinforce faith in military witness. A curse can help the unjust, *sinners,* to power, *§10.5.* Consider a case put before a just God on Hitler's behalf to put hated folk to death, *God's people,* for offending faith in an Aryan master race, *§9.2.* Hitler was certainly against a Jewish master race backed by God's might, *see §8.1 on Ezekiel.* However, such an idea of a Jewish master race may defame both a just God and just Jews? *Luke 22, 25-30, John 13.* Only by faith in Justice is 'Israel' to stand, *Zechariah 4, 6, §8, Isaiah 28, 11-19, §15, Isaiah 10, 20-22 & 1, 15-20, §8.6, Isaiah 7, 9-14, §11.6.* Even unjust global alliances for 'God' are to fall, *Isaiah 24.* Where do the just stand on Justice?

12.6 A gentle or violent God? Where is it safe to stand?

'God's word' sees this world as in principalities subject to curse-law of local gods or demons, *§8.3*. Angels and God's Spirit vie to offer God's just salvation from death and lies, *§7.3, Daniel 10, 12-14, Micah 4, 5, §8*. Justice is a gift from God to check rule of unjust rival gods over sinners, *§1, §4, Psalms 82, §8.3& 98*. God's might is a guarantee of Justice against evil gods so tyrants or crooks will die out by a just case related to 'God's word':

the lord reigns, let the earth be glad;
let the distant shores rejoice.

clouds and thick darkness surround
him;
righteousness and justice are the
foundation of his throne.
fire goes before him
and consumes his foes on every side.
his lightening lights up the world;
the earth sees and trembles.
the mountains melt like wax before
the lord,
before the lord of all the earth.
the heavens proclaim his
righteousness,
and all the peoples see his glory.

7 all who worship images are put to
shame,
those who boast in idols—
worship him, all you gods!

zion hears and rejoices
and the villages of judah are glad
because of your judgements,
o lord.
for you, lord, are the most high over
all the earth;
you are exalted far above all gods.

psalm 97, 1-9

This declares a just God's victory over unjust gods who slave to worship images and idols, false gods, war, *§8.3*. It augurs the Christ's reign, *§11.1*, so may depict second coming of gentle Jesus as Lord, *Matthew 24, 23-30, §10.11*. See *§11.5* on *Revelation 19, 11-21 & 6, 1-10*:

take my yoke upon you and learn from
me, for i am gentle and humble of
heart, and you will find rest for your
souls.

matthew 11, 29

The Lord comes veiled in clouds, *§9.4*. Earthquakes and fires deal death to foes on every side. It is a fearful picture for any in the dark, *Exodus 14, 19-20, 1 Kings 19, 11-13, §10.2, Isaiah 35, 4-6, §8.1*. Is it read as God or gentle Jesus flaming enemies? It depends on a just case put forward to cover deaths in a faith about Justice for which a just God is veiled in clouds, *§9.4*. That case must relate to mortal ideas of justice else God could not win a title-contest except by unjust force.

Crime drives mortals to pass and police laws which may not justify the laws with God, *§11.5.* For crooks pass laws for unjust gods to stop God, *Micah 4, 5, Isaiah 53 & 24, Luke 21, 12-28, §9.1.* Criminal 'justice' faces a death-sentence as in Egypt, *§5,* for taking a tyrannical 'Almighty' who lays down his law by force, *e.g. to punish for sin.* God's mercy, *Isaiah 1, 15-20, §8.6,* is to wean from criminal 'justice' to faith in Justice by straightening paths to God, *§11.6.* Some can rise above tyrannical views of 'God', *Proverbs 1, 20-33, §9.7.6.*

In *Psalm 97* above, God or the Christ may at first sight appear direct killers of crooks. It recalls *Psalm 11, §9.1,* saying God hates those who love violence yet sets (*violent?*) retribution on them: *fiery coals and burning sulfur in hell.* It recalls *Ezekiel 28, 18-19* on a deity who deals in horrible deaths. But a just reading may say God's enemies are not in God's direct jurisdiction to kill, *Micah 4, 5.* They are free to live and die by the law of unjust idols or gods that they love, that God offers to save from, *Jeremiah 2, 11-13 & Psalm 73, 10-12, §11.1, Micah 4, 5, §8.* We may only truly comprehend salvation by seeing stress to the earth or death-fires at God's coming, *1 Kings 19, 11-13, §10.2,* as by hand of unjust gods on sinners in their thrall, *the god's servants.* The gods thereby protect their servants who reject God's pardon, *by full enmity to God's servants,* from the 'reforming' sight of God, *Exodus 33, 14-20, §10.8, Job 42, 5, Philippians 3, 8-12.*

If the just are entitled to query any deaths, it has to be clear Justice is done: deaths justly merited, *Isaiah 66, 24, §1.13.* The perfect solution may require many to go into hell thinking death-fires vindicated their faith in Satan as one true 'God'. A curtain of flames may enable all to see foes burnt in a division into God's heaven and Satan's 'heaven' and 'hell' inside God's hell. Outsiders to hell and 'hell' then inherit a 'truth' in line with faiths they bet their lives on. Who sees just fault in that? The Christ is then perfect Justice by a spirit of judgement and spirit of fire, *Isaiah 4, 4 & 10, 17-23*:

and if your eye causes you to sin,
pluck it out. it is better to enter the
kingdom of god with one eye than to
have two eyes and be thrown into
hell, where

" 'their worm does not die,
and the fire is not quenched.'

everyone will be salted with fire."
mark 9, 47-49

The Christ is to witness to an atoning covenant with God to cover scarlet sins for criminals where even Moses, David, Elijah are claimed by Satan as criminals, *Isaiah 1, 15-20, §8.6.* See *§10.8, §10.10* on their crime. Now a false prophet offers God's forgiveness to sinners in contempt of God's law but Moses looks to the Christ to do it right, *Deuteronomy 18, 17-22, §11.5.* Does Jesus? Jesus says the letter of God's law stands, *Matthew 5, 17-20, §8.1,* but sinners cannot live up to the letter as puts all under a death-sentence, *§15, 2 Corinthians 3, 6, §10.13.* A first principles explanation is in *§11.3.* Jesus also says there is a prison where the last penny in punishment for sin is exacted as purgatory for some and death in hell for others, *§10.11, Isaiah 61, 1, Matthew 18, 21-25.* He advises to escape that prison sentence by taking God's pardon or offer of forgiveness for sins in relation to the Christ's teaching. That teaching is to be observed as a vital part of the covenant with God:

"you have heard that it was said to the people long ago, 'do not murder, and anyone who murders will be subject to judgement.' But I tell you that anyone who is angry with his brother will be subject to judgement. Again, anyone who says to his brother, 'Raca,' is answerable to the Sanhedrin. But anyone who says, 'You fool!' will be in danger of the fires of hell.
"Therefore, if you are offering your gift at the alter and there remember that your brother has something against you, leave your gift there in front of the alter. First go and be reconciled to your brother; then come and offer your gift.
"Settle matters quickly with your adversary who is taking you to court. Do it while you are still with him on the way, or he may hand you over to the judge, and the judge may hand you over to the officer, and you will be thrown into prison. I tell you the truth, you will not get out until you have paid the last penny.

Matthew 5, 21-26

To show anger against or call God's servant a fool may side with Satan against God. It carries risk of being made a full citizen of hell. Christian diplomacy is to avoid such traps yet oppose teaching thought to reject just reason, *Isaiah 24; James 3, 1-2; 1 Peter 3, 15-16.* Jesus teaches to try to save souls from hell not to condemn. But then, what adversary takes a careless 'Christian' to court for anger at brothers? seeking to have them thrown into hell for calling brothers fools? *§11.6.* It is surely a 'Christian' servant of hell's rival unjust vision of 'the Christ' exploiting truthful witness that the, *ready to forgive*, brothers must give?

"For God so loved the world that he gave his one and only Son, that whoever believes in him shall not perish but have eternal life. For God did not send his Son into the world to condemn the world, but to save the world through him.

John 3, 16-17

My brothers, if one of you should wander from the truth and someone should bring him back, remember this: Whoever turns a sinner from the error of his way will save him from death and cover over a multitude of sins.

James 5, 19-20

Jesus says not to judge, *§11.6, Matthew 7, 1-5 & 18, 21-35, Romans 10, 6-7* above, unless ready to be judged on similar terms. It is a strategy for annulling the death-sentence on mortals for 'crime'. The 'faithful' best not tar 'the wicked' for hell, *as by inquisition*, or canonise 'saints' for heaven, *§10.7.* Can the just presume on God's judgements or mercy? *§10.7, Romans 5, 7, §11.4.*

But the righteousness that is by faith says: "Do not say in your heart, 'Who will ascend to heaven?' " (that is to bring Christ down) " or 'Who will descend into the deep?' " (that is to bring Christ up from the dead).

Romans 10, 6-7

For suppose Satan runs a 'heaven', *his quarters*, inside God's hell, *§10.11.* He may then tempt to faith in his 'heaven' and so to damn or canonise souls relative to it. Might his 'Christians', *Isaiah 24*, be adversaries to drag angry 'Christians' into court to claim for his 'heaven' and 'hell'. The above is then a legally folded form requiring care like *Revelation 19, 11-21, §11.5.* The chief adversary to indict 'Christians' and take into hell for sins is thereby Satan, *§9.7.4, Revelation 12, 7-12.* The faithful stand against by ways compatible with the just Christ and God *for the age, Isaiah 7, 9-14, §11.6*:

Discipline yourselves; keep alert. Like a roaring lion your adversary the devil prowls around, looking for someone to devour. Resist him, steadfast in your faith, for you know that your brothers and sisters throughout the world are undergoing the same kinds of suffering. And after you have suffered for a little while, the God of all grace, who has called you to his eternal glory in Christ, will himself restore, support, strengthen, and establish you. To him be the power for ever and ever. Amen.

1 Peter 5, 8-11 (NRSV)

Existence of a bilateral spiritual world is essential to some ideas of a just God, *§7.12,* as next.

12.7 A Just God may licence a bilateral spiritual world

A just God is no tyrant so is for freedom of faith, *§11.3,* and lacks a will to curse life, *Lamentations 3, 33, §8.1.* That is a conjecture on a 'just' God to imply life is only cursed by other life's wish, *e.g. wish to curse enemies who curse back, §8.2.* For that God's blessing, we best not react to foes in ways to give their 'justice' jurisdiction, *Micah 4, 5, Matthew 5, 43-45, Romans 12, 14-21.*

This God might, *in some circumstances,* give adolescent life its choice of guardian spirits, *Genesis 3, 2-5, §7.4,* even for rebel gods who read its wish to sin as a wish for a 'justice' to depose God, *Isaiah 24, 21-22, Micah 4, 5, §8, Matthew 26, 52, Galatians 4, 1-9, §5.10.* Rebel gods seek power of 'lesser' life to feed their lifestyle, *chapter 11.* God's overall Justice then sets blessings and curses to court-readings of life's wishes, *§9.11, Deuteronomy 30, 17-20, §7.8.* If we aspire to a 'just' God of this kind, it obliges faith to a bilateral spiritual world where God and rival gods spiritually contest mortals, *§8.2, §9.1.*

If God and the devil, *mightiest of unjust gods,* contest mortals then unjust gods keep mortals by floating cases which God's plan must prove unjust. Meanwhile, we work in twilight zones, *dark spiritual bubbles,* for unjust gods, *§10.6, §11.4.* Now injustice can only exist if life is under 'justice' not agreed to. It is defined in account of all systems of 'justice', *ways of life,* open to mortals. That needs keys to gates of consent to enter or leave a 'justice' system, *i.e. let God or unjust gods into life, Psalms 1 & 24.* One theory is that God will take human form as 'the Messiah' to show the gateway to Justice to folk jailed in the dark by rebel 'justice', *Isaiah 9, 2-7, §11.1, John 10, 1-10, §10.* Jesus claims to be that Son of Justice: the only one able to walk the judicial path to free mortals as wards or prisoners to guardian spirits, *Matthew 12, 26-32, §9.8, §9.1, Galatians 4, 1-9, §5.10.*

open for me the gates of righteousness;
I will enter and give thanks to the Lord.
this is the gate of the Lord
through which the righteous may enter.
I will give you thanks, for you
answered me;
you have become my salvation.
the stone the builders rejected
has become the capstone;
the Lord has done this,
and it is marvellous in our eyes.
this is the day the Lord has made;
let us rejoice and be glad in it.

psalm 118, 19-24

Job testified that a just heart does not use inability to understand a curse on life to argue that God is unjust, *Job 1, 22.* Rather, 'the just' heart under test puts faith in a just God to lighten the dark on a path to escape the curse for blessings of heaven, like Job, *Job 1, 8*:

"... I know that my Redeemer lives,
and that in the end he will stand upon the earth.
And after my skin has been destroyed,
yet in the flesh I will see God;
I myself will see him with my own eyes—I, and not another.
How my heart yearns within me!
If you say, 'How we will hound him,
since the root of the trouble lies in him,
you should fear the sword yourselves;
for wrath will bring punishment by the sword,
and then you will know that there is judgement."

Job 19, 25-29

Is Jesus Job's redeemer?: the gate of consent to Justice, *John 10, 1-10, §10.* Now to shun the gate asks injustice, *i.e. evil's cursing wrath*, yet to try to open it is also cursed to evil's tests of, *i.e. curse on*, just faith, *§7.5, Galatians 3, 10-13.* Many are cursed more than they understand, *Luke 13, 1-9 & Isaiah 24, §11.5*, or wish on enemies:

With the tongue we praise our Lord and Father, and with it we curse men, who have been made in God's likeness. Out of the same mouth come praise and cursing. My brothers, this should not be.

James 3, 9-10

Thus, a curse on life is not proof there is no 'just' God. It may show rival systems of 'justice' exist whose gates of consent are veiled by some case in a duel of good and evil. The duel is enacted to evil's wish to curse life, *even 'good'*, by disputing loyalties. It puts will for good or evil to test as why God's salvation to Israel is conditional, *Isaiah 1, 15-20, §8.6*, and even the Messiah is tested by injustice, *Isaiah 53.* It may imply inner spiritual conflict, see below, whereby in one spirit a mortal asks a 'justice' to bless but in another asks a 'justice' that curses, *§9.1, §7.3, 2 Peter 2, 9, Matthew 5, 44-45.* God's relief to tortured minds is to clear the gateway to Justice, *§7.3, §10.10.* If gates of consent become plain, mortals can divide by ideas of 'justice', *ways of life*, for division into hell and heaven where all get the 'justice', way of life, asked, *§9.1.* The 'just' may see hell's cursing 'justice' is to torture and punish sinners, *Matthew 10, 28, §7.10.*

If God is just, folk are only cursed for disloyalty to God so *for sin against God.* That one-sentence theory implies salvation is by a just gateway to God's forgiveness for sin and that God wishes to forgive sins to save mortals:

> If we confess our sins, he is faithful and just and will forgive us our sins and purify us from all unrighteousness. If we claim we have not sinned, we make him out to be a liar and his word has no place in our lives.
>
> 1 John 1, 9-10

It need not be God's nature to 'punish' sin, *§8.1*, if sin is the gateway to systems of 'justice' under rebel gods to punish sin? For only a rebel spirit tempts to sin, *disloyalty to God, James 1, 13-15, §10.5*, and if it leads into systems to punish sin, those systems/jails are also disloyal so run by and for evil spirits who tempt to sin. Hence, to seek God, mortals must master their personal demons, evil spirits, that drag into sin, *Genesis 4, 6-7, §10.5.* They may pray for God's Spirit to circumscribe or exorcise evil. God then sees evil spirit as a Godly soul's enemy, *seeking to possess and curse-punish for sin.* It jails souls in the dark by cases claiming to one day fulfil our wish to sin as children, *Luke 20, 9-16, §7.10, §9.1.* Mortals then best desert childish idols in religion, art, science for the call of a safe room in heaven, *John 14, 2.*

Via Paul, Jesus may ask to let go of childish passions of the sinful nature, *Galatians 5, 17-21, §7.11*, for faith, hope, love as adult values. But if faith, hope, love, can be applied at idols, *1 Timothy 6, 10, §1.14*, they are not good in themselves but to be proven by a Godly object:

> Love is patient, love is kind. It does not envy, it does not boast, it is not proud. It is not rude, it is not self-seeking, it is not easily angered, it keeps no record of wrongs. Love does not delight in evil but rejoices with the truth. It always protects, always trusts, always hopes, always perseveres.
> Love never fails. But where there are prophecies, they will cease; where there are tongues, they will be stilled; where there is knowledge, it will pass away. For we know in part and we prophesy in part, but when perfection comes, the imperfect disappears.
> When I was a child, I talked like a child, I thought like a child, I reasoned like a child. When I became a man, I put childish ways behind me. Now I know in part; then I shall know fully, even as I am fully known.
> And now these three remain: faith, hope and love. But the greatest of these is love.
>
> 1 Corinthians 13, 4-13

Choice of spirits proffers a future in two houses, one for souls who by God's help prove loyalty to God, so depart sin for knowledge of God, *Isaiah 11, 6-9, §7.6, e.g. for a spiritual circumcision of a sinful nature, Jeremiah 9, 25-26 & 31, 31-33, §8.3.* The other house is for souls devoted to regimes in hate, fear and love of idols that curse to punishment yet as a chosen or preferred way of life, *§9.1.* The just Christ then offers a 'peace' free of fear, hate and curse to deliver from the evil one of the Lord's prayer, *Matthew 6, 5-14*, who is Satan in *Job 1, 8-12 & 2, 1-6*, and the curse or 'hand of our enemies' spoken of by Zechariah at John the Baptist's birth:

his father zechariah was filled with the holy spirit and prophesied:

"praise be to the lord, the god of israel,
because he has come and redeemed his people.
he has raised up a horn of salvation
for us in the house of his servant david
(as he said through his holy prophets of long ago)
salvation from our enemies
and from the hand of all who hate us—
to show mercy to our fathers
and to remember his holy covenant,
the oath he swore to our father abraham:
to rescue us from the hand of our enemies,
and to enable us to serve him without fear
in holiness and righteousness before him all or days.

and you child, will be called a prophet of the most high;
for you will go on before the lord to prepare the way for him,
to give his people the knowledge of salvation
through the forgiveness of their sins,
because of the tender mercy of our god,
by which the rising sun will come to us from heaven
to shine on those living in darkness
and in the shadow of death,
to guide our feet into the path of peace."

luke 1, 67-79

The opening conjecture on a 'just' God's nature thus implies we are cursed and in the dark by personal evil spirits who dress souls in a duel of good and evil, *§9.1.* We inherit familiar evil spirits, *a sinful nature, Exodus 20, 4-6, §7.9, Psalm 51, 1-12, §10.10,* as a 'gift' of the gods, *§10.5,* like a Siamese twin conjoined to souls. It may claim our name, *e.g. act as our ghost.* It is a parasite to feed in evil passions, *Galatians 5, 17-21, §7.11,* passed on at death. The inner spiritual conflict it can wreak, *if resisted,* is laid bare for Israel in Paul's texts, *§10.10, Acts 9, 15, §10.4,* allowing a just theory of soul and spirit over 'science' and religion, *§10.5, chapter 10.*

12.8 **Seeking the Christ puts mortal-ethics on trial**

The professional ethics of scholars start with a rule of law that defers to just process in areas, *§1.* Scholars of no faith in life after death may be freer in their ideas of 'justice' than scholars of faith in a 'just' or 'unjust' resurrection, *§9.7.5, Isaiah 30, 1-15, §9.12.* The most fettering idea of 'justice' may be to a 'just' resurrection, *Psalm 2, §9.4.* Justice, if it exists, upholds full right to life against those who uphold Death's unjust rule, *§6.3, Luke 21, 17-19, Romans 5, 7, §11.4.* To hypothesise that Death is 'natural' or final may abet tyrannies, *§1, Wisdom 2, Daniel 7, 19-23,* e.g. present Death as for annulling rights set by one idol for power to another, *§11.1, §6.1, Psalm 115, 17 & Mark 12, 27, §11.1.*

Unjust scholars justly rule if the will of the people after a fair education, *Deuteronomy 30, 17-20, §7.8.* Alas, the unjust skip a fair education to brainwash and deny rights to popular hate-groups in power bids, *Wisdom 2.* Put another way, testing injustice from a devil, *chapter 6,* causes unjust scholars to defend unjust rights to friends with right to curse hated enemies. The 'problem of evil' is that evil takes power by citing 'worse' evil as an enemy only evil can, *in truth,* fight using the weapons of evil, *§8.2, §11.5*:

"... what good is it for a man to gain the whole world, yet forfeit his soul? or what can a man give in exchange for his soul? if anyone is ashamed of me and my words in this adulterous and sinful generation, the son of man will be ashamed of him when he comes in his father's glory with the holy angels."

mark 8, 36-38

The just fight by just means against foes who deny just rights, *e.g. uphold right to lie for unjust political groups, §1.3, Proverbs 28, 5, §8.1 & 17, 23.* A just God saves from the unjust, *heals spirits broken by injustice,* if under test they turn from evil, *§7.5, Psalm 30 & 51,17.* He stands for just witness against a curse of unjust enemies who may even claim 'God's word' to their cause, *Psalm 73,* reading it to condone injustice like murder, *§11.6, §9.7.6.* Idolatry based on 'God's word' is popular, *Isaiah 24,* enough to make it a sealed book, *Daniel 12, 9-10, §3, Isaiah 35, 4-6, §8.1, 2 Peter 3, 15-16.* Faith in an 'unjust' resurrection is a spiritual calling, *§10.13, Isaiah 30, 1-15, §9.12, Proverbs 28, 5, §8.1.* Spiritual adultery, *to know and bed with evil,* is a right that a just God respects, *Genesis 3, 2-5, §7.4, §8.4, §11.*

The hearts of just and unjust fix differently on 'God's word' in a quest to do God's will, *§9.1*, be vindicated, *Psalm 24, 3-10.* Glory may go to souls who stand by Justice despite testing humiliation by enemies, *Isaiah 53, Romans 8, 31-36, §11.4*, including spiritual attack with feelings of shame, *§7.6, §10.5, §10.9, §10.10*:

you have made us a source of
contention to our neighbours,
and our enemies mock us.
psalm 80, 6

the lord is good to those whose hope
is in him,
to the one who seeks him;
it is good to wait quietly for the
salvation of the lord.
it is good for a young man to bear the
yoke while he is young.

let him sit alone in silence, for the lord
has laid it on him.
let him bury his face in the dust—
there may yet be hope.
let him offer his cheek to the one who
would strike him,
and let him be filled with disgrace.

for men are not cast off by the lord
forever.
though he brings grief, he will show
compassion,
so great is his unfailing love.
lamentations 3, 25-32

Now if a just reading of 'God's word' exists to uphold Justice, do not look to the unjust to find it! To test readings in open courts will not put the author of Justice on trial. It puts courts on trial. If they cannot tell just from unjust cases, they rob of Justice, *Romans 2, 17-24, §8.5.* The just risk humiliation by witness to just readings in court, *Luke 21, 12-28, §9.1.* The unjust do the same for unjust readings but may hold a veto on earthly justice due to right to 'injustice', *§11.6, Isaiah 24, 1-6, §11.5, Psalms 97 & 98, Luke 18, 1-8, §11.6, Acts 18, 9-17, §11.3.* Unjust courts and miscarriages of justice exist to respect wish of the unjust, *§11.6.*

If the Jewish Christ is God's justice and word, *Isaiah 9, 6, Deuteronomy 18, 17-22 & John 14, 6-10, §11.5*, He is the gateway to Justice. If Jesus is that Messiah, the New Testament is trustworthy on Justice. If not, is it trustworthy on Satan's 'justice'? Either way, the trial of Jesus is where just and unjust theories of God meet. The trial is a showcase for rival ideas of God's law and the just nature that servants of God need in relation to authority. To study ideas of justice around the trial may not prove Jesus is the Christ, *1 John 4, 1-3, §10.3*, but should clarify just and unjust ideas of the Christ in witness to God, *Isaiah 1, 15-20, §8.6.*

Suppose Jesus is the Messiah then after Jesus' death the fall of the Jerusalem temple was by a curse on it for rejecting God. It was partly built under a curse-discount from Satan, *a guiding relief from occupational stress,* to let unjust priests mature in a spirit to defy God, *Genesis 15, 13-14, §7.8.* They rejected Jesus as leaders of 'Israel' but did not break Jesus' faith in God, *Job 19, 25-29, §7,* so the temple was cursed to ruin for failing evil, *Luke 19, 37-44.* Afterwards, security might appear to rely on Satan's capricious 'justice' or wrath to defend, *Isaiah 10, 20-22, §8.6 & 42, 16-25, §1.16,* but it is God's defence of 'Israel's' prophesied path to turn back to God that defends, *Isaiah 1, 15-20, §8.6.* Satan must keep Israel as a blind hostage against God entering their world, *§10.8, Isaiah 28.* Leaders of faith in a military solution may assist in that, *§11.5, Wisdom 2, 11-12, §9.2.* Does faith in military might despise the Messiah and pact to Death by a poor grasp of Justice? turning *from the Spirit of God to a spirit of tyrannical might*:

not by might nor by power, but by my spirit,
says the lord almighty.
zechariah 4, 6

jesus said to her, "i am the resurrection and the life. he who believes in me will live, even though he dies; and whoever believes in me will never die. do you believe this?"
"yes, lord," she told him, "i believe that you are the christ, the son of god, who has come into the world."
john 11, 25-27

God made 'Israel' to head a path to Justice that focuses on the just Christ: to be a holy nation of priests for God, *Exodus 19, 5-6, §7.9.* Israel is to one day find and offer forgiveness for sins by a faith in 'God's word' that, *by Archangel Michael's help, Revelation 12, 7, §8.1, Daniel 12,* gets past simple faith in unjust ways, *§9.7.6*:

if you, o lord, kept a record of sins,
o lord, who could stand?
but with you there is forgiveness;
therefore you are to be feared.

i wait for the lord, my soul waits,
and in his word i put my hope.
my soul waits for the lord
more than the watchmen wait for the morning,
more than the watchmen wait for the morning.

o israel, put your hope in the lord,
for with the lord is unfailing love and
with him is full redemption.
he himself will redeem israel
from all their sins
psalm 130, 3-8

Judaic ethics hope for just reason in witness to the Christ, *Psalm 122*, to decry shameful ideas of 'God', *Isaiah 25, 8, §11.1, §9.7.6.* Thus, 'Israel' must one day show just fault with 'Jesus' else turn to 'Jesus' as God, *Isaiah 9, 6.* Where else but a court is just fault shown? Unjust 'justice' cannot be ended by force if that is oppression according to God and Satan, *Isaiah 42, 18-21, Matthew 12, 15-21.* Does the Christ teach Justice solely by rod of His mouth? *Deuteronomy 30, 17-20, §7.8, Isaiah 11, 1-5, §11.1, 2 Thessalonians 2, 8*, and warn that unjust powers of any kind are cursed to ruin by evil if they fail to break faith in Justice? *§11.5*:

in the last days
the mountain of the lord's temple will be established
as chief among the mountains;
it will be raised above the hills, and peoples will stream to it.

many nations will come and say,

"come, let us go up to the mountain of the lord,
to the house of the god of jacob.
he will teach us his ways,
so that we may walk in his paths."
the law will go out from zion, the word of the lord from jerusalem.
he will judge between many peoples
and will settle disputes for strong nations far and wide.
they will beat their swords into plowshares
and their spears into pruning hooks.
nation will not take up sword against nation,
nor will they train for war anymore.
every man will sit under his own vine
and under his own fig tree,
and no one will make them afraid,
for the lord almighty has spoken,
5 all the nations may walk in the name of their gods;
we will walk in the name of the lord
our god for ever and ever.

micah 4, 1-5

By *Micah 4, 5* above, God respects right of fairly educated peoples to be cursed to death by their chosen god's law. That fits with Jesus advising against power by rebellion as unjust and cursed, *Matthew 26, 52-56, §8.7.* Jesus' God then seeks victory by advocacy in just law or reforms, *Psalm 98.* It obliges God's servants to obey local authority except where rulers seek to outlaw witness to God, *§11.5.* A government may only take offence at a 'just' God by tyranny, say, faith that a curse on the world is lifted, *not worsened*, by attacking God's people. Many feel a compulsion to use force for 'God' even to put to death a 'weak' Christ who will not wage war except by rod of His mouth. Strong leadership?

12.9 Jesus' trial: 3 types of theory to licence a 'just' God

Jesus is the Jew who to witness to a 'just' God submitted to trial by Pilate as a path to meet prophecies, *§8.1, §9.7.5*. Only if the trial was unjust can Jesus have been the innocent victim *Isaiah 53* asks. He met prophecies from entering Jerusalem on a colt, *Matthew 21, 1-11*, to quoting *Psalm 22, 1*, 'My God, my God, why have you forsaken me?', *John 10, 14-16, §11.5*. He went to great pains in a one-off bid to be vindicated as the Christ by 'God's' will or law, *Psalm 24, 3-10*:

"Put your sword back in its place," Jesus said to him, "for all who draw the sword will die by the sword. Do you think I cannot call on my Father, and he will at once put at my disposal more than twelve legions of angels? But how then would the Scriptures be fulfilled that say it must happen in this way?

Matthew 26, 52-54

Then Jesus went with his disciples to a place called Gethsemane, and he said to them, "Sit here while I go over there and pray."
He took Peter and the two sons of Zebedee along with him, and he began to be sorrowful and troubled. Then he said to them, "My soul is overwhelmed with sorrow to the point of death. Stay here and keep watch with me."
Going a little further, he fell with his face to the ground and prayed, "My Father, if it is possible, may this cup be taken from me. Yet not as I will, but as you will."
Then he returned to his disciples and found them sleeping. "Could you men not keep watch with me for one hour?" he asked Peter. "Watch and pray so that you will not fall into temptation. The spirit is willing, but the body is weak."

Matthew 26, 36-41

The trial is a key area in 'Christian' ethics. Prophetic fulfilment limits the pitch for rivals on a suffering platform perhaps just to garlanding 'Jesus' with popular works of the devil to license fake second comings, *Matthew 24, 23-30, §10.11*. Jesus implies one theory of the trial to a just God but many raising an unjust 'Jesus' on the cross for an unjust 'God'. A third class of theory may deny the Christ suffers in the flesh to defeat evil, *1 John 4, 1-3, §10.3*. Truth may out by just questions, *e.g. how can it be a just God's will to base eternal justice on an unjust trial to convict the one innocent? §9.7.5, Isaiah 53, 8, Acts 8, 33*. It needs an answer in context of many such questions about 'unjust' acts ascribed to God in 'God's word'. Is there a just reading to clear a just God? *§4, §8.1*. The Passover can be another problem area.

The Passover festival poses the question: *how can it be a just God's will to kill babies*? It celebrates God's judicial will for Pharaoh to cull Hebrew babies, *§11.5*, then, *in reply*, God's judicial (*and personal?*) will to cull Egypt's first-born, *more babies, §7.9, §10.8*. The anti-tyranny principle, *§5*, says no one dies till proven party to crime as seems to require enough of a life, *Isaiah 14, 13-16.* But mortals may be born to hereditary evil handicaps to knowing God, *a sinful nature*, so, *arguably*, are parties to crime at birth, *§10.5, Exodus 20, 4-6, §7.9, Psalm 51, 1-12, §10.10.* The sinful nature is to compel to sacrifice babies to unjust gods giving jurisdiction, *§7.8, Micah 4, 5.* Unjust gods can any time kill babies in their care *until* parent's rebel by turning to a just God who may then hold some in life, *Exodus 20, 4-6, §7.9, Luke 13, 1-9, §11.5.* Unjust gods then culled the first-born in Egypt, *not God*, to punish Egypt for not ending the Hebrew path to God. Hence, a just God's will might be to stop killings of babies in general, never join in?

Jesus' birth was met by a prophesied punishment or cull of evil babies, *Matthew 2*, to compromise or cull the newborn God of *Isaiah 9, 6.* It tested Joseph's and Mary's will to save Jesus from unjust gods, not sacrifice:

"she will give birth to a son, and you are to give him the name Jesus, because he will save his people from their sins."
matthew 1, 21

for the lord will vindicate his people and have compassion on his servants.
psalm 135, 14

What just quality of Jesus is reflected in God's word to explain God's will for an unjust trial to condemn the innocent? Perhaps unjust trials are an unjust god's will, *Satan*, whereby prophecies of the trial imply Satan is billed in God's law and word as 'God's hand' or (*indirect*) will, *§4, Job 1, 11-12 & 2, 5-6, see §8.1, §9.7.5.* God did not then kill babies at the passover, *§7.9,* and 'God's word' is a bilateral covenant to God or Satan by choice, *§3, §9.7.* Just faith then rises to a bilateral view of divine law above a spiritual war, *§7, Proverbs 1, 20-33, §9.7.6.* Jesus saw it, *Luke 10, 17-21, §7.13.* Just faith may deduce Satan exists to jail mortals by hereditary sinful natures gifted by him, *§9.1, §10.5,* in a plan to depose a just God in a duel of good and evil, *§8.2, §8.4, §8.5, §8.6, Wisdom 1, 12-16, §1.2.* A just God's *direct* will at the trial was thus mercy to the innocent, *Matthew 12, 7, §9.7.5 & Hosea 6, 6, §8.1.*

The crucifixion or Passover may goad a conscience, *Romans 5, 7, §11.4*, to seek a just reading of 'God's word' that lets a just court rule. But the sinful nature goads to tyrannical 'justice', *e.g. to a tyrannical deity who sets death for breaking his law.* Such faith enters courts not to explain Justice but to threaten 'God's wrath' if questioned. Confronted by many threats of wrath, a just court can ask casework to licence a faith or science fit to define 'justice'? Note that even faith in a 'secular' tyranny touts tyrannical ideas of 'God' for its case that no just God exists for 'civilisation', *§2, Psalm 2, §9.4; Isaiah 14, 12-21, §8.3; 2 Peter 2, 19, §11.4.*

Many Jews turned to Jesus but few Jewish authorities. Jesus declared the latter slaves to Satan's spirit: *led by unjust spirits to murder Jesus for power of 'Israel' against a just God.* Below it says they believed Jesus really did do miracles, cast out spirits, raise the dead:

When he had said this, Jesus called in a loud voice, 'Lazurus, come out!" The dead man came out, his hands and feet wrapped with strips of linen, and a cloth around his face. Jesus said to them, "Take off the grave clothes and let him go." Therefore many of the Jews who had come to visit Mary, and had seen what Jesus did, put their faith in him. But some of them went to the Pharisees and told them what Jesus had done. Then the chief priests called a meeting of the Sanhedrin. "What are we accomplishing?" they asked. "Here is this man performing many miraculous signs. If we let him go on like this, everyone will believe in him, and then the Romans will come and take away both our place and our nation."

John 11, 43-48

Finally the temple guards went back to the chief priests and the Pharisees, who asked them, "Why didn't you bring him in?" "No one ever spoke the way this man does," the guards declared. "You mean he has deceived you also?" the Pharisees retorted. "Has any of the rulers or of the Pharisees believed in him? No! But this mob that knows nothing of the law—there is a curse on them." Nicodemus, who had gone to Jesus earlier and who was one of their own number, asked, "Does our law condemn anyone without first hearing him to find out what he is doing?"

John 7, 45-51

To keep power against Jesus' miracles and teachings, *Matthew 11, 2-15,* they said he/He did it in league with Satan as a threat to the gullible and 'God's' temple:

But when the Pharisees heard this, they said, "It is only by Beelzebub, the prince of demons, that this fellow drives out demons."

Matthew 12, 24

Jesus in turn saw the priests as slaves of Satan: *the Lord to condemn the innocent in unjust trials, Isaiah 28, John 8, 39-47.* Both sides imply spiritual prejudice blinds to injustice in religion or science, *Acts 26, 9-18, §8.3.* Even Jesus' disciples and family were part blinded, *Mark 3, 21 & 6, 1-5, Matthew 26, 52-56, §8.7.* Satan is cast as a blinding light, *§4.9,* who denies a just God, *§9.7.4, Isaiah 24.* Jesus thus addressed two spirited Israels and bids mortals seek a just salvation by the Christ's willing death as a sacrificial atonement for sin, *§11.4, §9.7.3.* That is Jesus' bilateral proposal on God's Justice above.

Jesus was tested by two Jewish mobs. One wished to make king by force, *John 6, 14-15,* the other to kill but could not detain, *Luke 4, 28-30 & 19, 45-48, John 10, 33-39, §8.1 & 58-59.* Neither could authorities detain so they awaited Jesus' coming to Jerusalem (*for Satan?*) to fulfil prophecies, *Mark 10, 32-34, Luke 13, 31-35.* Priests there furiously sought a 'just' case against Jesus to avoid 'God's' curse on injustice, *John 7, 49* above. They wanted a confession, *Matthew 22, 15-22, §11.5*:

> Jesus entered the temple courts and, while he was teaching, the chief priests and the elders of the people came up to him.
> "By what authority are you doing these things?" they asked. "And who gave you this authority?"
> Jesus replied, "I will also ask you one question. If you answer me, I will tell you by what authority I am doing these things. John's baptism—where did it come from? Was it from heaven, or from men?"
> They discussed it among themselves and said, "If we say, 'From heaven,' he will ask, 'Then why didn't you believe him?' But if we say, 'From men'—we are afraid of the people, for they all hold John was a prophet."
> So they answered Jesus, "We don't know."
> Then he said, "Neither will I tell you by what authority I am doing these things.
>
> Matthew 21, 23-32

They tried a blasphemy charge of claiming to be God's Son, *John 10, 33-39, §8.1.* The charge was intended to empower their 'just' Lord above to have Jesus arrested and put to death. By Jesus' account that may be their bilateral proposal on 'Justice': *the God they ask for.* Jesus acted, *John 18, 19-24,* to finesse them into deferring to Pilate to crucify for their 'just' Lord above (*for Satan?*).

12.10 **Jesus' trial licenses a bilateral spiritual world,** *§7*

Jesus claims mortals are tested by spirits they may hold to as divine but are not. Hence, Caiaphas prophesied Jesus had to be eliminated to save Jews from a curse:

> then one of them, named caiaphas, who was high priest that year, spoke up, "you know nothing at all! you do not realise that it is better for you that one man die for the people than that the whole nation perish."
> he did not say this on his own, but as high priest that year he prophesied that jesus would die for the jewish nation, and not only for that nation but also for the scattered children of god, to bring them together and make them one. so from that day on they plotted to take his life.
> therefore jesus no longer moved about publicly among the jews. instead he withdrew to a region near the desert, to a village called ephraim, where he stayed with his disciples.
> when it was almost time for the jewish passover, many went up from the country to jerusalem for their ceremonial cleansing before the passover. they kept looking for jesus, and as they stood in the temple area they asked one another, "what do you think? isn't he coming to the feast at all?" but the chief priests and pharisees had given orders that if anyone found out where jesus was, he should report it so they might arrest him.
>
> john 11, 49-57

Jesus agreed to die to save Jews from a curse but in order to appeal to God to overrule the death as unjust for a resurrection to lead spiritual war for souls against spirits Caiaphas spoke for, *1 Peter 3, 22, §8.3*:

> for it is commendable if a man bears up under the pain of unjust suffering because he is conscious of god.
> but how is it to your credit if you receive a beating for doing wrong and endure it?
> but if you suffer for doing good and you endure it, this is commendable before god.
> to this you were called, because christ suffered for you, leaving you an example, that you should follow in his steps.
>
> "he committed no sin,
> and no deceit was found in his mouth."
>
> when they hurled insults at him, he did not retaliate; when he suffered he made no threats.
> instead, he entrusted himself to him who judges justly.
> he himself bore our sins in his body on the tree, so that we might die to sins and live for righteousness;
> by his wounds you have been healed.
> for you were like sheep going astray, but now you have returned to the shepherd and overseer of your souls
>
> 1 peter 2, 19-25

Caiaphas evidently read *Deuteronomy 18, 17-22, §11.5,* to see Jesus as a false prophet to be put to death to clear a path for the real 'Christ' to make Israel a power, *John 11, 45-48, §9.* One or both spoke in a lying spirit, *2 Chronicles 18, 18-27.* Their readings live on because 'the church' is to witness to the synagogue that Jesus' Father's offer of mercy to Israel stands, *Isaiah 28, 11-18.* No matter who the Christ is, the conflict is proof of a bilateral covenant to God's word, *§4, Isaiah 10, 20-22, §8.6 & 28, 18, §7.4.* Jesus implies Caiaphas was allied with the wicked through the inspired writer of Acts:

"men of israel, listen to this: jesus of nazareth was a man accredited by god to you by miracles, wonders and signs, which god did among you through him, as you yourselves know. this man was handed over to you by god's set purpose and foreknowledge; and you, with the help of wicked men, put him to death by nailing him to the cross. but god raised him from the dead, freeing him from the agony of death, because it was impossible for death to keep its hold on him.

acts 2, 22-24

but in your hearts set apart christ as lord. always be prepared to give an answer to everyone who asks you to give the reason for the hope that you have. but to do this with gentleness and respect, ...

1 peter 3, 15

Jesus was tested by injustice in a bid to fulfil prophesy and save sinners, *§9, Isaiah 53.* Now injustice cannot be a just God's personal will. From the cross, Jesus quoted *Psalm 22, 'My God, my God, why have you forsaken me?* showing God did not lead to an unjust death, *§9.7.6.* By divine skill at Justice, *Isaiah 9, 6,* the Christ arguably sees the path to save sinners, *John 10, 14-18, §11.5: sees a just case to assure of it.* We need to see the case, *Psalm 22, 1; Isaiah 1, 15-20, §8.6,* to see how evil is defeated? *§15, §11.4, §13.10.* The Christ gives His God a just case to save sinners from Death, *Isaiah 28, 18, §7.4.* Jesus chose to go to death offering no defence (*indicting the courts's authority, John 19, 11, §7.10*), 'a lamb to slaughter' as in *Isaiah 53,* turning the cheek, *Lamentations 3, 25-32, §8.* He saw it as right *for the situation,* and Caiaphas saw it right to take Jesus' life for 'the Lord'. Jesus was to endure agony of Death three days, *a kind of wrestling bout?,* to ratify a pre-existing case to save souls, *Hosea 6, 1-2, Matthew 27, 62-66.* He is either the strongest to ever live, or, a weak soul to warlike enemies, *§8, 1 Corinthians 1, 18-24, §10.13.*

Now Jesus says God's sheep recognise Jesus' voice even if they need to hear it many times on some points, *Matthew 18, 21-22*, as Israel might exemplify. He warns Israel not to dote on rivals whose idea of Justice denies the test of suffering to death, *Isaiah 53*. Yet freedom of faith entitles sinners to call for and be offered every type of 'Christ' that may 'save' into hell's 'heaven' by alternative 'justice', *§9.7.4*:

"I tell you the truth, the man who does not enter the sheep pen by the gate, but climbs in by some other way, is a thief and a robber.
The man who enters by the gate is the shepherd of his sheep. The watchman opens the gate for him, and the sheep listen to his voice. He calls his own sheep by name and leads them out. When he has brought out all his own, he goes on ahead of them, and his sheep follow him because they know his voice. But they will never follow a stranger; in fact, they will run away from him because they do not recognise a strangers voice." Jesus used this figure of speech, but they did not understand what he was telling them.
Therefore Jesus said again, "I tell you the truth, I am the gate for the sheep. All who ever came before me were thieves and robbers, but the sheep did not listen to them. I am the gate; whoever enters through me will be saved. He will come in and go out, and find pasture. The thief comes only to steal and kill and destroy; I have come that they may have life, and have it to the full.

John 10, 1-10

Was Caiaphas a robber and thief of souls in God's temple? He is said to have plotted to arrest and take Jesus' life. The way to see if he was 'just' is to look at a just God's word for Caiaphas' proposal of just law to unseal it, *§8.1, Daniel 12, 9-10, §3, Psalm 22, 1, Isaiah 1, 15-20, §8.6*. Now the anti-tyranny principle, *§5*, says a just God cannot directly kill for blasphemy. God may not licence a 'faithful', *give charisma*, to serve God in that type of 'justice'. Thus, if Jesus had been killed on a blasphemy charge, courts could not licence it as God's direct will. The crucifixion does not prove a blasphemy charge as some may not see, *Proverbs 28, 5, §8.1*. Jesus indicted the synagogue of the day as largely unjust, *Matthew 23, 27-39*, yet asked coexistence and sound teaching not rebellion or disunion. The synagogue elected to defend itself from Jesus' teaching and deity, *Acts 26, 9-18, §8.3*, by a counter-proposal of 'God's' justice that entitled to oppress for blasphemy against God, *Acts 26, 11*, and build a divide to keep rival ideas of 'justice' out:

then jesus said to the crowds and to his disciples: "the teachers of the law and the pharisees sit in moses' seat. so you must obey them and do everything they tell you. but do not do what they do, for they do not practice what they preach. they tie up heavy loads and put them on men's shoulders, but they themselves are not willing to lift a finger to move them"

matthew 23, 1-4

and so i tell you, every sin and blasphemy will be forgiven men, but the blasphemy against the spirit will not be forgiven.

matthew 12, 31

Jews and Christians today do not attend one temple and debate just law because some on both sides are spiritually led to persecute the other. Are they, *in effect*, leaders to shepherd all in poor ideas of 'justice'? *1 Corinthians 6, 1-9, §10.7.* If God is for progress by fair debate, segregation is poor witness to God, *Isaiah 30, 1-15, §9.12.* If God is perfect Justice, *Isaiah 1, 15-20, §8.6; 2 Corinthians 10, 3-5, §8.2*, mortals can put faith in a 'just' science of truth related to evidence with God's word as key evidence, *§5.* There is then no licence for charismatic tyrants or priests to reserve their 'justice' from cross-examination in courts.

Jesus disputed the nature of 'justice', *so of Moses*, with, *it is claimed*, rebellious Jewish priests in unjust spirits. Now rebellion is in every religion, *§8.5*, so just courts cannot empower a faith of the day as basis for Justice unless it recasts as a proposal of Justice beyond reasonable objection, *Proverbs 1, 20-33, §9.7.6.* A just God makes the highest science on earth a progressive skill in 'justice' to unseal 'God's word'. Justice is to indict faiths that usurp 'God's word' and law, *§9.7.6.* Just courts cannot avoid the issue if 'God's word' offers a just salvation from a curse to death, *§6.1.* For what is 'justice' if not to deliver from lie or violence leading to death? Justice is to save from tyrannical sciences that curse, *§10.2*, from unjust suicide bombers, from ideas of 'justice' led by spiritual drunks who defame a just God. If courts limit 'justice' to standards not defending life from such evil's, it is fair only if the people's informed wish, *Isaiah 24, Luke 13, 1-9, §11.5.* 'God's word' alleges a powerful lobby in 'God's' image, *§9.1, §10.5*, that cannot abide Justice, *Proverbs 28, 5, §8.1*, leading into hell. Meanwhile, a curse of association, *§9.7.2*, gives kin a right to tie the knot with a global curse to death and reject a just God's mercy for all, *Luke 9, 5.* Truth? or too offensive to call?

12.11 Sex and marriage metaphors to daily spiritual life

'God's word' uses sex and marriage metaphor to cover how mortals relate with God or rebel gods, *e.g. Satan.*

Because Israel's immorality mattered
so little to her, she defiled the land
and committed adultery with stone
and wood.

... ...

13 Only acknowledge your guilt—
you have rebelled against the LORD
your God,
you have scattered your favours to
foreign gods
under every spreading tree, and have
not
obeyed me, ' " declares
the LORD.

"Return, faithless people," declares the
LORD, "for I am your husband. I will
choose you—one from a town and
two from a clan–and bring you to
Zion.
Then I will give you shepherds after
my own heart, who will lead you with
knowledge and understanding. In
those days, when your numbers have
increased greatly in the land,"
declares the LORD, "men will no longer
say, 'The ark of the covenant of the
LORD.' It will never enter their minds or
be remembered; it will not be missed
nor will another one be made. At that
time they will call Jerusalem The
Throne of the LORD, and all nations will
gather in Jerusalem to honor the name
of the LORD.

Jeremiah 3, 9, 13-17

Spirits might even sire mortals? §*8.3: e.g. 'heroes of old', Genesis 6, 1-4, §8.3 & 18, 14*, or a virgin-birth Son to God? *Isaiah 7, 9-14, §11.6.* If sex is spirited, it is part of religious prejudice for playing house with and divorcing spirits, *§7.3.* Mortals are born to spirit-bubbles of personal inherited formative spirits, *§9.1, Galatians 4, 1-9, §5.10, §10.5, §10.13.* House-spirits spit at rivals for a soul, *§7.5, Matthew 12, 26-32, §9.8, §10.2, Jeremiah 10, 23-24 & 2 Peter 2, 19, §11.4.* Thus, if the Godly stray to idols or unjust gods that is spiritual prostitution/ adultery. Body prostitution or adultery is also spiritual, possessive, if to a high totem, *§10.4*:

"You shall not commit adultery."

Deuteronomy 5, 18

For the prostitute reduces you to a
loaf of bread,
and the adulteress preys upon your
very life.

Proverbs 6, 26

Flee from sexual immorality. All other
sins a man commits are outside his
body, but he who sins sexually sins
against his own body. Do you not know
your body is a temple of the Holy
Spirit, who is in you, whom you have
received from God?

1 Corinthians 6, 18-19

Sex metaphors for evil spirits cast them not as fairy lights but inner red mists. The very superstitious may drop dead with fear at, *or feel compelled to try*, what 'God's word' warns are deadly sins. Now as regards spiritual adultery, God seems eager to forgive His people in *Jeremiah 3* above. But *Deuteronomy 22* below, sets a death-sentence on body-adultery. However, God then revokes the death-sentence in *Hosea* below where He asks Hosea to forgive his wife for adultery as may empower God, *as husband of Israel*, to forgive Israel's spiritual adultery. God asks to chuck out 'holy' relics, *e.g. sacred fruitcakes*, that unjust spirits hook by:

If a man is found sleeping with another man's wife, both the man who slept with her and the woman must die. You must purge the evil from Israel.
Deuteronomy 22, 22

The Lord said to me, "Go show your love to your wife again, though she is loved by another and is an adulteress. Love her as the Lord loves the Israelites, though they turn to other gods and love the sacred raisin cakes."
Hosea 3, 1

The on/off death-sentence for adultery makes God seem capricious or a non-absolute 'just'? Rather, death was set by Satan in a spell as 'God's hand' or acting 'God' of Israel? *§10.8.* A just God, *whose platform is mercy*, was entitled to in turn repeal it for Hosea's people, *cf. Abraham and Isaac, §7.8.* Thus, to victimise for physical adultery may be proof of spiritual adultery?:

The teachers of the law and the Pharisees brought in a woman caught in adultery. They made her stand before the group and said to Jesus, "Teacher, this woman was caught in the act of adultery. In the Law Moses commanded us to stone such women. Now what do you say?" They were using this question as a trap, in order to have a basis for accusing him. But Jesus bent down and started to write on the ground with his finger. When they kept on questioning him, he straightened up and said to them, "If any one of you is without sin, let him be the first to cast a stone at her." Again he stooped down and wrote on the ground.
At this, those who heard began to go away one at a time, the older ones first, until only Jesus was left with the woman still standing there. Jesus straightened up and asked her, "Woman, where are they? Has no one condemned you?"
"No one, sir," she said.
"Then neither do I condemn you," Jesus declared. "Go now and leave your life of sin."
John 8, 3-11

Jesus could not tell teachers of 'the law' that Satan set the death sentence, *using Moses, §10.8*, because God respects freedom of faith on 'God's' nature in a title-contest, *§4.* Nor could Jesus condone a death-sentence on body adultery if aiming to clear Israel of a death-sentence on spiritual adultery. His reply to teachers of the law had to be justly exact, reserving full truth for freedom of faith but implying that to put to death for adultery is sin, *under judgement.* All adultery is sin:

some pharisees came to him to test him. they asked, "is it lawful for a man to divorce his wife for any and every reason?"
"haven't you read," he replied, "that at the beginning the creator 'made them male and female,' and said, 'for this reason a man will leave his father and mother and be united to his wife, and the two will become one flesh'? so they are no longer two, but one. therefore what god has joined together, let man not separate."
"why then," they asked, "did moses command that a man give his wife a certificate of divorce and send her away?"
jesus replied, "moses permitted you to divorce your wives because your hearts were hard.
but it was not that way from the beginning.
i tell you that anyone who divorces his wife, except for marital unfaithfulness, and marries another woman commits adultery."
the disciples said to him,
"if this is the situation between a husband and wife, it is better not to marry."
jesus replied, "not everyone can accept this word, but only those to whom it has been given. for some are eunuchs because they were born that way; others were made that way by men; and others have renounced marriage because of the kingdom of heaven. the one who can accept this should accept it."

matthew 19, 3-9

for this reason a man will leave his father and mother and be united to his wife, and they will become one flesh.
the man and his wife were both naked, and they felt no shame.

genesis 2, 24-25

Genesis 2 above is a folded legal form to respect either of God or 'God' spiritually joining a couple, *§9.1.* A marriage made in heaven is unashamed of just readings of God's word, *Genesis 2, 25* above, ashamed of unjust readings, *Isaiah 24, Mark 8, 36-38, §8.* Satan marries in shared sin, *1 Corinthians 6, 16-17* above. A marriage made in hell may gain a pass over from an evil curse for services, *§10.4, for spiritual adultery, Isaiah 24.* Spirit-charisma is no proof of God but may mark a path, *§8.5.*

Jesus taught that to commit adultery in the heart may be sin enough to draw a death-sentence, *Matthew 5, 21-26, §6.* That need not be as easy as some fear as it implies firm loyalty to evil spirit. It betokens a spiritual place for sex both in love God and neighbour philosophy and unjust sciences of reproduction, *§9.1.* Jesus taught that marriages (*ones having one good partner?*) can be dissolved on grounds of adultery, *Luke 18, 29-30.* Such divorce focuses not on the physical adultery but underlying spiritual adultery. For if one partner is for heaven, the other hell, a divorce is just to respect both. It makes marriage a testing and possessive spiritual battleground for heaven and hell:

If any brother has a wife who is not a believer and she is willing to live with him, he must not divorce her. And if a woman has a husband who is not a believer and he is willing to live with her, she must not divorce him. For the unbelieving husband has been sanctified through his wife, and the unbelieving wife has been sanctified through her husband. Otherwise your children would be unclean, but as it is, they are holy.

1 Corinthians 7, 12-14

Do you not know that he who unites himself with a prostitute is one with her in body? For it is said, "The two will become one flesh." But he who unites himself with the Lord is one with him in spirit.

1 Corinthians 6, 16-17

The perfect marriage is made in heaven as a temple to God, *Proverbs 1, 8-10, Ephesians 6, 1-4*, sealed in God's Spirit, maybe reinforced in sexual feelings to defend from evil spirits tempting to adultery. Do such marriages abound? All marriages may be tested by evil spirits with hot and cold feelings to form unstable liaisons, as may make marriages that break to compromise people. But in *Hosea 3* above, God is ready to forgive sins involved to save souls from evil.

A good home is a temple to a just God for parents and children even if outer temples to 'God' are clouded in spiritual adultery. Even adulterous male priests might be saved by a wife's greater fidelity to God at home. Women may man the home as a spiritual stronghold to foster a loving family as backbone to progress that brings Justice, *Psalm 98.* That stronghold is compromised, *lost if Paul is right, §10.4,* if women join men as priestesses in adulterous religion. Perhaps few marriages are made purely in hell or heaven but on paths with options to go either way.

12.12 Jews for and against Jesus: spiritual prostitution

Jews who think Jesus is the Christ are to teach the Christ's ministry to Israel has a deep forgiving basis:

> But God demonstrates his own love for us in this: While we were still sinners, Christ died for us.
> Since we have now been justified by his blood, how much more shall we be saved from God's wrath through him!
> For if, when we were God's enemies, we were reconciled to him through the death of his Son, how much more, having been reconciled, shall we be saved through his life! Not only is this so, but we also rejoice in God through our Lord Jesus Christ, through whom we have received reconciliation.
> Romans 5, 8-11

Jesus says He went to the cross to save Jews who at the time slept with evil as God's foes, *criminals.* He wished to save them from 'God's wrath', *Satan,* as a bitter pill to swallow, *Isaiah 25, 8, §11.1, Daniel 12, 9-10, §3.* Jews against Jesus, *Job 19, 25-29, §7,* seek a rival brand of 'justice' to a rival 'God'. Scholars not perversely unjust may help all by resolving antagonistic spiritual prejudices into rival proposals on God's justice:

> They took Jesus to the high priest, and all the chief priests, elders and teachers of the law came together.
> Peter followed him at a distance, right into the courtyard of the high priest. There he sat with the guards and warmed himself at the fire.
> The chief priests and the whole Sanhedrin were looking for evidence against Jesus so they could put him to death, but they did not find any. Many testified falsely against him, but their statements did not agree.
> Then some stood up and gave this false testimony against him: "We heard him say, 'I will destroy this man-made temple and in three days will build another, not made by man.' " Yet even then their testimony did not agree.
> Then the high priest stood up before them and asked Jesus, "Are you not going to answer? What is this testimony that these men are bringing against you?"
> But Jesus remained silent and gave no answer.
> Again the high priest asked him, "Are you the Christ, the Son of the Blessed One?"
> "I am," said Jesus. "And you will see the Son of Man sitting at the right hand of the Mighty One and coming on the clouds of heaven."
> The high priest tore his clothes. "Why do we need anymore witnesses?" he asked. "You have heard the blasphemy. What do you think?"
> They all condemned him as worthy of death.
> Mark 14, 53-64

Religion to a just God is to offer Justice to pave the way for God's coming in triumph, *Psalm 98.* Justice is life and mercy to overrule a curse to death on life, *§4, §7.* The trial of Jesus was arguably led in evil spiritual forces who could level no charge other than that Jesus claimed to be the Christ or King of the Jews. It felt a blasphemy to the high priest but his opinion, *spiritually reinforced or not*, is not enough to define Justice, *Job 19, 25-29, §7.* 'God's word' is to a mixed crowd in 'Israel' on the nature of Justice, *Jonah 3 to 4.* Jesus thinks 'Christians' a mixed bunch, *Matthew 24, 5.* The true God of Israel or true Christ is with some proposal of Justice that only the 'just' may abide with, *Proverbs 1, 20-33, §9.7.6.*

To deny Jesus justly is to define 'God' differently than the real 'Jesus' does, *§9.7.5.* Jesus cast Israel's authorities of the day as poor at Justice, needing God's mercy via a just atonement for sins, *Isaiah 1, 15-20, §8.6.* Some priests do not want Justice as happy to serve a tyrannical 'God's' law in the temple, *§9.8, Isaiah 25, 8, §11.1, Romans 2, 17-24, §8.5.* The Old Testament allows for their rule by likening 'Israel' to a religious prostitute when sleeping with false gods, *§8.4, Jeremiah 3, Hosea 4, 7-19.* Did Jesus seek to snare 'God's temple' in spiritual prostitution? *injustice*, or oppose spiritual prostitution in it? Do the perverse and unjust rule in much established religion as sinners? *§10.4*:

"what do you think? there was a man who had two sons. he went to the first and said, 'son, go and work in the vineyard.'
" 'I will not,' he answered, but later he changed his mind and went.
"then the father went to the other son and said the same thing. he answered, 'I will sir,' but he did not go.
"which of the two did what his father wanted?"
"the first," they answered.
jesus said to them, "I tell you the truth, the tax collectors and the prostitutes are entering the kingdom of god ahead of you. for john came to you to show you the way of righteousness, and you did not believe him, but the tax collectors and the prostitutes did. and even after you saw this, you did not repent and believe him.

matthew 21, 28-32

To indict spiritual prostitution in religion raises strong feeling. Jesus expected all 'Christians' to be tested by it, *§8.6.* For spiritual prostitutes as chosen 'Christians', *Jew or Gentile*, may unite in brotherly love, *§8.4, §9.7.4*, or, war for their spiritual prejudices against just truth.

Jesus says all need God's mercy by a just atonement for sin that is deep enough to invert status. Thus, prostitutes or ill-regulated tax-collectors who accept it may be better in heaven's eyes than priests who fight its introduction! *Luke 18, 10-14, Isaiah 29, 22-24, §8.6.* It implies established folk can be barely 'just', *as to make 'murder' root of their 'justice'*, as an idea discomforting to idolaters, *Romans 5, 7, §11.4.* Jesus leaves room for Jews to return to God later, *Isaiah 1, 15-20, §8.6,* even via purgatory, *§10.11, Romans 11, 15-31, §7.10.* He supported the metaphor of the house of Israel as a vineyard. On Israel's vines grow souls as good or bad grapes. The bad grapes include leaders at bringing a curse on 'Israel' to desolation, *Isaiah 25, 2-5*:

I will sing for the one I love a song
about his vineyard:
my loved one had a vineyard on a
fertile hillside.
He dug it up and cleared it of stones
and planted it with the choicest vines.
He built a watchtower in it and cut
out a winepress as well.
Then he looked for a crop of good
grapes, but it yielded only bad fruit.

"Now you dwellers in Jerusalem and
men of Judah,
judge between me and my vineyard.
What more could have been done for
my vineyard than I have done for it?
When I looked for good grapes,
why did it yield only bad?
Now I will tell you
what I am going to do to my vineyard:
I will take away its hedge,
and it will be destroyed;
I will break down its wall,
and it will be trampled.
I will make it a wasteland,
neither pruned nor cultivated,
and briers and thorns will grow there.
I will command the clouds not to rain
on it."

The vineyard of the Lord Almighty is
the house of Israel,
and the men of Judah
are the garden of his delight.
And he looked for justice, but saw
bloodshed;
for righteousness but heard cries of
distress.

Isaiah 5, 1-7

To not witness for or against Jesus may be sin to delay God but nothing God has not allowed for, *Psalm 98.* Are Jesus' disciples or their enemies the bad grapes to curse Israel? Put another way, is the New Testament God's word and Justice to Israel? If 'God's word' is not to serve unjust spiritual prejudice, '*faith*', *§9.7.4,* Jews can study the New Testament to show 'just' fault or merit, *§9.* To whom is just casework not light relief from the Spirit? *Isaiah 24, Psalm 38, 19, Matthew 20, 1-16.*

Jesus developed on the metaphor of a vineyard growing souls, *Luke 20, 9-16, §7.10*. He saw it as rented out to tenant-farmers, *Galatians 4, 1-9, §5.10*, who refuse to release souls belonging to God's Son: the rightful heir to the farm. He implies the evil tenants conspire to float a 'just' case to murder 'God', *Isaiah 9, 6*, out of their envy, *Psalm 2, §9.4*:

> For he knew it was out of envy that they handed Jesus over to him. While Pilate was sitting on the judge's seat, his wife sent to him this message: "Don't have anything to do with that innocent man, for I have suffered a great deal today in a dream because of him." But the chief priests and the elders persuaded the crowd to ask for Barabbas and to have Jesus executed.
> Matthew 27, 18-20

Now Pilate's wife's dream led her to a plea for mercy for the innocent man. Was the dream spiritual duress to steer Pilate? He was said to know Jesus was handed to him out of envy. Jesus' word ascribes envy to spiritual pull of Satan in the hereditary sinful nature, *John 10, 33-39, §8.1, Galatians 5, 17-21, §7.11*. If 'our' sinful nature is a familiar evil spirit, *§7, §10.5*, the authorities acted as spiritual prostitutes. There is another way to see it. The parable in Luke ends with teachers of the law and chief priests supposing Jesus aimed the parable at them, *Luke 16-19*. But were they wicked enough to deliberately put to death God's Son and heir? Rather, they could not accept Jesus was God's Son, *Matthew 12, 7, §9.7.5 & 21, 23-32*, above. That leaves the tenants in the parable who knew Jesus to be God's Son and heir as Satan and rebel gods. The tenant-farmers are thus rebel gods, *demons allied with Pilate's gods*, that Israel is accused of spiritual prostitution with, *§7.3, §8.3*.

If rebel gods farm mortals as food, *grapes or sheep*, in spiritual food chains, *§10.5, §11.2*, the idea of losing juicy stock to God's Son could cause envy. That envy then spiritually filled authorities against Jesus' popularity, *John 10, 33-39, §8.1*. The gods also inspire superstitious fear at God's invisible approach, *§7.3*, and sacrifice to demons, *§7.8, §10.13*. The priests felt by duress of evil-spirit-guardians that Jesus aimed the parable at them, *§7.1*, but that may be a half truth. The trial may oblige all to accept a bilateral spiritual contest for souls, *§7*, with rival proposals on God's just nature. That truth is rooted in Israel, *Romans 11, 15-31, §7.10*.

12.13 Spiritual horns of the righteous and wicked

If mortals live as slaves or wards to familiar spirits, they only find truth if a spirit of truth sends it with Justice, *Isaiah 11, 1-10, §11.1, Zechariah 4, 6, §8, Joel 2, 28-32, §7.11, John 16, 7-11, §7.11.* The message of Justice can only come after a just ruling on entitlement of mortals to it as with Daniel, *§7.3.* It may then be sent to folk holding out against a conspiracy of unjust 'science' and religion to rule the world, *§1, Isaiah 24, Matthew 5, 3 above.* Those folk witness against the unjust and their plans to secure tyrannies on earth.

Conspiracies of the unjust abound to meet mortal right to know evil, *Genesis 3, 2-5, §7.4.* They must run their course and shape the path along which the message of Justice can come via its mortal servants, *Daniel 2, 30.* For if all unjust conspiracies are led by Satan in spirit, *Revelation 12, 7-12, §7.1,* he will guide the unjust to set a path for Justice as counter-intuitive to the just mind as possible. The devil thereby ensures the message of Justice can be tested and perverted to a message of injustice to claim his goats for hell at Judgement Day, *Isaiah 30, 1-15, §9.12, 1 Corinthians 1, 18-24, §10.13.*

Blessed is the man
who makes the Lord his trust,
who does not look to the proud,
to those who turn aside to false gods.
Many, O Lord my God,
are the wonders you have done.
The things you planned for us
no one can recount to you;
were I to speak and tell of them,
they would be too many to declare.

Sacrifice and offering you did not desire,
but my ears you have pierced;
burnt offerings and sin offerings
you did not require.
Then I said, "Here I am, I have come—
it is written about me in the scroll.
I desire to do your will, O my God;
your law is within my heart."

I proclaim righteousness in the great assembly.
I do not seal my lips,
as you know, O Lord.
I do not hide your righteousness in my heart;
I speak of your faithfulness and salvation.
I do not conceal your love and your truth
from the great assembly.

Do not withhold your mercy from me, O Lord;
may your love and your truth
always protect me.
For troubles without number surround me;
my sins have overtaken me, and I cannot see.

Psalm 40, 4-12

Justice is life and truth, *§4*, as why a just God or Son of same nature, *Isaiah 9, 6*, may be vital to life in creation, *chapter 11*. Idolatry opts for 'injustice' as may translate into a death-wish by a just case, *§4, Wisdom 14, 27-31, §9.5*. For mortals, the ultimate event in just science may be the open coming of God or Son to rule in person, *Psalm 98*.

To deliver Justice to mortals under injustice is only easy if their evil handicap is not much, *Romans 5, 7, §11.4*. Tyrannies and war show evil as fierce and possessive, *Proverbs 28, 5, §8.1*. Strong witness to God may need spiritual clothes from God, *§9.1, Isaiah 6*. Both God's and Satan's servants are said to have horns: *Psalm 75, 10*, to butt for their ideas of 'justice'. The horns betoken spirits of 'justice' whereby tyrants butt for might as right, *Wisdom 2, 11-12, §9.2*, and those for a just God butt for just process, *Luke 1, 69, §6*:

in the third year of king belshazzar's
reign, i, daniel, had a vision, … … …
…
5 as i was thinking about this,
suddenly a goat with a prominent
horn between his eyes came from the
west, crossing the whole earth
without touching the ground. he came
toward the two-horned ram i had
seen standing beside the canal and
charged at him in great rage. i saw
him attack the ram furiously, striking
the ram and shattering his two horns.
the ram was powerless to stand
against him; the goat knocked him to
the ground and trampled on him, and
none could rescue the ram from his
power. the goat became very great,
but at the height of his power his
large horn was broken off, and in its
place four prominent horns grew up
toward the four winds of heaven. …
… … …
… … …
20 "the two-horned ram that you saw
represents the kings of media and
persia. the shaggy goat is the king of
greece, and the large horn between
his eyes is the first king.
the four horns that replaced the one
that was broken off represent four
kingdoms that will emerge from his
nation but will not have the same
power.
"in the latter part of their reign, when
rebels have become completely
wicked, a stern-faced king, a master of
intrigue will arise. he will become very
strong but not by his own power. he
will cause astounding devastation and
will succeed in whatever he does. he
will destroy the mighty men and the
holy people. he will cause deceit to
prosper, and he will consider himself
superior. when they feel secure, he
will destroy many and take his stand
against the prince of princes. yet he
will be destroyed but not by human
power.

daniel 8, 1, 5-8, 20-25

In the above, Daniel describes how one tyranny butts another to 'liberate' people. Tyrannies can only end if faith in Justice is not butted out. Meanwhile, folk may live as slaves to spirits of 'justice' under a spiritual war where tyrannies only fall by rulings in God's court. The rulings may oblige Satan, *supreme tyrant of tyrants and God's wrath*, to cull tyrannies that fail to break faith in Justice. Satan is meanwhile occult behind a veil of natural and political causes that allow freedom of faith for ideas of 'justice'. The 'just' act as if by God's Spirit against tyrannical 'justice' led by rebel gods, *Micah 4, 5*, who organise lesser evil spirits to feed on mortals in the sinful nature, *§7*. When a tyranny falls by war, the war may be a horn of the devil to take credit from unsung souls who held out for Justice. Tyrannies ascribe a hollow victory in propaganda to their heroes or idols rather than give credit to a just God, *§9.5, §9.6*.

The horn of Justice is said to be rooted in Israel but 'Israel' seems patchy at 'justice':

In fierce anger he has cut off every horn of Israel.
He has withdrawn his right hand at the approach of the enemy.
Lamentations 2, 3

"Do not hate your brother in your heart. Rebuke your neighbour frankly so you will not share in his guilt."
Leviticus 19, 17

When every horn is cut off in Israel as above, Israel is not butting for God nor the angry devil who curses Israel for failing him, *Isaiah 28, 19-20*. Enemies seek to establish Israel's loyalty to injustice under test, *Isaiah 24, 14-23*. Poor witness to neighbours gives enemies a claim as in *Leviticus 19, 17* above. But even good witness may meet a curse of association with sinners as why the Messiah may first come to die for sinners He wishes to save, *§9.7.2*, and why mortals must die by 'God's wrath' pending God's full salvation in the battle of good and evil.

Evil wages war by 'injustice' but calls it 'justice' whilst God wages 'war' by perfect Justice. Daniel above implies no one will win security by 'injustice', *Luke 13, 1-9, §11.5*. A remnant of Israel is prophesied to return to Justice by end-times. By *Daniel 8* above, Justice is by allegiance to the Prince of princes. Israel can only stand by faith in Justice indexed to virgin birth of a son, *Isaiah 7, 9-14, §11.6*, God's Son, *Psalm 2, §9.4*. It cannot stand in error on the Messiah.

Survival of the fittest is an idea of 'justice' to let the mighty feel superior, *Daniel 8* above. The 'justice' of 'natural' science can supply virgin births to order and sire 'superior' mortals by genetic or cyborg science, But in supernatural science, sins of 'parents', *e.g. wish for amoral genius*, are inherited, *§9.11, Exodus 20, 4-6, §7.9*, for a breed with demonic spiritual horns. It implies a demonic cult to evolutionary 'science', *§9.2.*

Israel is to be courted by ideas of Justice, *§4*, most of which may be tyrannical, *Daniel 7, 23-28, Revelation 13 & 17.* The tyrannical can help take a promised holy land by force, *Zechariah 4, 6, §8.* War may impart no love or understanding of Justice to evil as why war is an institution. Did David defeat Goliath by an understanding of Justice? or because he led the path to Justice? David lived at an early stage in 'God's word' but we have it all. It asks to spread Justice to cause nations to give up war, *Micah 4, 1-5, §8.* Tyrants may see that as a weakness to test, *Isaiah 24, 14-18, Daniel 7, 23-28.* By their butting, we look for leaders able to turn injustice or wrath back on evil. The Messiah alone may be strong enough to do that, *Isaiah 53.* His horns are not tyrannical, *Revelation 13, 11-17 & 14, 9-11, §9.7.4*, yet the treacherous may read 'God's word' to give Him tyrannical horns that justify their own:

> Then I saw a Lamb, looking as if it had been slain, standing in the centre of the throne, encircled by the four living creatures and the elders. He has seven horns and seven eyes, which are the seven spirits of God sent out into all the earth.
>
> Revelation 5, 6

Demons are cast as horned spiritual dragons, *Revelation 12, 7-12, §7.1*, see box *§6.10*, with fiery breath and scales of pride, *Job 41, NKJ Bible.* The king of the proud is Leviathan as may denote Satan's spiritual body on earth, *Isaiah 27, 1, Revelation 12, 17 to 13, 18*:

> "He (Leviathan) looks down on all that are haughty; he is king over all that are proud."
>
> Job 41, 34

The scales that fell from Paul's eyes in *Acts 9, 18* may be satanic spiritual armour: pride that veils sight of God, *Acts 26, 9-18, §8.3*, darkening love for neighbour. Paul gave up one set of armour and horns to put on another by the Spirit of Jesus' 'God', *§10.10*, as follows.

12.14 Spiritual armour or clothes according to Jesus

To perceive that spirits exist is assurance enough for some that 'God' exists. But if unjust lying spirits exist as God's enemies, they comfort in unjust faiths, *§7, James 4, 6-10, §10.5, §10.3, Isaiah 24.* Just faith is asked by a just God, *§9.7.2, §11.6,* to avoid simple unjust faiths that anchor a curse to apocalypse, *Proverbs 1, 20-33, §9.7.6, Isaiah 24.* God is said to be in fruits of the Spirit, *§9.1,* that show ability to do God's will in testing situations. In practice, the Messiah alone may walk a perfect just path against injustice whilst others are more like sailing ships tacking through spiritual weather systems on zig-zag paths to God or 'God', see box, *§7.5.* Paul and Ezekiel testify that rapid spiritual promotion to serve a deity can be traumatic, *§10.10.*

Mortals begin in Satan's house as an abode for crooks under a death-sentence. He counts sinners as his criminals to punish, *§4, Luke 4, 5-6, §1.15; 1 John 5, 19, §6.10, Mark 8, 36-38, §8.* David says we are clothed for a life of sin from birth, *Psalm 51, 1-12, §10.10.* If we do not like Death, we can appeal to God for salvation, *§7.* But by serving tyranny, ephemeral riches and power can be had under a fickle curse-discount granted to help societies mature as a testing curse on God's servants, *§4, §9.7.4, Psalm 73, Luke 13, 1-9, §11.5.* The way of more by curse-discount wealth is a gamble to ruin the planet, *§10.1, Matthew 16, 26.*

Apart from the first people, *said to be Adam and Eve in Paul's texts,* only God's Son who is God in nature, *Isaiah 9, 6,* may not be born clothed in sin by ancestral inheritance under the law, *Genesis 4, 6-7, §10.5, Exodus 20, 4-6, §7.9, Isaiah 7, 9 &14, §11.6*:

> then isaiah said, "hear now, you house of david! is it not enough to try the patience of men? will you try the patience of my god also? therefore the lord himself will give you a sign: the virgin shall be with child and will give birth to a son, and will call him immanuel. he will eat curds and honey when he knows enough to reject the wrong and choose the right.
>
> isaiah 7, 13-15

The above child of Justice must not follow Adam and Eve to take living spirit-clothing from Satan, *§10.9,* whatever the temptation or injustice, else Satan will claim a just case for eternal jurisdiction of all mortals to depose a just God.

Satan and God offer house-styles in spiritual clothing, *§9.1, §10.5, Genesis 3, 7-9, §11.3, Isaiah 61, 10, Zechariah 3, 1-4.* Paul describes clothes for God's house as the armour of love, *1 Corinthians 13, 4-13, §7*:

But since we belong to the day, let us be self-controlled, putting on faith and love as a breastplate, and the hope of salvation as a helmet. For God did not appoint us to suffer wrath but to receive salvation through our Lord Jesus Christ.
1 Thessalonians 5, 8-9

If the wrath of evil can enter and ravish heaven, *Isaiah 14, 12-21, §8.1, Revelation 12, 7-12, §7.1*, God's spiritual armour might be eternally necessary, *Luke 7, 28, §11.4, Isaiah 11, 6-9, §7.6, 1 Corinthians 13, 4-13, §7.* Those not bridled, *§10.5*, in God's spiritual armour might find God's heaven uncomfortable:

Do not be deceived: Neither the sexually immoral nor idolaters nor adulterers nor male prostitutes nor homosexual offenders nor thieves nor the greedy nor drunkards nor slanderers nor swindlers will inherit the kingdom of God. And this is what some of you were. But you were washed, you were sanctified, you were justified in the name of the Lord Jesus Christ and by the Spirit of our God.
1 Corinthians 6, 9-11

To reject evil may leave poor in spirit where God is not well taught, *§9.1, Matthew 5, 3* below. The above says no *practising* idolaters, liars, sorcerers, adulterers, homosexuals, (*or heterosexuals by Matthew 22, 30*) or swindlers gain the kingdom. Yet some who were are forgiven and dressed in privileged knowledge of God to seal against temptation, *§10.10, Isaiah 11, 6-9, §7.6*:

... the head cannot say to the feet, "I don't need you!" On the contrary, those parts of the body that seem to be weaker are indispensable, and the parts that we think are less honourable we treat with special honour. And the parts that are unpresentable are treated with special modesty, while our presentable parts need no special treatment. But God has combined the members of the body and has given greater honour to the parts that lacked it, so that there should be no division in the body ....
1 Corinthians 12, 21-25

Blessed are the poor in spirit,
for theirs is the kingdom of heaven.
Matthew 5, 3

God's mercy is deep, *§11*, giving the penitent a place in God's kingdom, in a spiritual body under the Christ as King, *§11.1*:

But God demonstrates his own love for us in this:
while we were still sinners, Christ died for us.
Since we have now been justified by his blood,
how much more will we be saved
from God's wrath through him!
For if, when we were God's enemies, we
were reconciled to him through the
death of his Son, how much more, having
been reconciled, shall we be saved
through his life! ... ...
Therefore just as sin entered the world
through one man, and death through sin,
and in this way death came to all men,
because all sinned— for before the law
was given, sin was in the world. But sin is
not taken into account when there is no
law. Nevertheless, death reigned
from the time of Adam to the time of Moses,
even over those who did not sin by
breaking a command, as did Adam, who
was a pattern of the one to come.

Romans 5, 8-10, 12-14

Some sinners are so steadfast in sin as to be sons of the devil. God's enemies belong with Satan so inside his fiery furnace, *hell.* There, people still weep and get angry as part of hell's order, *Matthew 13, 36-43, §9.1.*

"Blessed are those who wash their
robes, that they may have the right to
the tree of life and may go through
the gates into the city. Outside are the
dogs, those who practice magic arts,
the sexually immoral, the murderers,
the idolaters and everyone who loves
and practices falsehood.

Revelation 22, 14-15

... to him who is thirsty I will give to
drink without cost from the spring of
the water of life. ... ...
But the cowardly, the unbelieving, the
vile, the murderers, the sexually
immoral, those who practice magic
arts, the idolaters and all liars— their
place will be in the fiery lake of
burning sulfur. This is the second
death.

Revelation 21, 6, 8

Might this imply dark realms outside hell where weeping and anger linger? *Luke 13, 23-30.* There is also a parable about wedding clothes to fit for the kingdom of heaven that refers to dark outer realms:

jesus spoke to them again in parables, saying: "the kingdom of heaven is like a king who prepared a wedding banquet for his son. he sent his servants to those who had been invited to the banquet to tell them to come, but they refused to come.
"then he sent some more servants and said, 'tell those that have been invited that i have prepared my dinner: my oxen and fatted cattle have been butchered, and everything is ready. come to the wedding banquet.'
"but they paid no attention and went off— one to his field, another to his business. the rest seized his servants, mistreated them and killed them. the king was enraged. he sent his army and destroyed those murderers and burned their city.
"then he said to his servants, 'the wedding banquet is ready, but those i invited did not deserve to come. go to the street corners and invite to the banquet anyone you find. so the servants went out into the streets and gathered all the people they could find, both good and bad, and the wedding hall was filled with guests.
"but when the king came in to see the guests, he noticed a man there who was not wearing wedding clothes. 'friend' he asked, 'how did you get in here without wedding clothes?' the man was speechless.
"then the king told the attendants, 'tie him hand and foot, and throw him outside, into the darkness, where there will be weeping and gnashing of teeth.'
"for many are invited, but few are chosen."

matthew 22, 1-14

The wedding clothes betoken affinity to God's Spirit. Why would the King not know how some souls got into heaven? Perhaps the division of souls by flames into hell and heaven, *§6*, is led by Satan taking those he can but leaving some who appear marginal to sow trouble in heaven. The man with no wedding clothes is then a 'friend' but who may lack affinity for wedding clothes so be vulnerable to evil: a sleeping servant awaiting Satan's call. If God never kills, *as by casting souls into hell*, would He set a place for such souls outside hell? The sleepers may give Satan a just right to continue spiritually contesting heaven? The 'attendants' are then evil spirits testing for souls who will eventually declare that they prefer to be tied 'hand and foot' in hell's clothes. Evil spirits prey on them to confirm in evil and take into hell. Hell is for souls to whom sight of the source of life is distressing as goes with inability to bear God's spiritual armour, *Matthew 25, 14-30*. Job testifies that sight of God can at first be humiliating even for a 'righteous' sinner, *Job 42, 5-6*. To wear God's spiritual armour may be eternally necessary to keep evil at bay.

12.15 The relation of God's law to faith (*spiritual prejudice*)

Jesus' death respects at least two rival camps on God's justice among Jews. The camps show faiths that may be just or unjust. Unjust ideas of 'justice' bait spiritual pits to trap the impure of heart, *Psalm 57, 6*:

if a man digs a pit,
he will fall into it;

if a man roles a stone, it
will role back on him.

proverbs 26, 27

But all can struggle on to God by 'just' casework, *Isaiah 1, 15-20, §8.6, 2 Corinthians 10, 3-5, §8.2.* It may save from pitfalls. A question each seeker of a just God faces is how their spiritual prejudice or faith meshes with God's law? *Isaiah 7, 9-14, §11.6 & 26, 2, Habakkuk 2, 4.* Jews fear a curse on faith that makes a fetish of God's law to break the eternal covenant, *Isaiah 24*:

very well then , with foreign lips and strange tongues
god will speak to this people,
to whom he said,
"this is the resting place, let the weary rest";
and, "this is the place of repose"— but they would not listen.
so then, the word of the lord to them will become:
do and do, do and do,
rule on rule, rule on rule;
a little here, a little there—
so that they will go and fall backward,
be injured and snared and captured.

therefore hear the word of the lord, you scoffers
who rule this people in jerusalem.
you boast, "we have entered into a covenant with death,
with the grave we have made an agreement.
when an overwhelming scourge sweeps by
it cannot touch us,
for we have made a lie our refuge
and falsehood our hiding place."

so this what the sovereign lord says:

"see, i lay a stone in zion,
a tested stone,
a precious cornerstone for a sure foundation;
the one who trusts will never be dismayed.
17 i will make justice the measuring line
and righteousness the plumb line;
hail will sweep away your refuge the lie,
and water will overflow your hiding place.
your covenant with death will be annulled;
your agreement with the grave will not stand.
when the overwhelming scourge sweeps by,
you will be beaten down by it.
as often as it comes it will carry you away;
morning after morning, by day and by night,
it will sweep through."

isaiah 28, 11-19

The above implies many hope to be vindicated by observing commandments or ritual, *by formalities.* Apparently, that need not show faith in a just God or a sense of Justice. There can be pride in obeying God's law and in fine ritual as if securing the eternal covenant but in reality a pact to injustice and death. See *§8.3* on circumcision, *Psalm 50, 5.* Fastidious obedience to God's law can be a spiritual pit in covenant to Satan, *Isaiah 10, 20-22, §8.6,* a form of prejudice God is to save 'Israel' from. God lets freedom of faith for evil even in temples, *Genesis 3, 2-5, §7.4.*

Suppose that in *Psalm 118, 19-24, §7,* the tested stone for a sure foundation for Zion is the Christ. It decodes as that the just Christ will face test by injustice to save sinners from evil. The Christ's earthly life may be to pass Satan's tests to free sinners, *§10.9, Isaiah 53.*

Greater love has no one than this, that he lay down his life for his friends. You are my friends if you do what I command.

John 15, 13-14

The Justice of the stone is to annul Israel's blind pact to a 'justice' that curses to death for not obeying rules perfectly. Legalistic priests for living up to the law may seem strong but lack understanding, *Matthew 23.* In *Isaiah 28* above, Israel is urged to seek the just faith by which it can stand, *Isaiah 7, 9-14, §11.6.* It invokes mercy for not living up to God's law as implies a section of law to release from laws that curse for sin, *i.e. laws to define an atonement for sin, §9.7.5.* Many wish to see foes punished for sin so is God's mercy vindictive? *Jonah 3* to *4.* If sinners cannot strictly obey God's law, each may face a death-sentence in punitive law, *Ecclesiastes 7, 20, Psalm 32 & 51, 1-12, §10.9.* Sins a just God is not entitled to forgive reject the jurisdiction of His Spirit, *Psalm 32, 8-11, §10.5, Matthew 12, 31, §10.*

God urges to an atonement for sin to escape a curse on sin. He urges to covenant by a sacrifice to God yet not of critters or thanks, *Psalm 50, 2-23, §11.4.* The Christ will teach, *Deuteronomy 18, 17-22, §11.5.* The case that Jesus taught justly is hard, *Proverbs 1, 20-33, §9.7.6.* The case that Jesus taught blasphemy cannot presume God kills for it, *§5,* as may oblige all towards Jesus in spirit. Sin is atoned for by love and faithfulness, *Proverbs 16, 6, §8.4,* and Jesus says no greater love exists than lays down its life for friends. His God's love is of that degree in reality, *§8.2, Isaiah 9, 3 & 53*:

now we know that whatever the law says, it says to those who are under the law, so every mouth may be silenced and the whole world held accountable to god. therefore, no one will be declared righteous in his sight by observing the law; rather, through the law we become conscious of sin.
but now a righteousness from god, apart from the law, has been made known, to which the law and the prophets testify.
this righteousness from god comes through faith in jesus christ to all who believe. there is no difference, for all have sinned and fall short of the glory of god, and are justified freely by his grace through the redemption that came by christ jesus.
god presented him as a sacrifice of atonement, through faith in his blood. he did this to demonstrate his justice, because in his forbearance he had left sins committed before hand unpunished— he did it to demonstrate his justice at the present time, so as to be just and the one who justifies those who have faith in jesus. …

… … …

for we maintain that a man is justified by faith apart from observing the law. is god the god of jews? is he not the god of the gentiles also? yes, of gentiles too, since there is only one god, who will justify the circumcised by faith and the uncircumcised through that same faith.
do we then, nullify the law by this faith? not at all! rather, we uphold the law.

romans 3, 19-26, 28-31

This says directly what *Isaiah 28* implies: none are made righteous in God's sight by observing the law. It equates faith in Justice to faith in the Christ who gives His life as the atoning sacrifice for sinners, *§10.* It declares a relationship between God's law which defines sin and *the* faith based on love for God and neighbour by which to atone for sin, *Psalm 89, 14 &11, 7, §8.1, Proverbs 16, 6, §8.4, 1 John 5, 3, §8.1, Matthew 5, 18-20, §8.1.* Yet it explains little beyond it being a just God's will. Faith is left a matter of spiritual prejudice for or against the Christ's teaching on 'God's word', *Isaiah 9, 6, Deuteronomy 18, 17-22 & John 14, 6-10, §11.5.* It even leaves room for faith in an antichrist who takes Jesus' name to try to pervert justice, *Isaiah 24, Matthew 24, 4-5,* and for faith Jesus' death proves Jesus blasphemed. If the case that God deals death for blasphemy is itself simple prejudice, *§5,* just courts may not uphold it.

It seems the just science to Jesus' ministry is based on a God who respects freedom of faith for good and evil, *chapters 9, 10, 11,* as is briefly summarised next.

By the argument in *§7* and elsewhere, this world may be under a just God during a bilateral spiritual contest for power. This world allows life to make proposals of 'justice' based on faith and to compete by them to prove the 'justice' fit to inherit creation. A just God is infallible but does not deny life the right to enact laws as enemies to put God to the test in a duel of good and evil, *§8.2*. For the contest, Satan is supreme evil god whose proposal of 'justice', *Micah 4, 5*, may claim from God the right to arbitrarily punish for sin, *disloyalty to God*, as a discipline to replace God's Spirit, I*saiah 11, 6-9, §7.6.*

To escape eternal punishment for sin, souls must justly ask to give up sin for discipline of God's Spirit by some case in law to limit ongoing punishments for sin as unjust. But if the devil's proposal is rigorous, arbitrary levels of punishment on sin, *i.e. tyranny*, may be just, *§9.1, Luke 13, 1-9, §11.5.* Such a proposal is ruined only if he is trapped into punishing a non-sinner for sin and brought to book for it. If the only non-sinners about, *Ecclesiastes 7, 20*, are God and Son, *the Christ of same nature, §11.1, Isaiah 9, 6*, the just basis to God's word may rest on both being put to test to save sinners. Meanwhile, their promise to help may keep sinners alive but cursed in sin, *Romans 3* above. The Christ's ministry is then to gather sinners 'loyal' to the Christ, *to God's nature*, whilst not sinning against God to fall subject to Satan's justice, *Isaiah 7, 13-16.* He preaches God's offer to forgive sins pending a full case in law to limit and end punishments for sin on subjects.

The Messiah's ministry is to establish a power-base for God's offer of mercy. The offer may threaten to sweep the world forcing Satan to either concede or challenge right of God and Son to forgive sins. The options for challenge are first to indict sinners turning to God as of unsound mind, *hypocrites, e.g. unwilling to stop sinning as makes liable to draconian punishment for sin, §7.5, Psalm 40, §9.7.1, §10.8.* Secondly, he may indict the Messiah as likely to sin if tested by temptation, intimidation or punishment so likely to become a fallen sinner subject to Satan with the rest. Satan then legally demands that the Messiah or Christ who is God, *Isaiah 9, 6*, is put to test in his bid for eternal power covered in prophesy, *§7.10, Isaiah 53.* That is a deep proposal on God's justice in a title contest implied by Jesus and Paul yet not always plain to respect freedom of faith for good and evil, *Genesis 3, 2-5, §7.4.*

12.16 **Conclusions: the prisoners of the grey cells** *(§6.16)*
Mortal life may pass under a spiritual contest evidenced in powerful unruly thought, faiths or prejudices, *e.g. superstitious fear of a sentient order that rules good or bad fortune in life, §10.1, §10 to §14.* Each soul is contested on the spiritual house or clothing it feels at home in, *§1, §7, §9.1, §10.5.* It is born to personal inherited spiritual clothing, *Exodus 20, 4-6, §7.9,* even to pass life as a blind slave to unjust familiar spirits that feed on mortals by fictions, *§7.3, §10.5, Jeremiah 10, 23-24 & 2 Peter 2, 19, §11.4.* The reward and curse of higher forces drives mortals to faith in 'natural' or supernatural causes, *§2, §10.1.*

Natural science insists the mechanisms to good or bad fortune are not playthings of spiritual forces. But there is a shortfall in rigor to such faith, *chapter 1, §9.8.* It may be a totemic spiritual prejudice, *§2,* whereby the natural mind raises 'rational' idols, *great men and theories,* in drives to free society of other religious prejudices. But whilst supernatural science hangs above their heads, they may raise their own superstitious fear to astronomical heights, *§1.7* to *§1.15, §10.1,* as new religion. To expose such prejudice, *chapter 1, §10.1, §2,* turns a falling house of natural science into evidence of supernatural reality, *§10.13, §11.6.* If the house is a lie in violation of Justice, *§2,* its nemesis is a just science of the supernatural, *§4, §7, §10.5.* Just science defines prejudice to be faith in any unjust science or religion that organises as a conspiracy to pervert justice, *§2.* That is an axiom of just law only true in a just universe though it is not true in the minds of its crooks.

Many accept civilisation rests on an idea of 'justice'. Tyrannies assert standards of 'justice' less than 'the just' find acceptable, *§1.* They belay courts by subversion or might, *Wisdom 2, 11-12, §9.2.* Subversives issue propaganda on 'sound' cases to prove 'the just' wrong on 'justice', *§6.4.* Their cases may establish an unjust universe where courts are expected to deny rights to rival ideas of 'science' as unfit. But if 'the just' prevail, *support their faith by a sound case in truth related to evidence,* all tyrannies fall as conspiracies to pervert justice. The proof of a just universe is that no prejudice has a sound case in truth related to evidence to take over a just court. If tyrannies rule earthly courts despite 'the just', *Revelation 13,* 'the just' might appeal to a higher just God's court, *Daniel 7, 23-28.* Only a just God may guarantee Justice, *chapter 6.*

'The just' think it not ethical for the unjust to seize power before an unjust universe is proven yet to 'the unjust' it is the right way to proceed, *Wisdom 2, 11-12, §9.2.* They take power by injustice to play king of the castle by instinctive or spiritual prejudice against the rise of 'just' science, *§2.*

The BBC program 'On Wings of Angels' shows a respected tyranny in science. As late as the outbreak of the second world war, there was no firm evidence for 'evolution'. A young scientist with religious inclinations was hired on a contract to seek evidence for evolution by a professor hoping to undermine authority of the church. The research scientist was to be judged by success at framing the theory. Suppose he had come to the conclusion that the theory was false but on the time scale involved could not produce results in any direction? A just mind might respect that as of an independent mind deserving support. But a tyranny simply disposes of rebellious servants who fail it, *sees their contract is not renewed,* to bring in new blood till given what it wants. It is corruption of the scientific method to 'justify' vanity and deceit by research league tables and 'noble' prizes. The researcher did succeed in giving the professor what he wanted but later became a priest in the church, seeking love as a higher Justice.

Tyrannies will run education if courts allow prejudice in research and education, *e.g. propaganda claiming to revile all 'prejudice', §1.* They fall when unjust 'sciences' are found to lack a sound case in truth related to evidence to deflect charges of conspiracy to pervert justice. Those unjustly cast out by 'the system' may seek a just defence. Should any tyranny succeed in disproving the axiom of just law, it submits society to its rule, *§1.* Life may then revolve around a blueprint to incarnate a supreme tyrannical god, *the devil, §6.16, §9.2*, as a religious aim, *§13.*

To some it is wrong of 'the fit' to think they can break any law for advantage, *if they can get way with it, §2.* 'The fit' simply do it, not broadcasting intent. 'The just' may query entitlement of 'natural' science to grounds in education, research or media as a possible conspiracy to pervert justice. But it needs a sounder 'just' theory as alternative, *§3, chapter 11*, against men of unjust science who are inspired mathematical or 'theological' scientists but conceptually unjust, *§1.7.* Newton's nature is oft thought naive in regard to his efforts to bring religious data into models of the universe, *§1.9.* He was perhaps less successful in ordering the religious sphere (*or does that falsely represent Newton's work? §6.16*) but not privy to a wider range of religious data available today.

Newton maybe read scriptures to see mathematically carved images of material reality might be used as idols in neglect of spiritual spaces overlying matter and men. Idolatry is described as the root of all evil, *Psalm 97, 7, §6, Wisdom 14, 27-31, §9.5.* Idols incite prejudice to establish tyrannies, *§9.5.* Tyrannies are the 'justice' of the unjust who may enter power-sharing agreements with rival tyrannies, *§1, Isaiah 24, 14-20.* Justice is their common enemy to be despised, *unknown or unwanted,* for inflaming the unjust as an excuse 'civilised' idolaters need to bar Justice to all. It produces miscarriages of justice like at the trial of Jesus. Pilate's court refused to adjudicate in a religious dispute on the nature of truth and stood by a 'justice' to placate angry rebellious mobs, *§1.3.* It perhaps sentenced the world to ages of injustice but as what the world or mob ask for, *Luke 23, 28-43, §9.7.2*:

> "you are a king, then!" said pilate.
> jesus answered, "you are right in saying i
> am a king. in fact for this reason i was
> born, and for this i came into the world,
> to testify to the truth, everyone on the side
> of truth listens to me."
> "what is truth?" pilate asked. with that he
> went out again to the jews and said, "i
> find no basis for a charge against him. but
> it is your custom for me to release to
> you one prisoner at the time of the
> passover. do you want me to release
> 'the king of the jews'?"
> they shouted back, 'no not him! give us
> barrabus!" now barrabus had taken part
> in a rebellion.
>
> john 18, 37-40

If the public are fed propaganda in schools by unjust 'science' or religion, just science must break through against a trauma of falling idols, *§9.5, §9.6.* The proof for a just God offered here may empower courts to adjudicate by seeing if a reasonable objection exists? If there are none that a just court can uphold, this proof of a just God may stand *ex silentio.* Parties to such a case pledge by their own code of 'justice' via the global scientific or religious theory of reality by which they propose to define 'justice' to society. There are theories and folk whose 'justice' is gross but who cannot see it else keep quiet about it till test brings it out, *§2, §9, Isaiah 29, 13-16, §1.5.* Why should courts not put the theories that vie for minds to test? *§1.*

Why should the 'just' not put texts claiming to be a just God's word on trial to clarify their 'just' basis? At the least, it may stop folk defaming their faiths. For theology is defined as faith in Justice, *§7.* Are there key areas to 'God's word' to serve as basis for a just reading of the rest? *§3, §8.1.* A just God's word, *Proverbs 8, 8-9, §8.1,* is opened in proportion to knowledge of Justice, *§3.* To lack knowledge of Justice makes it a sealed book in simple unjust readings, *Proverbs 1, 20-33, §9.7.6.* Unjust spirits then make folk drunk on unjust readings of 'God's word', *§10.2, §11.6, §10.5.* Justice is to uphold just truth against spiritual drunks who may seem erudite or enlightened to one another but rob of Justice. A little 'justice' is a lot to mortals:

But to the wicked, God says:
"What right have you to recite my laws
or take my covenant on your lips?
You hate my instruction
and cast my words behind you.
When you see a thief you join with him;
you throw in your lot with adulterers.
You use your mouth for evil
and harness your tongue to deceit.
You speak continually against your brother
and slander your own mother's son.
These things you have done and I kept silent;
you thought I was altogether like you.
But I will rebuke you and accuse you to your face.

"Consider this, you who forget God,
or I will tear you to pieces,
with none to rescue:
He who sacrifices thanks offerings honors me,
and he prepares the way
so that I may show him the salvation of God."

Psalm 50, 16-23

An adulterer in God's temple sleeps with rival unjust gods, *§12,* as a thief to rob of 'justice', *§1.* They might read the above as 'God' endorsing a tough stand against mundane crime and body-adultery? But any tyranny dictates law and order by oppression in an unjust spirit, *Isaiah 28, 11-19, §15 & 30, 1-15, §9.12,* as may rob of Justice, *Romans 2, 17-24, §8.5.* Priests of tyranny can be reactionary or progressive, *Isaiah 24,* by a 'justice' to freeze or burn out just ideals. The integrity of the wicked is loyalty to a tyranny: *e.g. unquestioning faith in 'holy' ideals.* But no tyranny can be perfectly loyal to a god of tyranny so rebel gods punish the tyrannical for disloyalty, *e.g. for failing their plans to depose a just God.* There may then arise a mightiest of evil gods as the definition of the devil, *§1, Isaiah 14, 13-14, §1.2 & 14, 12-21, §8.3.*

The true scientific method gives priority to areas of evidence not fitting an unjust theory to avoid prejudice and for a creditable relation to ideas of just law, *§1.* Professionals should be wary of theories of an unjust evolutionary universe if some facts do not fit. Facts at odds may include oddball creatures, mechanisms and religion, *§9.3.* To focus on facts that an unjust theory fits is religion, *p1, §13, §10.13.* Even to falsely discount religion and spirits is religion, *§10.1.* True science honours the key problems, *chapter 1*, that may mark a path from unjust science to just science.

Now 'God's word' suggests every unjust religion or science in the end stumbles at the tested stone for Zion. Is that stone the true Christ? *Isaiah 28, 11-19, §15, Psalm 118, 19-24, §7, 1 Peter 2, 4-8.* True scientists show due care about God and the Christ as they are said to pledge a coming of Justice to save the world, *§6, Isaiah 35, 4-6, §8.1,* just progress, *Isaiah 28, 17.* The science to justly qualify every unjust theory is then led by a just God in person or Spirit, *Joel 2, 28-32, §7.11.* A just proof of God can then unify 'science', religion and 'justice' against tyrannies in research or education as an omen of God's coming. Bids to establish a 'just' science end up as paths to God. The path from Descartes to God is shown in *chapters 1 to 11.*

Science is hedged in by facts about 'the supernatural', *§10.1.* It is not necessarily impartial to see material science as distinct from 'superstition', *chapter 1, §2.1, §4.10.* Consider quantum theory, *§1.8, chapters 4 & 5.* Theories of the quantum mechanical wave-function and its collapse border on the supernatural. The wave-function is a mathematical object, *representing a real system.* It is formulated to yield values to measurements on the system. It is said to collapse if experimentally probed yet there is no mechanism to explain why? But the formulas work and lack of mechanism need not trouble scientists clinically interested in measurements or power. But some suffer visions of reality based on the theory. It seems the consciousness of the observer may intervene (*like magic*) to collapse a wave-function. Further, all the universe may tie into a wave-function so a conscious experimenter can, *in principle*, 'set' a path for the universe, see box *§1.8.* It sounds the science for megalomaniacs yet may be true in a supernatural universe under a just God who respects life's freedom of faith, box *§10.1.* The megalomaniac to watch for may be incarnated, invoked, as in *§6.16.*

If God respects freedom of faith, the course of 'our' world and 'science', *§1.9*, respects faiths of all parties to it under some evaluation principle that sums over all faiths *§7.12, §8.2.* If the wishes of life are nevertheless predictable to God then it is God's will. But there is then no objective reality, *§5.6.* The results of experiments into 'reality' reflect faiths even of distant friends and foes under a dispute between God and Satan. No 'science' will take all power without a consensus, see box *§10.1, Matthew 17, 14-20, §5.3.* Every superstition is valid in places under it. Reports of deadly curse-magic or faith-healing by a god's blessing can be as true as material 'science'.

Jesus implies God could not do much faith healing in Jesus' home town as family and friends had poor faith in God, *Isaiah 9, 6, Mark 6, 6, §9.8.* It implies God's evaluation principle over faiths gives sceptics a local veto on clear evidence for God. 'Natural' science finds no clear evidence of faith healing by God because it collects statistics for an army of sceptics. Statistical science is thereby a curse on rival religious faiths, *1 Chronicles 21, 1-7, §11.5.* It may drive faith healing back to a third world where it dies out as sceptical 'science' moves in. Sceptics thereby wield a secret power of lawlessness, *§1, §4.10.* Their 'science' is a religious bid for power as may tyrannically deny careers to scientists interested in 'anomalous' effects of consciousness on reality, New Scientist *26 November 1994, p34-38.* 'Normal' daily reality may be set by the conscious faiths of people and guardian spirits.

Statistical fact gathering is then a religious ritual to bar spiritual comforts to rival faiths. There is compensation by medicines, sanitation, powers granted under a higher just science of curses and blessings to empower unjust science to rule by 'wish of people'. A curse is enacted by Satan on an unjust science to empower its tyranny as why Godless 'science' is not so clever, *Wisdom 14, 27-31, §9.5, §1.15, §2.* Supernatural laws confiscate comforts around unjust idols as part of a test of faith in a just God. The unscrupulous prophesy a cornucopia by unjust 'sciences' but deliver apocalypse. To run 'science' as a giant experimental power-bid, *crossing fingers that it will not end the world,* is criminally negligent if not insane, *chapter 6.* Such gambles are accepted by 'the fit', *§6.1, §6.2,* in atomic tests, deadly disease science, *§1.13,* because they have faith in an unjust world where their survival is at stake, *§9.2.*

'Natural' science says life is about a choice of poverty in a dark age house lacking services, or of wealth in houses lit by the services of science. It is survival by 'science' else extinction in a hostile 'natural' universe? Supernatural science offers choice of a house under God's blessings, *Psalm 23*, or a house lit by the curse on unjust sciences to war, earthquake, pestilence, famine, comets, muggers, drug-addiction, inherited genetic or other disease, etc.. An unjust science tries to justify itself by fighting the curse that the devil places on it to empower it. Extinction by the devil's wrath is the fate of every unjust science and religion that fails to depose God for Satan, *Isaiah 30, 1-15, §9.12 & 24.*

To survive or escape the power-bids of the unjust needs faith in Justice, *Psalm 98*. Sceptics seek invasive powers to leave nowhere for the just to hide from a curse on unjust science, *except with God.* It is not safe to hide if souls are cursed for not witnessing to sceptics for God, *§13*. It is a matter of accepting the devil's curse-discounts on offer, *§9.8*, and trying to make 'science' more just, hoping to ride out a curse on unjust science and religion till Justice comes, *Psalm 98*.

Material scientists may doubt consciousness affects matter yet flows of matter most vital to human comfort are obviously directed by minds, *chapter 4*. It seems naive to deny mind over matter whilst (*unconsciously?*) waving material limbs about in emphasis of the idea. But faith in unconscious matter can be a form of superstitious fear, *§10.1*. To argue 'science' is matter over mind can ward off fear of the supernatural like a rabbit's foot wards off fear of ill-luck, *§4.10*. If it forms a power-bid for positions on public funds, courts may ask to see a sound case for it.

Suppose material science is superstition, *even a cult*, with characteristic curse and curse-discounts. It then belongs in ranks of other superstitions like ancestor worship, Vodou, new age religion, Buddhism, idolatry, Judaism, Christianity, Islam. Darwinian science may belong in the tradition of animal and other sacrifice to totems, *§10.4*. It does not respect rival religions if it sees them in evolutionary terms as backward pursuits of superstitious minds. That is vanity if such 'science' is itself spiritual but the ethics to it, *§12.2*, allow 'the fit' to be sly and hide their true views for power, *§9.2*. Why would many fail to recognise feelings for their daily work as spirited? *§6.5*.

Scientists, philosophers, politicians, may be in the dark under spiritual forces if, *in Newtonian terms*, the point of application of a spiritual force is subjectively internalised, *§1.10*. Spiritual compulsion then feels a personal ambition, *natural, 'free', Galatians 5, 17-21, §7.11, §10.2, Psalm 1.* To see spiritual reality, the point of application of a spiritual force must alter to be subjectively external giving awareness of a higher just or unjust spiritual reality that shepherds, *Psalm 23*:

O Lord, you have searched me and you know me.
You know when I sit and when I rise;
you perceive my thoughts from afar.
You discern my going out and my lying down;
you are familiar with all my ways.
Before a word is on my tongue you know it completely, O Lord.

You hem me in—behind and before;
you have laid your hand upon me.
Such knowledge is too wonderful for me,
too lofty for me to attain.

Where can I go from your Spirit?
Where can I flee from your presence?
If I go to the heavens, you are there;
if I make my bed in the depths, you are there.
If I rise on the wings of the dawn,
if I settle on the far side of the sea,
even there your hand will guide me,
your right hand will hold me fast.

If I say "Surely the darkness will hide me
and the light become night around me,"
even the darkness will not be dark to you;
the night will shine like the day, for darkness is as light to you.

For you created my inmost being;
you knit me together in my mother's womb.
I praise you because I am fearfully and wonderfully made;
your works are wonderful,
I know that full well.
My frame was not hidden from you
when I was made in the secret place.
When I was woven together in the depths of the earth,
your eyes saw my unformed body.
All the days ordained for me were written in your book before one of them came to be.

Psalm 139, 1-16

Mortals are not perfect in good or evil but relate as sinners to good and evil spirits, *§9.1, §10.5.* They are spiritually dressed by guardian spirits whose influence they may take for granted, *§11* to *§14, Galatians 4, 1-9, §5.10*: spirits that slave or guide in the ways of life or death, *Jeremiah 10, 23-24 & 2 Peter 2, 19, §11.4.*

There is enough evidence for spirits to enable theories of soul and spirit to cover religious experience, *e.g. §8.5, §10.5.* Real forces guide minds corresponding to terms like 'spirit', 'God' or 'devil', *§8.3, §12.1.* A coherent just reading of 'God's word', *§3,* would imply prophets who never knew one another knew a common just spirit, *§1.2.* Spirits are then intelligent 'just' or 'unjust' forces to sacrificial religions, *§7.8, §2.* They compel to unjust idols, *chapter 5,* as to 'natural' science, *§10.13, §2.* The peak in evidence that spirits exist may be a unique theory to submit all unjust sciences to just law, *§2,* forming a just proof for God. The theory given here shows that mortal lack of insight into Justice implies a bilateral spiritual world as reasonable truth, *§7.* Just science can compete with unjust science or religion for hearts and minds. The grip of unjust religion or 'sciences' suggests marriages to spirits are very hard to break. People get carried away in denial that they live as slaves to spirits, *§11* to *§14.*

Just science raises models of soul and spirit, *§10.5, §7,* where souls are wedded to familiar guardian spirits in spiritual cells often cut off from God, *John 14, 2.* That personal cell is where a soul feels at home, *is let to relax,* in a spiritual ecology that tucks up souls in a security blanket of familiar spirits, *§7.2.* Spirits possess or guide mortals as proteges, *§10.2.* The blanket is of angels, demons, evil spirits, right up to God and Satan. It colours a personal outlook on life, *§10.5.*

Just science sets mortal life in a penal colony under a governor who jails them as his criminals under a death-sentence, *§4, Luke 4, 5-6, §1.15.* Mortals either seek release else agree to his curse that slaughters or afflicts. The prison is to spiritually tax or farm souls for life-forces to feed a kingdom of evil spirits, *§10.5, chapter 11.* Earthly tyrannies give consent in kind to the farm, *Luke 20, 9-16, §7.10.* Mortals prey on mortals and farm 'lesser' life for parts or food as consent in kind. They would have no future were it not for a reforming governor outside who promises truth and 'paradise' if prisoners vote him in, *Job 28, 20-22, §9.4.* To secure the prison, *Isaiah 8, 19-22, §10.11,* the governor shapes punishments and privileges like wealth, fame, power, *a curse-discount to model prisoners,* for helping keep life in the dark on the new governor's offer, *§11.5, Psalm 73.* Ephemeral comforts go to many who think they are more blessed than is true, *Isaiah 28, 14-20, Luke 13, 1-9, §11.5.*

God's offer of reform forces Satan, *Luke 4, 5-6, §1.15*, to update living conditions in places. Morale in the prison is lifted and diverted in plans to improve the world by arts and sciences that make it easier not to flee to God in desperation. The schemes are in one sense to keep the governor in power and God out, *§9.1*, but in another, are gifts from God to whom thanks is due for underlying progress to Justice.

Some cells offer comforts, say, are decorated in grey wallpaper for joy and pride in unjust teaching, *James 4, 6-10, §10.5*. Others get red wallpaper to signify violent feelings which defend unjust teaching. Others get blue wallpaper to signify affliction, *e.g. depression or leprosy as a reward on faith in unjust teaching not high enough for privileges of the grey cells*. Prisoners of the grey cells help deny prisoners in blue rooms fair education on spiritual reality but arguably stop 'justice' falling to lower levels. It is evil if souls in blue rooms are forcibly subjected to barbaric treatment for mental illness in ignorance of spiritual reality: *e.g. lobotomy, ECT or drugs, §9.9* to *§9.11, Luke 14, 34-35*. The prison is about crime and punishment. The reforming governor needs faith in Justice to grow, *Jonah 4*, to clear the 'truth' as His mandate to pardon and guide out of crime, *§4, Psalm 98, John 4, 23-24, §11.1 & 8, 31-59 & 16, 13, §9.4*.

Those in the prison seen as mundane crooks by others may live in, say, green cells. But any who use their grey cells to oppose knowledge of God's justice are crooks, *§4, Luke 23, 28-43, §9.7.2*. Some in green cells might be victims of injustice due to blinding by the grey cells but does that exonerate? *§9.7.2*. If 'truth' sets free, it may give crooks strength to resist spirits who drag into crime or degradation. It is about finding conscience enough to heed good spirits against evil, *§10.5*. Is that more likely in the grey or green cells? If God is not for rebellion, many a 'justice' system may permit paths of reform towards just truth, *§11.5*.

The grey, green, blue, red cells express prejudices on reality that indicate a sinful nature, *Psalm 2, §9.4, Galatians 5, 17-21, §7.11*. The sinful nature is a ball and chain given all souls to hinder a turning to God. It is an evil spirit-shepherd, *§10.5*, feeding in human weakness for sin whereby unjust teaching is possessive, addictive. To bend to the sinful nature carries a curse to injustice from Satan as a cross in discomfort to carry in bids to escape lies and injustice for Justice.

The pilgrim's progress is to journey from green, blue, red, grey cells to God who adds, say, gold wallpaper for a guilt-edged cell. The guilt-edged cells aspire to Justice but live with doctrinal error in a twilight zone, *§10.6.* Evil is not troubled when souls travel from red, blue, green rooms if no further than their grey cells. Evil has right to set bad luck on the pilgrim's path, *illness, depression,* if 'truth' crosses it and is denied, *Isaiah 24.* In general, the wallpaper is spiritual feedback to amplify or damp thought-feelings that fit for heaven and hell, *§9.1, John 16, 7-13 & Galatians 5, 17-21, §7.11, Luke 7, 21-25, §10.10, 1 Corinthians 13, 4-13, §7.*

For safety, the guilt-edged cells must offer 'justice' to friend and foe in Satan's prison. Foes may pass laws to defend locals from unjust witness, even jail for it. Only Satan forcibly exorcises or slaves the unwilling. Thus, if the girl below was a willing slave of rebel gods, Paul had to respect that to stay out of jail, *Romans 14, 4*:

... a slave girl who had a spirit by which she predicted the future. she earned a great deal of money for her owners by fortune-telling. the girl followed paul and the rest of us shouting, "these men are servants of the most high god, who are telling you the way to be saved." she kept this up for many days. finally paul became so troubled that he turned around and said to the spirit, "in the name of jesus christ i command you to come out of her!" at that moment the spirit left her.

when the owners of the slave girl realised that their hope of making money was gone, ... they brought them before the magistrates and said, "these men are jews, and are throwing our city into an uproar by advocating customs unlawful for us romans to accept or practice."

the crowd joined in the attack against paul and silas, and the magistrates ordered them to be stripped and beaten. after they had been severely flogged, they were thrown into prison, and the jailer was commanded to guard them carefully. upon receiving such orders, he put them in the inner cell and fastened their feet in the stocks.

about midnight paul and silas were praying and singing hymns to god, and the other prisoners were listening to them. suddenly there was such a violent earthquake that the foundations of the prison were shaken. at once all the prison doors flew open, and everybody's chains came loose. the jailer woke up, and when he saw the prison doors open, he drew his sword and was about to kill himself because he thought the prisoners had escaped. but paul shouted, "don't harm yourself! we are all here!"

acts 16, 16-28

The girl kept affirming Paul's witness to locals which surely helped so did that give Paul a case to exorcise? The evil spirit obeyed and left her (forever?) but Paul was then jailed as if for an unjust trespass against local evil. Perhaps locals more receptive to God were in the jail within the outer jail? *Matthew 25, 39-40.* Anyhow, the case to test-punish Paul and Silas did not hold for long. The quake was Satan's release to let their witness to a just God continue outside the jail.

Those against the reforming governor can go on many kinds of exciting or mysterious expeditions for the existing governor. But he enacts a curse to death on servants who fail him as the wages of sin, *Isaiah 14, 12-21, §8.3, Psalm 2 & 149.* Jesus thus echoes and develops on *Jeremiah 7, 4-10, §9.10* about a life with no sound foundation, *Luke 6, 46-49.* If a 'science' or religion, *any unjust sect*, cannot stand in earthly courts as just, will it fare better at Judgement Day without a sound atonement for sins? *Isaiah 1, 15-20, §8.6, §15, Psalm 1, Revelation 7, 9-17.* Justice and censorship is a tough area if a just God is for freedom of faith, *§3, Isaiah 30, 1-15, §9.12, Matthew 10, 16-23.* Scholars best not serve faiths that are obviously unjust, *§1, §1.3.*

The path to peace may be via an educational program that cannot be fairly divorced from a just God. Folk often hear voices in scripture calling them to kill or punish for 'God'. They often hear a call to drugs or crime. A fair education may be the best chance most have to avoid blue or green cells. Fair education may be an essential part of social justice and essential to a just division into heaven and hell by tastes in 'justice'.

If scholars are tacitly against Justice, *§1,* they may teach a grey way of life fit for hell. For instance, the theory of evolution looks remarkably unjust, *§2,* without a solid case for it as truth related to evidence. In 'Testing Darwinism', Phillip Johnson, *a professor of law specialising in logic of evidence*, says trial rigor may show the case mostly circular arguments or propaganda. Trial rigor may shrink any unjust religious faith, *§9.* Should a fair education lay out options in 'justice' and let souls choose a way of life they wish to inherit? The just truth may be that many wish for Satan as their unjust deity, *violating the eternal covenant,* to invoke a curse on unjust faith, *Isaiah 24, Proverbs 1, 20-33, §9.7.6.* For some, 'truth' sets free of a hell within, *§3.6,* but for others, 'truth' is a violation of 'freedom', *§1.*

13.1 Justice and the Father of Rebellion: Paradise Paved

It is a reasonable truth that a perfect God of love is a just God who respects life's wishes? *§11.3.* A just God does not make an imperfect world: *one where life can sustain a just case that God does not respect its wishes.* Yet if wishes of life conflict in a world, God cannot fulfil every wish or prayer. A just God may then respect life's wishes subject to laws community leaders agree with God, *Matthew 17, 14-20, §5.4.* Some leaders may ask God's law for a heavenly kingdom, others want to take jurisdiction of all other life in a power bid, *§11.1.*

In theory, this God's archenemy is a devil who plots to frustrate life's wishes so to imprison. The devil would act by just cases put to God to jail life in respect of any wish to be disloyal to God: *to jail it for sin against God, §12.7.* His jail runs regimes of sin to depose a just God, *§9.1: to play God with life by lying to it, §11.6, §12.16.*

> the Lord sets prisoners free, the Lord gives sight to the blind, the Lord lifts up those who are bowed down, the Lord loves the righteous.
> psalm 146, 7-8

This just theory suggests social chaos on earth reflects a legal contest to own souls whose zenith may be the Day of Judgement when either a just God saves souls from prison, *Psalm 34, 22, Job 19, 25-26, Romans 8, 31-36, §11.5,* or the devil takes for loyalty to a prison of lies, *§12.16,* as its food supply or harvest, *§11.2, Matthew 13, 24-30, Job 16, 19-22 & 19, 23-27, 1 John 2, 1-2.*

Now very first life should be perfect relative to a perfect God because imperfect and perfect cannot coexist at the point of creation. God plans for creation to be directed by life's wishes thereafter. The idea God makes imperfect life to perfect by evolution denies the premise of a perfect mind, so, would be *prison culture.*

The first life is by direct wish of a perfect God so has to be perfect. It remains perfect whilst it agrees with God. However, life is only life, *more than a puppet,* if it has free-will to disagree with God and neighbours. For life to really be life, it must rebel against God or neighbours for a while. It then falls from perfection to a state of imperfection, sin, for a time. After a fall into imperfection there are two paths life might try to regain perfection. The first path is to end acts of rebellion by acceding to God's leadership or will.

The other path to 'perfection' is to organise a rebellion to seek a new kind of perfection, a fitness better than a just God. That is a wish to evolve in sin, *injustice*, to depose a just God, *§9.1.* The path of evolving to be fit calls to eternal failure, *delusion or lie*, if God is perfect, *§9.3.* However, life might want it anyway as a preferred lifestyle: *auto-evolution.* If auto-evolution is a wished for lifestyle of rebellion, *its only 'fulfilment' in sin*, it must be enabled in creation by a God who respects life's wishes.

Now a just God cannot lead rebellion against Himself so allows life ability to be gods of auto-evolution. The devil must then arise to fulfil life's wish to rebel, *John 18, 37-40, §12.16.* The limits to rebellion against a God of eternal life are at death & destruction, *Proverbs 8, 36, §6.1*, so the devil will lead a death or glory bid to sacrifice life in rebellion's way, *§7.8.* He is a wished for father of rebellion to sons of evil, *Matthew 13, 36-43, §9.1*, invoked to depose Justice, *Isaiah 14, 12-21, §8.3.* Can he be proved god of this world? *chapter 6, §9.7.5*:

People can take death, destruction and doubt God exists as proof we have all possible free-will from God. But there must be a just case by which God rules we wish for death and destruction before heaven with God. A just God needs to see a legal death-wish from folk before submitting them to death and evil, *Job 28, 20-22, §9.4.* That brings a quick proof for Satan.

Many mortals do not accept death and destruction are their wish, though some revel in them. Some say it means there is no just God. They prefer not to think evil exists because life rebels against God. However, to swear injustice means there is no just God may rebel against God by raising the so-called 'problem of evil'. That oath may be the devil's own creed so he may keep a rebellion going by clinically inflicting injustice to drive sin against God to develop/evolve.

Now if mortals are so blind or imperfect, *free*, as to doubt a just God exists, they can hardly justify their way of life to God in court, *Job 42, 1-6.* Where then is the legal mind acting for people to argue for death & destruction on them to a just God? It could be a real mind, or a virtual mind if God discerns it to be evolving among people to one day justify terms under which we now live. But real or virtual, it pleads to a just God for death & destruction on us. That defines the devil as god of this world in real or virtual form, *§8.2.* He is leader and guardian of our rebellion against God in God's court, *Job 1 & 2, Revelation 12, 7-42, §7.1.*

If we turn to scripture, God and Jesus argue with the devil, Satan, in places like, *Job 1 & 2, Luke 4, 4-6*, where the devil is real with authority over people. Both New and Old Testaments preach God saves from Death & Destruction as evil spirit allies of Satan, *§9.4.* If 'God's word' is rightly read to see a real devil exists then ideas of a virtual or mythical devil are lies, more rebellion in loyalty to the devil, *§10.4.* To refuse a just reading of the word may exemplify the devil snatching truth from minds, *Luke 8, 11-15, §5.4*, or God respecting a twilight zone, *§10.6.* That may be proof enough for many of a personal devil, and the text outside supports the case.

Rebellion is about denying a perfect God in petty or capital sins. The capital sinner walks by theories of progress to crown the perfect evil, *e.g. incarnate Satan, §9.2.* That is where evolutionary theories lead under a just God, *§6.16; §9.2; 2 Thessalonians 2, 10-11; Isaiah 1, 28.* It shows mortals the type of God-centred universe we live in, one where God *respects life's wishes*, and the stage in rebellion creation is now at.

Now if sin or evil is a state open to all life, any flaw in a soul might lead to a decay into evil on a time scale to eternity. A perfect God would know if life created perfect is going to rebel and become or give birth to His enemies. Creation may have to pass through birth pains of a rise of evil, *Romans 8, 22, Matthew 24, 3-15*, whilst life explores ways not eternally sustainable.

It might seem God cannot fulfil evil's wish for God not to exist. However, if God is source of all life, that wish is a death-wish, *Proverbs 8, 36, §6.2.* God might design for evil to legally admit its death-wish and so respect even evil's wishes in the long run. Some evil has a death-wish but in denial of it. It abhors God's influence so sets its heart in a dark capsule of hatred to God, *§12.13, Isaiah 8, 19-22, §10.11.* It builds a cell to defend its heart from God. From inside its prison, it leads on paths of rebellion that may end with it admitting or stating its death-wish as explained next.

Evil's faith is that God is imperfect because this is a 'flawed' world where evil is discontent. To blame God for evil and discontent is evil's faith or creed. It must spread its faith, *discontent*, for a power-base. Hence, it attacks 'good' by injustice to feed faith that evil would not exist with power to curse if God was perfect, *Psalm 107, 1; Job 1, 22; 1 Thessalonians 5, 15-18.* Evil leaders enact curse-laws *on evil* to defend evil hearts from God. They enact laws to suspend a just God's right to stop injustice like 'natural' disasters on evil. Thus, capital evil legislates for 'acts of God' on evil, *Psalm 82, §8.3.*

To justify evil in a legal bid for power, evil needs to prove in God's courts that evil exists by God's negligence in creation. Thus, a just God must never create or rule life in ways to give evil a sound case in law to condemn God as unjust. For evil will hone its laws, *Micah 4, 5*, to put creation and God to test. It will target any life made solely by God's will though only the very first being may be in that category, *§2.*

The devil thus rides out on a case in law against God to test and indict life in God's creation. He seeks to gather evidence for God being imperfect, *§6.7, Revelation 12, 10, §7.1.* God then designs for due process in creation to rebut any evidence cited by evil. That may be God's only design option if He aims never to be a dictator, *to respect life's wishes*, and if life less than God but with all possible free-will is not unconditionally good. A just God then creates perfect life but with free-will to rebel and right to 'best' leadership of an evolutionary rebellion in dispute with a just God.

Now any valid model of the cosmos is to cover spirits and their interests, *§7.12, §10.1, §12.1.* 'God's word' in a just reading is potentially *the* authority on that, *§12.3.* In *Genesis* a perfect beginning for people is claimed but as a third phase of life after a second phase of ministering spirits. The latter are said to be angels loyal to God and angels in rebellion: *demons.* Demons might hold compromised angels in their prisons, *2 Peter 2, 4.* But all the second phase is seen cheering creation of the third phase in Job below. It claims there that 'God's word' is, *in its just reading*, essential to a true theory of origins as does *2 Peter 3, 3-6, §9.3*:

then the lord answered job out of the storm. he said:

"who is this that darkens my counsel
with words without knowledge?
brace yourself like a man;
i will question you,
and you shall answer me.

"where were you when i laid the
earth's foundation?
tell me, if you understand.
who marked off its dimensions?
surely you know!
who stretched a measuring line across it?
on what were its footings set,
or who laid its cornerstone—
while the morning stars sang together
and all the angels shouted for joy?

job 38, 1-7

After this origin, ministering spirits crop up, *Matthew 13, 36-43, §9.1,* under varied titles or names, see *§8.3* on morning stars. Angels and demons are then partisan forces over mortals from beginnings, *Genesis 3, 22 & 4, 7 & 6, 2-4 & 11, 7 & 18, 1 to 19, 3 & 28, 12 & 32, 1.* They act as guardians of folk for God, *Psalm 91, 11-12, Matthew 18, 10* and demonic gods of folk in rivalry to God, *1 Kings 11, 33, 2 Kings 23, 10-13, Jeremiah 32, 34-35, Psalm 106, 36-38, Psalm 82, Revelation 9, 20-21.* But angels and demons are not the very first life.

13.2 **1st life: Our Mother in heaven: the Messiah**

The first life in God's creation has a joyful birth far from any rise of evil. It is immortal if a God of love is only directly responsible for life that wishes to live. It is one being if God respects its right to wish for more life or not. If it wishes for more life, its loyalty to God may later be tested by a rebellion as in *§1*, seeking to prove God negligent in creation. Evil will indict God and the first being for the existence of evil. The first being must never wish God did not exist or had not made it.

The being least likely to raise barriers to God is one for whom God is its love and satisfies its wishes. Its place is then with God in Spirit. The being most fit to live in God's Spirit is the image of God as the most perfect life God could give birth to. God can be sure such life can enjoy blissful communion with God. Identity with God makes it coeternal with God and Spirit. Old Testament scripture shows a first being:

the lord brought me forth as the first
of his works, before his deeds of old;
i was appointed from eternity,
from the beginning, before the world
began.
when there were no oceans, i was
given birth,
when there were no springs
abounding with water;
before the mountains were settled in
place,
before the hills, i was given birth,
before he made the earth or its fields
or any of the dust of the world.
i was there when he set the heavens in
place,
when he marked out the horizon on
the face of the deep,
when he established the clouds above
and fixed securely the fountains of the
deep,
when he gave the sea its boundary
so that the waters would not
overstep his command,
and when he marked out the
foundations of the earth.
then i was the craftsman at his side.
i was filled with delight day after day,
rejoicing always in his presence,
rejoicing in his whole world
and delighting in mankind.
"now then, my sons,
listen to me;
blessed are those who keep my ways.
listen to my instruction and be wise;
do not ignore it.
blessed is the man who listens to me,
watching daily at my doors,
waiting at my doorway.
for whoever finds me finds life and
receives favour from the lord.
but whoever fails to find me harms
himself;
all who hate me love death."

proverbs 8, 22-36

This first being clearly wished for more life. She has a female gender role as joint parent with God to people as sons. She calls herself 'wisdom', *Proverbs 8, 1-9, §8.1 & 9, 1-6.* But people have free-will to ignore Her instruction. To hate Wisdom, *Wisdom 7, 15* to *10, 5,* is to love death, so, to show a death-wish. To heed or love Her is blessed by God to eternal life. Wisdom must be an ally of the Messiah if He is the eternal King of life.

Now the Messiah is 'Ancient of Days', *Micah 5, 2, §7.9, Daniel 7, 9-22, Isaiah 11, 1-10, §11.1,* to be called God, *Isaiah 9, 2-7, §11.1,* as fits the account of a first being, *Wisdom.* Is the Messiah Wisdom in changed gender role? It fits scripture where Jesus is God's Son & King, *Psalm 2, 6-7,* exact image of God, *Hebrews 1, 3, §7.10, John 12, 44-50,* first being, *John 8, 58, 1 Peter 1, 2,* mother to 'Israel', *Matthew 23, 37,* blue-print for all life, *Colossians 1, 15-17.* Was Jesus then Mary's mother but became her son so she could become Jesus' brother in heaven? Compare *Proverbs 8* above & *John 1* below:

In the beginning was the Word, and the Word was with God, and the Word was God. He was with God in the beginning.
Through him all things were made; without him nothing was made that has been made. In him was life, and that life was the light of men. The light shines in the darkness, but the darkness has not understood it.
There came a man who was sent from God; his name was John. He came as witness to testify concerning that light; so that through him all men might believe. He himself was not the light; he came only as a witness to the light. The true light that gives light to every man was coming into the world.
He was in the world, and though the world was made through him, the world did not recognise him. He came to that which was his own, but his own did not receive him. Yet to all who received him, to those who believed in his name, he gave the right to become children of God — children born not of natural descent, nor of human decision or a husband's will, but born of God.

John 1, 1-13

Judging by life on earth, more life leads to a world like this in rebellion, lacking clear sight of God. The first being perhaps heeded a cry of unborn 'good' for life over an unborn 'evil' seeking to deny life to it. God's nature is then to act for 'good' by Justice against plans of evil, *the devil,* to cull 'good' by power of death, *§1.2, Isaiah 14, 12-21, §8.3, Romans 8, 19-22, §6.13.*

To depose a just God, a rebellion must establish right to own or possess life. To break free of rebellion, life must legally prove loyalty to God. One way to prove loyalty to a just God is for Him to offer law that to obey proves loyalty. Moses laid such a path but with such tradition comes sedition. Suppose folk are so harassed by a rebellion that they cannot live up to God's law or find its just sense, *Isaiah 28*. The law then clarifies why a rebellion owns life so the Messiah must head a new path out of a rebellion prison for law-breakers, *§12.7*.

If the first being has God's nature, *Isaiah 9, 6*, faith in His incarnation may prove loyalty to God above claims of a rebellion. It presumes a faith not puffed up in extortionate ways of rebellion, *§11.6, Habakkuk 2, 4*. The first being is the perfect Messiah to a rebellious world lacking clear sight of God where God's word is a sealed book, *Daniel 12, 9-10, §12.3*. He is to lead sinners on a just path to God that meets and caps God's law, *Deuteronomy 18, 15-19, John 14, 23-24*. That is what Jesus teaches via Paul, *Galatians 3, 21-24, §7.10, Colossians 2, 13-18, §8.3*. Prophecies say the Ancient Of Days takes human form and a punishment from sinners to free sinners, *Isaiah 53, 3-7, §7.10*:

your attitude should be the same as
that of christ jesus:

who being in the very nature god,
did not consider equality with god
something to be grasped,
but made himself nothing, taking the
very nature of a servant,
being made in human likeness.
and being found in appearance as a
man,
he humbled himself
and became obedient to death—
even death on a cross!
therefore god exalted him to the
highest place
and gave him the name that is above
every name,
that at the name of jesus every knee
should bow,
in heaven and on earth and under the
earth,
and every tongue confess that jesus
christ is lord,
to the glory of god the father.
philippians 2, 5-11

Why would the Messiah take human form? Is it due to rebellion lawyers denying right to save if the Messiah is another form of life? They may say such a Messiah has different interests to mortals and acts only to keep God in power. The Messiah is then a human pioneer of loyalty to God, *Deuteronomy 18, 17-22, §11.5, Isaiah 9, 2-7, §11.1, John 14, 6-10, §11.5*. A case to punish Him to validate a just path to God arises as next.

Rebellion is by faith that God is imperfect. It runs on sin against God so rebellion law is to induce sin, say, by tempting or punishing sinners. To punish for sin may change direction in sin or induce sin. It turns some to God, *Psalm 32, 8-11, §10.5.* To sin makes subject of a rebellion so it is rebellion law which sets punishments on sin against God, *§7.9.* To free of sin, God may offer knowledge of His Spirit to one day cloak life, *Isaiah 11, 6-9, §7.5.* Thus, punishment laws are a substitute for knowing God. Evil hones them to drive evil in work to prove God imperfect, *Isaiah 14, 20-21, §8.3 & 66, 24, §1.13*, which is hell's order, *Matthew 25, 41-46, §7.10.* Hence, God stands for mercy, *forgiveness for sins*, by laws of atonement veiled in their limits, *§12.15; Psalm 32; 1 John 5, 16-17, §9.7.2; 1 Timothy 1,13.*

Rebellion against the Almighty must be a legal regime to prison life for sin against God, *§1.* It upholds sin as evidence to indict God of negligence or weakness, *Revelation 12, 7-12, §7.1.* To prove negligence would convict God and the Messiah as to blame for all crime or injustice. That is grounds *in rebellion law* to put them to death as sinners if it gets power of them. The human Messiah then faces a just death if He sins against God. It would be God sinning against God as proof God is imperfect: *ending hope of a just salvation to sinners.* Some texts show a Messiah who does not sin yet steps outside God's blessing, *Psalm 22*, to take a punishment to death to save sinners. Is that a deeper demand of rebellion law for releasing sinners? *Isaiah 53, 3-7, §7.10.*

One way to explain it is in *§7.10.* If rebellion law can make subjects sin, why take it on trust that God incarnate, *the Messiah*, is any better? The rebellion then asks proof that God in human form, *Isaiah 9, 6*, is not a sinner. It asks to test the Messiah for sin against God under the worst punishment, *Wisdom 2, 12-24*, or spiritual duress its law sets on mortals, *Luke 4, 1-13, Matthew 26, 36-41, §12.9.* In rebellion faith, that torture is justified to clean the slate over alleged guilt in making a flawed world, *Isaiah 53, 10-12, Acts 3, 15.* But if the Messiah does not sin to the death, *Isaiah 53, 1-7, Luke 4, 1-13*, the rebellion murders a non-sinner. That sin may draw punishment in the rebellion's own law, *if it cannot fault other parts of God's plan.* Meanwhile, God may resurrect a sinless Messiah, *Acts 2, 22-39, 1 John 4, 9-10*, as spiritual leader for mortals out of the rebellion, *1 Peter 3, 17-22*, up to its fork into hell. But how does the rebellion develop to reach this situation?

13.3 **2nd life: Angels and Demons**

A perfect God implies lesser life is not so perfect. If it cannot relate well enough to the perfect, *let God sustain it*, it may die, *§11.1.* God is then the greatest and the least life able to exist eternally, *§2.2, Revelation 4, 11*:

"I am the alpha and the omega," says the Lord God, "who is, and who was, and who is to come, the almighty."
Revelation 1, 8

A just God's direct will is only to make life able to live, *to relate, §2.3*, come rain or shine like the first being or Messiah, *§2.* If the Messiah wishes more life, *leading to evil*, is that Her one free-will sin? *§1, Matthew 19, 17*, or God's will by identity? *§2, Isaiah 9, 6.* The Almighty is not a tyrant if His nature is to guarantee Justice to all, *§8.2, §12.4, Matthew 5, 43-45, §9.7.6 & 24-30, §2.3.* But a rebellion wants its 'justice' over all whereby God is implicitly a judge, *§12*, mediating over life's wishes in a power-struggle of fair and unfair 'justice', *§8.2, §12.7, Daniel 8, 1-25, §12.13.* For that, 'God's word' has just and unjust readings for freedom of faith, *§12.4.* Life then has free-will to choose the 'justice' of demons, *Isaiah 28, 11-19, §12.15*, or God, *Proverbs 1, 20-33, §9.7.6, 1 Corinthians 10, 20-21, §7.8.*

A just God aims to fulfil life in social bodies that show love of neighbours and God, *§2.2, §3.7, §11.1.* Ideally, life would not covet God's, the first being's or a neighbour's place. But life can only have its own place if varied in nature and less than God. It then seeks to live at a relational distance from God where, *if not tested by a rebellion*, it can be at home or content. Even if God set second life straight into optimum social bodies, free-will may imply rebellion to disorder, *§1.*

A systematic rebellion is to feed its gods or leaders in false status, *§6.10, §11.1.* It runs unfair competition for places. An evil 'rich' trap and rob a good and evil 'poor', *tax for life-forces, §11.2*, in a social inversion, *§6.4, §12.12.* Such a rebellion may have to run its course if reform, *not revolt*, is the way to curb rebellion against a just God, *1 Corinthians 7, 17-23, §11.5.* Rebellion is a path of 'progress' for status to evil, *§1, Jude 1, 6.* A just God offers a life personally and eternally sustainable relative to God and neighbour, *Acts 10, 34-35.* God is for friends to get to know and love their place relative to God, *§12.14, John 13, 1-11, Luke 14, 7-11 & 7, 28 &9, 46-48, Mark 10, 17-31*:

my brothers as believers in our lord jesus christ, don't show favoritism. suppose a man comes into your meeting wearing a gold ring and fine clothes, and a poor man in shabby clothes also comes in. if you show special attention to the man wearing fine clothes and say, "here's a good seat for you," but say to the poor man, "you stand there" or "sit on the floor by my feet," have you not discriminated among yourselves and become judges with evil thoughts? listen my dear brothers: has not god chosen those who are poor in the eyes of the world to be rich in faith and to inherit the kingdom he promised those who love him? but you have insulted the poor. is it not the rich who are exploiting you? are they not the ones who are dragging you into court? are they not the ones who are slandering the noble name of him to whom you belong?

if you really keep the royal law found in scripture, "love your neighbour as yourself," you are doing right. but if you show favoritism, you sin and are convicted by the law as lawbreakers. for whoever keeps the whole law and stumbles at just one point is guilty of breaking all of it. ... ...

speak and act as those who are going to be judged by the law that gives freedom, because judgement without mercy will be shown to anyone who has not been merciful. mercy triumphs over judgement!

james 2, 1-10 & 12-13

Second life must have a natal wish to live and see more life made to build its social bodies. The gift of a nature most happy at a distance from God and a wish to parent life at greater distances from God may be how evil arises by life's wish. Evil matures to blame God for its birth and actions in power-bids, *§1.* God need not dictate to any life beyond it having to choose a homeland as God's friend or foe, *§10.10, §12.14.*

'God's word' calls the second life angels. It does not say much on birth of angels but shows a race divided into two camps. Angels loyal to God are led by archangels like Michael, *Daniel 12, 1, §5, Jude 1, 9.* Angels against God turn into demons or morning stars under the devil. Morning stars appear to be spirits who vie with God to rule mortals. Some stars deceive about who the Messiah is and other things, *Isaiah 14, 12-14, §8.3, Revelation 2, 24-28.* The Messiah vies to be King of mortals, *Isaiah 9, 2-7, §11.1,* as the only morning star true to God, *Numbers 24, 17-19, 2 Peter 1, 19, Revelation 22, 16.* He may be King of angels loyal to God, *1 Peter 3, 22, §8.3.* Both angels and morning stars found the birth of a third life phase, *people,* agreeable at *Job 38, 1-7, §1.*

A theory of why and how a rebellion split the angels may draw on ways of mortals. For mortals enter the same rebellion against God as a fact of life, *§1,* yet from a different angle to the angels. Why would angels and demons agree to, *ask for,* the third phase of people?

Any life has to rebel against God or neighbours to know its free-will, *§1.* That may begin in troubling falls into dislike of God in a limited area. It seems to have led to loss of faith in a just God among angels so they fell into times of conflict on the meaning to angel-life. Now a troubled angel can ask a God who respects life's wishes for anything, *even a working philosophy of rebellion.* A perfect God may say no rebellion can depose God but rebellion is about lack of faith in God: *a wish to test God by works framing the hypothesis that God is untrustworthy, fallible.* Such faith founds the science of rebellion whether in heaven, *Revelation 12, 7-12, §7.1,* or its mirror on earth. On earth, it may build social houses on foundations of sand to suddenly fall, *§5.4.*

For God to make life with a natal death-wish, *hating God,* would show contempt of life. Even to will birth of life bound to turn evil and hate God may be contempt of life. Extreme evil is then born only by wish of lesser evil. Some may champion right of evil to life because they doubt God's judgement exactly as some mortals champion a Godless master race, *§9.2.* The master race is not Justice to life but a strong evil to replace weak. It invokes evil to justify its birth by proving God wrong about evil. For that, evil needs to realise a perfect crime to ruin God's justice, see box *§11.4.* God cannot directly will for crime to exist so crime must be by wish of a rebellion. God respects life's right to give birth to evil. The 'perfect' evil or devil is dedicated to evolving to put God to the test.

To summarise on the rise of evil, God grants free-will to angels who parent angels of god-like ability in spirit and law of rebellion. Thus, the devil, *also called Lucifer or Satan,* comes into being. He is 'perfect' evil, ready to gamble a just God is weak for allowing evil like himself too much. A just God may openly warn on rebellion's fate, *hell,* but rebellion is about ignoring God. Jesus says Satan is a thoroughbred liar and murderer, see below & *§12.5.* He says evil has a religious bent: *a genius to lie over a dogmatic base.* Thus, evil may misrepresent 'God' in religion or science for authority to back Satan's lies or 'truths' as 'natural', unquestionably right, *§9.7.4:*

jesus said to them,
"if god were your father, you would love me, for i came from god and now am here. i have not come on my own; but he sent me.
why is my language not clear to you? because you are unable to hear what i say. you belong to your father, the devil, and you want to carry out your father's desire. he was a murderer from the beginning, not holding to the truth, for there is no truth in him. when he lies, he speaks his native language, for he is a liar and the father of lies. yet because i tell the truth, you do not believe me!

john 8, 42-45

do you think i came to bring peace on earth?
no i tell you, but division. from now on there will be five in one family divided against each other, three against two and two against three.

luke 12, 51-52

If God respects life's wishes, the earth is by commission of leading angels which need not mean every angel or demon is fully informed if that prejudices Justice, *Ephesians 3, 7-11, §8.6, §10.4.* Jesus says rulers of the rebellion are not for turning, so mortals must polarise as good or evil, *sheep or goats.* He says Satan, *the most fit to lead rebellion against God*, was a liar and murderer *from the start.* Obviously(?), murderers are not born by a just God's *direct* wish, so, angel birth laws allow(ed) them to breed up evil gods, *§9.2.* The talent needed to lead a rebellion against Justice is to 'justify' murder by godly ability to spin a lingo of lies, *§12.4.* Now a key lie of evil when claiming divine licence is to bill 'God' as its *direct* parent, *§1, Psalm 82, §8.3, Matthew 13, 36-43, §9.1.* If Justice allows freedom of faith on evil's origin then faith about evil's father is a test of faith in God. Does Ezekiel imply Satan was God's Son?:

If *Ezekiel 28, 13-17* is taken as a parallel between the king of Tyre and Satan, *§8.1,* it says Satan was good at birth. It implies God made Satan a perfect angel who only turned evil after the earth was made? In that event, *John 8* above is read to say Satan was a murderer from the time he turned evil. But Ezekiel's scripture might then suggest this world was God's agency to draw Satan or others to murder? *James 1, 13.* That case is latent even if Ezekiel states another reason to Satan's fall. Has Ezekiel painted a latent image of a deity who is unjust? *a murderer and liar*? If so, it promotes Satan as one true god. If Ezekiel or other imply an unjust 'God' then are they false prophets whom God might save? Other reasons are given elsewhere to suggest Ezekiel may have been abused by Satan like Joshua, *§9.7.3, §10.10.*

The three phase model of life need not be adjusted to respect Ezekiel's scripture though there is freedom to try.

We are told that for sake of Justice, 'God's word' is a sealed book till end-times, *§12.3.* The path to open it is loyalty to God's King: the just Messiah and true Ancient of Days, *§8.2.*

13.4 The Way of Demons and Origin of Life on Earth

Evil is born to lead angels to question if their wishes are best met by keeping faith with God? Lord Satan offers to lead full rebellion in the faith that God is fallible. The choice is not a matter of cold logic, *§1.7.* God's respect for life allows life's reason to be a slave to faith: *what it wishes to believe from the heart.* Life is not then a slave to God's just reason or Spirit. It is subjective and God stands for love God and neighbour, *§3.7.*

Evil makes the future of angel-kind its issue. It can be voiced in questions on the value of free-will in relation to God. For if formal rebellion never arises, has God given life as much free-will as He could or made it a weak-willed puppet? What good is free-will if its only just use is to submit to God's will? It follows that a just God gives life right to amend its nature to cut links to God. It can dress in the armour of a god or science of rebellion, *§9.1.* Evil is then said to turn callous or scaly. The pride of mortals leads into social bodies under scaly dragons, *§6.7, Job 41, 15, Revelation 13.* A full change into evil, *§9.1,* may be as irreversible as full death.

Demons are spirits who reject God as direct source of their life-forces. They feed on life-forces from matter or other life. To feast on brother angels they ply with a philosophy of rebellion, *§11.2.* By philosophy, they may live as parasites feeding on life closer to God. Life closer to God needs to witness back to evil on a just God to hold its place, *John 7, 37-39, §11.1.* To be free of God, demons need an infinite vitality or power by life-force science, *chapter 11, Luke 11, 24-26, §5.3.* They take power of 'lesser' life to farm it in dogma that distances from God. The plans to depose God are fed by joy of flows of life-force channelled into sin. Evil's lust for power, *to sup life-forces from others,* may cause it to imagine God is a rival 'unjust' parasite.

Primary education in evil is by games that dare to minor crimes for a rush of life-forces that too soon dries up. King of the castle is a push and pull game played for real over heaven, *Revelation 12, 7-12, §7.1,* and earth, see on *Daniel 10* in *§7.3.* To sin against God is how angels can prove their free-will to one another. The more rebellious an angel is, the 'freer' it is. To the devil, the better an angel can sin, the stronger it is, see box *§11.4.* The rank or glory of a demon god is then by its strength to inspire crime or sin in weaker evil, to open it to wrath of the god, *Job 42, 5-6, Isaiah 1.*

Demons feed as spirits to tempt or stress a society, *§9.1, §9.4.* They push and pull into rebellion, *sin.* They may appeal firstly by a mutual spiritual rush of life-forces at some crime, *Genesis 4, 7.* That feeling opens the door to political dogmas of power struggle against God that spin out lies to excuse crime. The religion of sin as a measure of free-will, 'freedom' or 'independent mind' may be a time-bomb in creation to polarise life between faith in God and faith in right to crime. Such theory fits facts of life on earth, *§12.2.* It shows a just God respects life to the point of allowing all or some life all possible free-will for dispute:

"... you have heard that it was said, 'love your neighbour and hate your enemy.' But I tell you: love your enemies and pray for those who persecute you, that you may be sons of your Father in heaven. He causes the sun to shine on the evil and the good, and sends rain on the righteous and the unrighteous. If you love those who love you, what reward will you get? Are not even the tax collectors doing that? And if you greet only your brothers, what are you doing more than others? Do not even pagans do that? Be perfect, therefore, as your heavenly Father is perfect...."

Matthew 5, 43-45

To quash a rebellion by Justice, God needs an agreed law. Only by the justice of free-will consent can God arguably show love for enemies, *§12.4.* Evil then has right to try to finesse the Almighty on His just right to defend good from evil. It lets evil legally enact plans to depose God, *§8.2.* A duel of good and evil is then led by rebel gods as lawyers enacting laws to contest rule of life with God, *§11.3.* Rebel gods deny a just God's right to rule evil so they can farm lesser-evil for life-forces, *§11.2.* Apparent chaos in creation arises whilst a just God establishes agreed principles of law and order among life, *Micah 4, 5, §12.7.*

In principle, any life can join God's enemies. Thus, angels who stay loyal to God may be tormented by demons who say loyalty to God is of inferior angels lacking free-will. God can see which life is good or evil but evil seeks to test God and take power to 'free' even 'good', *Revelation 12, 7-12, §7.1.* Leaders across a divide in faith think in unlike ways. Their 'reason' is to 'protect' life from the other. But a perfect God's reason will remain 'the truth'. It follows that both good and evil best serve their causes by expert grasp of God's Justice. The devil is an evil master of God's Justice.

Suppose most life begins loyal to God. A rebellion then has to work to increase its numbers. If angels can parent angels, evil may try to outbreed good. It can also try to convert angels loyal to God. Suppose a rebellion increases or clones its numbers to more than half the angels, *Revelation 12, 4.* Is God then tied by a principle of respect for life's wishes to yield the future of creation to a rebellion? The weakness to a democratic proposal to depose God is that God claims to be the perfect source of all life-forces. To take rebellion too far may then show a death-wish, *be insane, Proverbs 8, 36, §6.2.* Thus, God's respect for life's wishes may be subject to sanity clauses, *chapter 6.* Sanity is in beliefs that value and sustain life. A just God may withhold power from the insane to defend sane life loyal to God. However, God then needs to justly prove His enemies are insane, *i.e. have a death-wish, Proverbs 8, 36, §6.2.*

Suppose God has made a creation where He has to say most life is insane or evil. Leaders of evil do not think they are insane so would indict God as an evil tyrant who lies to withhold power from the majority. A large revolt may hail itself as living evidence that God is a liar unable to respect or betoken life's wish. If such a case helps recruit for a rebellion, rebel gods will push it. But a just God may counter by offering enemies home rule: their own kingdom(s), *Micah 4, 5, §12.8.* That may establish hell as a land too dry to satisfy the thirst for evil vitality of leading demons.

At first sight it might appear a just God can hold a minority rebellion to peaceful persuasion. But a minor rebellion can make a case for violence *because it lacks support.* Rebel gods may declare evil is heir to God's creation by faith that God is unfair or unfit in its design. They then indict God for not having made creation to allow angels 'fair choice' of rebellion or loyalty to God. They may say angels loyal to God are naive and brainwashed by God. They can then rule that God is an illegitimate ruler and enact their own 'just' law for power of life to save it from God. The gods of evil then contest the jurisdiction of God's law not only over evil but over life loyal to God. They may enact forcible measures to imprison confused 'brothers' to free of delusions for the glorious future of angel-kind, *Jude 1, 6.* It is exactly as mortal rebels behave so as mortals might behave if in the gods' position against a 'weak' just God who respects life's wishes. Mortals oppress in the name of evil gods or idols.

The state of this world, *how rebellious folk act*, suggests a rebellion against God would try any scheme for power, *Isaiah 24, 14-23.* The only deity some want is an almighty tyrant to curse enemies. That is the god of rebellion, Satan, *§1.* His wrath may tear life that fails him to pieces, *Psalm 50, 16-21, Isaiah 14, 12-21, §8.3 & 24.* Rebel gods cannot tear a 'just' Almighty apart so instead enact rebel 'justice' against His rule, *Micah 4, 5, Psalm 82, §8.3.* They may enact laws all see are insane, *introducing power of Death*, but as means to a 'sane' end, *Wisdom 1, 12-16.* For evil can pledge to restore sanity after God is deposed, see on *Isaiah 55, 1-11, §11.1.*

Life wishing to rid of a just God who really is source of all life-forces has a death-wish, *Proverbs 8, 36, §6.2.* God may explain that to cut links to God, *cast off ability to repent of rebellion*, seals life in a capsule with a death-wish. Its remaining life is then to build and explore a burial tomb, *e.g. hell.* Once hell is sealed, life there begins to decay, *Psalm 82, 6-7.* On being told this, rebel gods may get angry. Is it God issuing death threats to bolster failing authority and stop angels rebelling? Rebel gods may counter that a just God is fallible in design if creation does not allow proof of His title with no unjustifiable loss of life. God is to prove His rule legitimate *before* sealing evil in hell even if evil 'justice' brings chaos meanwhile. God must first fairly convict the rebellion of a death-wish to prove He is not a tyrant clinging to power by saying foes are insane. That proof is necessary to save confused angels from death or murder in a rebellion, *Jude 1, 6.* Under a just God, life only dies *after* it legally declares a death-wish.

The rebellion must wait for God's proof of title before going to full rebellion else it admits its death-wish. The demand for God's proof may head off full rebellion. To fairly prove evil has a death-wish, God must humour that part of the rebellion's psyche in denial of its death-wish. He then gives evil what it asks on a path leading to it either legally admitting its death-wish or turning. The rebellion is to be hoist on its own petard. It wants proof angels loyal to God are not brainwashed. The answer is in a new world to which angels and demons submit fledgeling life of their own nature. The fledgelings are to be born and tested in the new world, *Job 38, 1-7.* They are born to an educating maze overseen by their angels and demons as partisan forces under God as guarantor of Justice, *Zechariah 1, 12-17.* That may be the true origin of life on earth.

13.5 3rd Life: Fledgeling Theory & God's Word to Israel

The earth seems made for fledgeling life related to angels and demons, *Psalm 8* below. In 'God's word', origins and relations to angels and demons are covered in a way to give freedom of faith on origins, *Wisdom 13, 1-9 & 2; 2 Peter 3, 3-6, §9.3.* The debate on origins shows the freedom of faith, *Job 38, 1-7, §1.*

In a title contest, angels and mortals loyal to God are allies. To reach mortals, angels may fight (*use a case that to know angels respects mortal wishes*) territorial demons over mortals, *§7.3, Daniel 10.* Much is written on our relations to evil spirits, *§7.8, §10.5,* less on relations to angels. But in *Psalm 91, 11-12,* some adults walk paths by angels, *§10.3,* and *Matthew 18, 10, §7.3* says some children walk by 'their' angels. In fledgeling theory, souls kin to angels *most* loyal to God are to be tested by evil for loyalty to God. The test is to witness to a just God over spirit and mortal foes who attack by injustice, *Psalm 66, 8-12.* The chosen people are of angel descent tested in a world 'made' by demon gods for deposing God, *Romans 8, 28-30, §11.4 & 11, 1-4, §13.10.*

In *Zechariah 3, 4, §10.10,* priest Joshua is in filthy garb under Satan then cleanly clothed by an angel for a tacit shift in doctrine from Satan to God, *§9.7.3.* The filthy garb may be metaphor for dress by evil spirit, *Genesis 3, 22, §11.4,* the fine garb for dress by the angel, *§12.14.* Spirit dress alters ways, *§9.1, Isaiah 11, 6-9, §7.6.* In dirty garb, Israel wages war by injustice, *§11.5, Isaiah 1, 15-20, §8.6.* Now if priestly error is to test all to time's end, *Isaiah 24,* must there be two Israels? *§9.7.3, §12.15,* dressed for heaven and hell? *§12.10, John 8, 42-45, §3.* If God's Jews are kin to angels, angels have right to try to dress them. Hence, archangel Michael is Israel's protector below but angels may only let enough sight of God to meet God's plan of mercy, *Daniel 10, Isaiah 28, 11-19, §12.15, Zechariah 1.* Israel may suffer in the dark so mercy can harvest angel lines of descent among the Gentiles, *Jude 1, 6, Romans 11, 25-32*:

> at that time michael, the great prince
> who protects your people, will arise.
> daniel 12, 1

> what is man that you are mindful of
> him,
> the son of man that you care for him?
> you made him a little lower than the
> heavenly beings
> and crowned him with glory and
> honour.
> psalm 8, 4-5

A just God does not offer proofs of title to creation that life cannot understand or agree to be bound by. Thus, proof of a just God's title is to hinge on life having fair choice between what a rebellion or just God stand for. It makes God and Satan joint deities in a free-will title contest over this world, *§8.1*. Both can dispute loyalties by claiming to be our 'just' God. 'God's word' appears coded to respect that, *§8.1, §12.3, Isaiah 14, 12-21, §8.3*. But at some stage of this world, a higher rebellion may arrive at its choice to defer to Justice else wager its life, *everything*, on victory, *Psalm 82, §8.3*. War may then rack heaven, *Revelation 12, 7-12, §7.1*, and a curse to apocalypse strike the earth, *Isaiah 24*.

An infallible God cannot give a free-will proof except at the behest of life on brink of full rebellion. For the 'fair choice' of God or rebellion hinges on how evil wishes to define evil for its power-bid. Evil gods must first formally define evil then ask God for a new world to offer life in it a fair choice of good and evil, *Genesis 3, 2-5, §7.4, Deuteronomy 30, 17-20, §7.8*. People are made for that choice in a world supervised by their angels and demons, *guardian spirits, §10.5*, where God's Spirit is reserved, *Job 28, 20-22, §9.6, Isaiah 11, 6-9, §7.6, Daniel 10, 12-14*. The first being as Messiah and King of angels may carry God's authority in this world, *Isaiah 9, 6*, salvation from God, *Proverbs 8, 22-36, §2*.

The essence to this world is that mortals have material needs administered by spirit-guardians they choose, *Deuteronomy 30, 17-20, §7.8, Wisdom 14, 27-31, §9.5, Isaiah 24, Micah 4, 5, §12.8, Galatians 4, 1-9, §5.10*. People are cursed and blessed under bonds to spirits that clothe them, *Genesis 15, 13-14, §7.8; 1 Chronicles 21, 11-17 & Isaiah 24, 1-6 & Luke 13, 1-9, §11.5, Matthew 12, 26-32, §9.8*. If all wish to dress as evil gods, *Psalm 40, 4, §7.9*, it deposes a just God. True evil is ready to try anything, *even invent and risk death, §1.2*, to depose a just God, *Psalm 82, §8.3*.

Rebel gods define evil by laws they enact to help mortal tyrants or priests rule on earth, *Micah 4, 5*. If evil does not claim to be infallible, evil can define evil as it goes along: *try any law that might depose God.* It thereby perfects the definition of evil in tests on mortals and also enacts the curse-law on evil for hell. Finally, evil may admit its death-wish rather than defer to God, *Proverbs 8, 36, §6.2*. God's design lets evil evolve to law asking to be shut in hell for failing to depose God.

Mortals are thus third life: fledgeling children of second life who asked for them to be born to settle a mutiny against God's title. This world is a stage set to give key mortals a fair choice between good and evil. No unjustified loss of life occurs if all are raised at Judgement Day and Death only rules after just sentence to hell. Until title is settled, both God and Satan have a claim to be the 'just' God of mortals. For sake of 'justice', 'God's word' is ambidextrous to let choose either Satan or God as 'God', *§8.1, §12.3.* Because evil has right to define evil, it is free to sow evil on earth to test good in the title-contest, *Isaiah 14, 12-21, §8.3*:

> Jesus told them another parable: "The kingdom of heaven is like a man who sowed good seed in his field. But while everyone was sleeping, his enemy came and sowed weeds among the wheat, and went away. When the wheat sprouted and formed heads, then the weeds also appeared.
> "The owner's servants came to him and said, 'Sir didn't you sow good seed in your field? Where then did the weeds come from?'
> " 'An enemy did this,' he replied.
> "The servants asked him, 'Do you want us to go and pull them up?'
> " 'No,' he answered, 'because while you are pulling up the weeds, you may root up the wheat with them. Let both grow together until the harvest. At that time I will tell the harvesters: First collect the weeds and tie them in bundles to be burned; then gather the wheat and bring it into my barn.' "
> Matthew 13, 24-30

If God *directly* made evil, *or turned life to evil,* would God not be a criminal? But if a just God does not sow evil folk, why think He *directly* made or sowed the devil? *§3.* The devil sows evil on earth to test and claim 'good' life. He legislates for mortals to inherit a sinful nature, *§9.1, §10.5, Exodus 20, 4-6, §7.9; Psalm 51, 1-12, §10.10, John 8, 42-45, §3.* Life is an edited edition of God (*source of all life*), *Mark 4, 13-25,* but Satan rules in expressions of God's nature edited to rebel, *to sin, Matthew 7, 24-29.* Evil has right to amend its nature for a fear of God that flees into hell, *Isaiah 66, 24, §1.15 & 14, 20-21 & 8, 19-22, §10.11.*

God is called to prove title against the devil's works, *Psalm 98, 1 John 3, 8.* If He respects life's wishes, He cannot spy on demons, *§9.1, Job 1, 6-7,* or stop life running wild with evil, *Job 28, 20-22, §9.4, Isaiah 11, 6-9, §7.6.* Yet, if Satan is legally God's left hand, *Job 1 & 2,* and sees all evil, God is all-seeing in a legal sense.

Reality is an issue for mortals to settle by their wishes. It is to be prospected for by hearts handed down by ancestors under inheritance laws that clothe in good and evil spirit, *§9.11*, penning by truth and lie. For freedom to choose 'reality', there is a haze over the area of origins. Many mortals inherit places far from the idea that life on earth is about whether God or Satan has title to creation? *to them.* It shows life is unbiased or 'free' to choose a path. The nature of good and evil, truth and lie, seem up for grabs. But if a just God exists, truth and lie map to just and unjust reason, *Proverbs 28, 5, §8.1, Matthew 7, 24-29, Isaiah 29, 13-16, §1.5.*

teach me your way, o lord, and i will walk in your truth;
give me an undivided heart, that i may fear your name.
psalm 86, 11

Schism is part of a title contest, *Isaiah 24, Luke 21, 12- 28, §9.1.* The Day of Judgement may divide sheep and goats by maps of reason they uphold as global, *§1.5, chapter 12.* A global theory sets a proposal on 'justice' to fit for heaven or hell, *Isaiah 5, 18-20, §8.1 & 30, 9-10.* Love of 'injustice' is with hell's 'God', *2 Thessalonians 2, 9-12, §9.3, Luke 12, 51-53, Matthew 10, 28.* The just Messiah is to indict unjust maps to save, *Isaiah 11, 4.* Only God's truth has a perfectly just base. The final proof of that may be a decay of life in hell to show evil builds on delusion and lie, has a death-wish.

Mortals feel for the truth under pulls of related spirits. Their reason may turn between devil or God on paths into alternative spiritual spaces, *§1.7, §8.6, Job 28, 20-22, §9.4.* In God's space are a variety of personal proofs for God, *Isaiah 1, 15-20, §8.6, 2 Corinthians 10, 5, §7.11, Luke 7, 35.* In the rebellion space are the beasts of reasoned 'injustice', *Daniel 7.* It may be possible to map out rival spaces to help a fair choice, *§12.2*, but evil cheats. It moves to establish lie or delusion above people's ability to object by power politics and a genius for lies, *Isaiah 30, 1-15, §9.12.*

God's servants then witness to God's map against unjust maps that tempt to an unjust 'peace' under 'God', *Luke 4, 5-6, §1.15.* God is with just reason to lead out of unethical systems set to depose God. There may be a leading unjust map for an end-time power bid, *§9.7.4, §10.11.* The last throw of the unjust may be a tyranny to end just faith in a gamble that it does not also end the world, *Daniel 8, 20-25, §12.13.*

13.6 Truth to mortals: 'God's word' and Grace

Paths into God's space of reason faithfully track the Spirit to a just God's word in areas, *§12.3*. Its main themes are hard to disprove and ask faith in 'justice' to escape the traps or pitfalls of evil maps, *§8.1*:

they will sing before the Lord, for he comes,
he comes to judge the earth.
He will judge the world in righteousness
and the peoples in his truth.
Psalm 96, 13

Do not snatch the word of truth from my mouth,
for I have put my hope in your laws.
Psalm 119, 43

Surely you desire truth in the inward parts;
you teach me wisdom in the inmost place.
Psalm 51, 6

Free me from the trap that is set for me,
for you are my refuge.
Into your hands I commit my spirit;
redeem me, O Lord, the God of truth.
Psalm 31, 4-5

Show me your ways, O Lord,
teach me your paths;
guide me in your truth and teach me,
for you are God my Saviour,
and my hope is in you all day long.
Psalm 25, 4-5

Lord, who may dwell in your sanctuary?
Who may live on your holy hill?

He whose walk is blameless
and who does what is righteous,
who speaks the truth from his heart.
Psalm 15, 1-2

These psalms testify to a path of truth (*a long journey into Justice, §9.11*), for leaving a rebellion against God, *§11.6*. God is to save from ties to evil that kill: *purify willing hearts, §10.10, §12.14.* Thus, God warns not to be an unjust power, *Isaiah 30, 1-15, §9.12 & 24; 2 Peter 2, 19-22, §7.11*, but evil thinks unjust is 'just'. 'God's word' is sealed to allow evil a fair choice of 'God', *Daniel 12, 9-10, §12.3*, by unjust readings that leave 'paradoxes'. Hence, God's foes reject God to seek power by Satan as 'God', *§12.3, Psalm 78, 2, Isaiah 28, 14-22, Luke 8, 10-18.* Evil duels with good to belay a just reading of God's word, *to mask it in and outside religion.* Unjust spirits thereby lead the blind, *Isaiah 42, 16-25, §1.16, §8.5, §10.5*, to establish in rebellion, *Isaiah 24*:

Because of rebellion, the host of the saints and the daily sacrifice were given over to it. It prospered in everything it did, and truth was thrown to the ground.
Daniel 8, 12

'God's word' uses the metaphor of a stumbling stone for a key area that the faithful heed for a path to full truth. Namely, *Isaiah 8, 11-17, §8.6* says the 'Lord Almighty' is a stone even Israel, *bearer of 'God's word'*, is to stumble over. Thus, Israel is to take up evil maps in disloyalty to God and be held in the dark for a while, *Isaiah 10, 20-22, §8.6.* To reject the stone is a pact to death and curse on blind servants, *Isaiah 42, 16-25, §1.16.* But in *Isaiah 28, 11-22, §12.15*, God talks not as the stone but of laying the stone in Zion. That fits with *Isaiah 9, 2-7*, or the New Testament, see *§11.1*, that say God's King, *the Messiah*, is same nature as God, also called 'Lord Almighty', *§8.2.* Thus, *Isaiah 8 & 28*, together say the stumbling stone is the Messiah, *God incarnate, §12.7.* The Messiah is to open 'God's word' for the just, *Deuteronomy 18, 17-22, §11.5; Matthew 16, 21-23; 2 Thessalonians 2, 9-12, §9.3.*

If the stumbling stone, *path to truth*, is God's Son and King, *Psalm 2, §9.4*, then *Isaiah 8* is veiled prophesy of Israel denying the Messiah, *Isaiah 53, Romans 9, 30-33; 1 Peter 2, 6-8, §6.17.* It is veiled to allow Israel a fair choice between good and evil. That fair choice is only proven against evil lawyers if Israel really is turned, *rejects the Messiah*, but later returns to Him. Similarly, 'Christians' for Jesus as the just Messiah may turn to an unjust antichrist they call 'Jesus' but later return to the 'just' Jesus, *Daniel 8* above, *§8.6, §12.9.* Now if the Messiah turns souls from evil maps, He is in essence God's truth or word incarnate, *Deuteronomy 18, 17-22, §11.5, John 1, 1-13, §8.2, & 14, 6-10, §11.5.* His foes are God's foes, *Satan's children*, as keen liars, *John 8, 31-59.* Evil maps thereby stumble over the Christ's true teaching, *§12.3, §12.9.*

The above illustrates a property of 'God's word' vital to a fair title contest. It has interlocked nets of verses to define 'truth'. The nets are gathered in for a proposal on the Justice under which *all* scripture is written, *§9.7.5.* A just heart finds just truth *in areas*, see *Psalm 51, 6 & 15, 1-2* above. But it is normal to gather in nets to support sin as allows God's foes to idolise 'God', *Psalm 50, 21, Jeremiah 7, 4-10, §9.10, Hosea 6, 6, §8.1.* 'God's word' respects freedom of faith even if its readers do not. In end-times, *if God is to win*, the high question to a title-contest is not whether 'God' exists but whether folk wish a deity in the image of Satan or God? *§9.7.4.* By chosen spirit-dress, *§9.1*, folk may look to 'the Messiah' in image of God or devil.

For a just God to establish His mandate to rule, cultural progress, *as the devil tries to block*, must make it easier to see some kind of 'God' exists. God's justice respects tastes in 'justice' for a division of kingdoms, *Micah 4, 5, §12.8, Matthew 25, 31-41, §11.4.* That mortals are truly free to take evil faiths or mores has to be established beyond doubt in a valid title-contest. The proof is by letting evil spirits slave souls to target evil faiths in twilight zones, *John 9, 4-5, §10.6.* Thus, first people, *Adam and Eve?*, rebelled against God to assert their free-will for evil, *§1.* Evil spirits then slaved their children, *Genesis 4, 7, §7.7,* for the test of Noah's loyalty to God after which the world was reset at the flood for new tests of faith. The world headed off to a clear choice in spiritual schools, *§9.4,* in the tree of knowledge of good and evil, *chapter 5.*

Mortals may be in trust to guardian spirits, *Galatians 4, 1-9, §5.10, Micah 4, 5, §12.8,* born to an educating maze in paths to full loyalty or full rebellion against God. The maze allows faith in auto-evolution, *infinite cultural rise,* or a just God. Mortals are not at first prejudiced by knowing they run a maze under a duel of spirits. That is proven by a twilight zone in which souls not made by 'natural' selection put faith in it. They rationalise dying as their price for progress, *§1.2, Proverbs 8, 38, §6.2.* Their temples are natural history museums: shrines to tablets of fossil stone from a god of evolution and cultural diversity, *§6.16.* It is a path to one day join Satan to openly dispute with God. The temple needs to see 'natural' violence for its freedom of faith. It thus invokes a curse to 'natural' disaster, religious violence and predator-prey behaviour, *Isaiah 11, 6-9, §7.6, Wisdom 14, 27-31, §9.5.* The problem of evil is that evil has to cite evil to justify its rule.

Those who preach life as a struggle to survive in a spiritless world may be proof of mortal freedom of faith. They help spirits enslave to lies that approximate the real world by narrow or false views of the life-cycle of birth, reproduction and death. Satan's hell offers many charming views on the meaning to death. The life-cycle is to enable tests of faith over individual lives and cultural progress, *Genesis 15, 13-14, §7.8.* Ambivalence to God condemns life to the maze. Does a just God set life span to speed salvation from evil gods on personal and cultural paths? *Genesis 6, 3.* By end-times, many mortals may show the mind-set of evil gods above them, *Psalm 8, 4-5 & 82, 6.*

The educating maze twists and turns between good and evil, *§8.5.*

Good and evil runs are inherited down cultural and family lines, *Exodus 20, 4-6, §7.9.* Spirits thus drive scientists in their labs. who see inheritance laws exist. But just intelligence is needed to see that a behavioural science based solely on material flags, *§9.2,* genetics, may be a lie, *§9.11, §10.13.* The inheritance laws that dress souls can be spiritually mediated, *§9.1.* They allow people suited to different parts of the maze to 'evolve', *Luke 7, 28-30.* To prove infallibility, God may set results of tests in sealed prophecy, *Revelation 5, 1-5, §7.10,* above unjust sciences, *Revelation 9, 20-21.*

Inter and intra-religious strife show the religious percolating into just and unjust maps of reason. 'God's word' is beset by unjust teaching to drag souls into maps of evil spirits, *§9.7.4.* But unjust religion can be attacked by angels inviting into God's maps, *§8.5.* God saves if personal and cultural tests establish His title to rule outside hell. All sinners are subject to claim by Satan as his subjects, *Revelation 12, 7-12, §7.1*:

"I live in a high and holy place,
but also with him who is contrite and lowly in spirit,
to revive the spirit of the lowly and
to revive the heart of the contrite.
I will not accuse forever,
nor will I always be angry,
for then the spirit of man would grow faint before me—the breath of man that I have created.
I was enraged by his sinful greed;
I punished him, and hid my face in anger,
yet he kept on in his wilful ways.
I have seen his ways, but I will heal him;
I will guide him and restore comfort to him,
creating praise on the lips of the mourners in Israel.
Peace, peace, to those far and near,"
says the Lord. "And I will heal them;
but the wicked are like the tossing sea,

which cannot rest,
whose waves cast up mire and mud.
"There is no peace," says my God,
"for the wicked."

Isaiah 57, 15-21

'Peace' is life with justice not where 'injustice' or Death rule, *Luke 1, 79.* There is 'no peace for the wicked' in or outside hell, *Isaiah 14, 20-21, Revelation 14, 11,* for they are sown to work for Satan to draw to hell's maps, *Psalm 1,* and Satan is God's wrath and punishment on them for failure, *chapter 8.* To see past Satan to God heals some so sin stops. The depth of Satan's veil over God's face may be such that a simple unjust reading of *Isaiah 57* above takes Satan as 'God', *§9.7.5, §9.7.6.*

13.7 Mortals in a Dark Prison under Satan

Spirits of truth ask for faith that creation is God's design. It is then 'good' in some just sense, *Genesis 1, 31*, that respects freedom of faith, *Isaiah 30, 1-15, §9.12, §12.3.* Satan's unjust 'faithful' may declare it 'good' in an unjust sense. True faith is to justify or pave the way for God's salvation, *Psalm 51, 22-23, Matthew 5, 3-10, §2.3,* empowering God to increase knowledge of God for all. God then comes to fairly indict works of the devil, *Psalm 37, 37-40, 1 John 3, 8*, as 'original evolution' may be, *§1, §9.3.*

Under a just God, people only reach the limits of rebellion and injustice, *hell*, if led to *consciously* rebel to God's face. Is even to crucify the Messiah who is God, *Isaiah 9, 6, §8.6*, conscious enough? *Isaiah 53, Luke 23, 34, §6.7.* To be led by an antichrist is cursed, *Isaiah 24 & 35, 4-6, §8.1*, but does it condemn at Judgement Day? *§10.11.* Those against Justice 'escape' it for hell's tyranny, *Micah 4, 5, §12.8.* There, Satan is 'God' of freedom fighters evolving in sin to depose Justice, *Isaiah 57, 20-21, §9.4, Job 1, 6-12, Luke 4, 1-13, Revelation 12, 10.* Death and destruction may rule in hell, *§7.4*, as pillars of evolutionary paths seeking powers to depose God, *Proverbs 8, 36, §6.2.*

In just law, mortals may be children who show an unconscious wish to join evil by sin against God. They sin if tempted or oppressed, *Genesis 4, 6-7, §10.5.* Demons thereby take custody by a plan to help them evolve in sin to full loyalty to evil. By blind sin, mortals pact to the devil's offer to perfect them in rebellion, *§1.2.* They then work under a curse to evolve as full members of the kingdom of evil, *§9.1, Isaiah 55, 1-11, §11.1.* It may be a long time before folk as children hear that 'truth', *Galatians 4, 1-9, §5.10.* If Satan could justly make it never, that deposes God.

God licences the devil's plan until mortals formally ask release from it, *Isaiah 28, 11-19, §12.15.* For the plan is to fulfil people's rebellious wishes by sending Death and Destruction to help them evolve to fully reject God, *§7.4, §9.1.* The plan is to punish or curse mortals for sin against God till they fully reject God. High consent is by sacrificial conduct, *Genesis 4, 7-11*, or everyday behaviour that shows a death-wish, *chapter 6.* Sacrifice of life is a price mortals arguably wish to pay for 'progress' to depose God, *§9.5, Isaiah 28, 18, Proverbs 10, 16, Wisdom 1, 16 & 2, 24, Romans 6, 23.*

God's strategy to check a rebellion and save sinners is simply to uphold impartial Justice, *Psalm 98*:

> the king said to him, "how many times must I make you swear to tell me nothing but the truth in the name of the lord?"
>
> 1 kings 22, 16

God also gives laws, *guidance*, to define loyalty to God and oblige rebellions to enact counter-laws to annul God's justice, *Micah 4, 5, §12.8.* That sets a rebellion on its path into hell, *Psalm 1.* The curse-laws of hell are willingly enacted by unjust gods to disprove God's laws on crime in power bids to break mortal-faith in God, *§11.3.* The power-bids attack the path to just faith as politically incorrect or a curse to crime and injustice, *Isaiah 24.* Pioneers of 'injustice' lay paths to hell, *Psalm 1, Proverbs 28, 5, §8.1*, by faith in an unjust world with right to 'crime', *chapter 12.* The path to heaven is by faith 'Justice' will prevail over 'injustice', *§12.7, Isaiah 11, 6-9, §7.6.* It is a contest of rival ideas of 'justice':

> woe to those who call evil good and good evil,
> who put darkness for light
> and light for darkness,
> who put bitter for sweet
> and sweet for bitter.
>
> isaiah 5, 20

Mortals fall under rebellion curse-law by disloyalty to God, *sin.* Sin is taken as backing rebellion and its curse to death and destruction. For curse-relief, folk then look to God else to tyrannical magical sciences in a quest for the tree of life, *§11.4.* It is said folk began to call on God as Death and Destruction bit, *Genesis 4, 25-26, §7.5.* There was a first wish to end a pact to evolve in sin for Satan. It empowered God to offer impartial Justice as may lock the rebellion in hell under its curse law: *the devil's rule.* Life in hell is spirit-dressed to Satan's image, *§9.1, Isaiah 66, 24, §1.13.*

'God's word' offers a path to salvation, *§8.1.* To respect all life, it must thread through the laws holding sinners in Satan's prison. For a title-contest is only fairly settled if life's wishes are respected. Any rebellion must allow a loophole for mortals to depart to God. Rebel gods may legislate for the smallest loophole and it may have been agreed with God, *foreseen*, before this world, *Genesis 15, 13-14, §7.8, Micah 5, 2, §7.9, 1 Peter 1, 20, Ephesians 1, 4-5 & 11-13.* The gods cannot accept God will win a title-contest whose course is by just regard to free-will of mortals in the dark.

Rebellion law sets penalties for sin to give citizens a purgatorial debt so they belong to it as to a jail till debt to rebellion is paid or atoned for. It is part of Justice, *Luke 18, 1-8, §11.6, Romans 13, 1-7, §11.5.* Subjects of the prison governor, *the evil one*, insist sin is paid for. To escape him, a first step is to forgive some trespasses, *1 John 5, 16-18, §9.7.2.* Heaven is the only place to escape to if God is ready to forgive sin against God, *Psalm 103, §12.4, Isaiah 1, 15-20, §8.6, Luke 15.* Thus, the Lord's prayer asks release from a rebel prison:

"and when you pray, do not be like the hypocrites, for they love to pray standing in the synagogues and on the street corners to be seen by men. I tell you the truth, they have received their reward in full.
But when you pray, go into your room, close the door and pray to your father, who is unseen. then, your father who sees what is done in secret, will reward you. and when you pray, do not keep on babbling like pagans, for they think they will be heard because of their many words. do not be like them for your father knows what you need before you ask him. "this, then, is how you should pray:

" 'our father in heaven,
hallowed by your name,
your kingdom come,
your will be done
on earth as it is in heaven.
give us today our daily bread.
forgive us our debts,
as we also have forgiven our debtors.
and lead us not into temptation,
but deliver us from the evil one.'

for if you forgive men when they sin against you, your heavenly father will also forgive you. but if you do not forgive men their sins, your father will not forgive your sins."
matthew 6, 5-15

God and the devil offer forgiveness for sin under laws of atonement. God cannot justly forgive faith in the 'God' of rebellion, *Proverbs 1, 20-33, §9.7.6, Isaiah 24, Hosea 6, 6, §8.1, Luke 13, 1-9, §11.5.* That 'God' gives curse-discounts, *blessings*, to false teachers, *§9.8*: to establish unjust religion in his spirit, *chapter 10, 2 Kings 17, 34-41, John 8, 42-45, §3.* It implies God forgives some sins against God easier than others, *§10.11, §12.6, Psalm 32.* The whole system is under God so pardon and punition are abbreviated as a just God's will, *§8.1*:

"... forgiving wickedness, rebellion and sin. yet he does not leave the guilty unpunished; he punishes the children and their children for the sin of the fathers to the third and fourth generation."
exodus 34, 7

Loyalty to God walks as if in His Spirit to resist sin, *Isaiah 11, 6-9, §7.6.* A just God has not right to forgive sinners who reject His Spirit, *Proverbs 8, 36, §6.2, Matthew 12, 31, §12.10.* If the Messiah walks with the Spirit, *Isaiah 9, 6, Deuteronomy 18, 17-22, §11.5, Isaiah 11, 1-10, §11.1,* forgiveness for sin needs loyalty to Him, *Job 19, 25-29, §12.7, Isaiah 53, Hosea 6, 6, §8.1.* Jesus taught that, and of a spirit of antichrist to turn the Messiah's word for rebellion, *§10.3, §9.7.4*:

"... I tell you the truth, all the sins and blasphemies of men will be forgiven them. But whoever blasphemes against the Holy Spirit will never be forgiven; he is guilty of an eternal sin."
He said this because they were saying, "He has an evil spirit."
Mark 3, 28-30

"... I tell you, whoever acknowledges me before men, the Son of Man will also acknowledge him before the angels of God. But he who disowns me before men will be disowned before the angels of God. And everyone who speaks a word against the Son of Man will be forgiven, but anyone who blasphemes against the Holy Spirit will not be forgiven..."
Luke 12, 8-10

A rebellion cannot forgive all sins whilst God reigns as it only rules over sin, *Mark 14, 48-49.* God may fully pardon, *Psalm 103, 1-4, §12.4, Matthew 10, 28, §7.10,* but it needs two things. Mortals must end a pact to evil by repentance of sin, and, make full atonement for past sin, *personal or hereditary,* see *Exodus 34, 7* above. A strong atonement might acquit for rebellion in a dark age, *§10.6, Isaiah 1, 15-20, §8.6,* or invert social status, *Matthew 21, 23-32, §12.12.* Evil gods set the nature of the atonement in rebellion law to keep God out and quiet, *Psalm 50, Job 1 & 2, Revelation 12, 7-10, §7.1.*

Now if God is source of life-forces, *chapter 11,* life needs to 'see' God in ratio to its type, *Psalm 63, 1, §11.2.* Too much or too little sight may enervate. Evil sees God via the life in its power, *§11.2.* It legally shields it from enough sight of God to break free, *Job 28, 20-22, §9.4, Job 42, 1-6, Acts 26, 9-18, §8.3.* Thus, the gods indict God as a being who inflicts His Spirit on life against its will, *Isaiah 11, 6-9, §7.6.* Forces of darkness may bar mortals as evil children from sight of a just God by a death-penalty on sin, *Exodus 33, 14-20, §10.8, Job 28, 20-22, §9.4.* But to see Satan pose as 'God' is 'fine', *§10.8.* The Messiah must enter a jail for sinners as their defence lawyer, *1 John 2, 1-2, §9.7.4, 1 Peter 3, 17-22.*

13.8 God's Justice and accursed Power-bids

Suppose God is perfect so the essential source of life-forces. That obliges all life to laws close enough to God's law, *e.g. 'commandments'*, for strength and vitality. There may be an optimum sight of God's law that rebel gods must allow subjects so they can feed the gods well. The gods seek vitality by taxing law-breakers, *sinners*, for life-forces, *§11.2*, but a lawless society may give a poor yield like the one cursed to die at the flood, *§7.7*, where God preserved Noah's line. After the flood came 'commandments' that unjust gods rule by, *Isaiah 29, 13-16, §1.5.*

Evil adopts the 'commandments' as its law since they define sins against God that hell punishes for. Hell can be pernickety about rules and sin, *§7.9, 1 Timothy 1, 5-9, §8.5.* God allows freedom of faith on the 'God' or 'justice' to 'God's word', *§12.3, Micah 4, 5.* The 'God' of the unrepentant is Satan as one to eternally punish and kill for sin in hell:

> Do not be afraid of those who kill the body but cannot kill the soul. Rather be afraid of the One who can destroy both soul and body in hell.
>
> Matthew 10, 28

> I will praise you, O Lord, with all my heart; before the "gods" I will sing your praise.
>
> Psalm 138, 1

> I know the Lord is great, that our Lord is greater than all gods.
>
> Psalm 135, 5

Satan punishes sin and lures into sin for power. His religion is to a 'God' who eternally punishes sin as a tyrant. Thus, *Isaiah 65, 17-20* is his pledge of a 'heaven' inside hell from which to rule a curse to death. *§9.7.5.* His religion overrules Justice as it offers salvation from sin (*the devil*). Those against a just salvation are cursed to die for it by 'God', *Isaiah 14, 12-21, §8.3 & 24 & 30, 1-15, §9.12.* 'God's word' gives that truth in its 'just' reading, *§12.3*, but 'unjust' readings support lie and sin, *the unjust devil*, as 'God', *Isaiah 14, 12-21, §8.3, §10.8*:

> To the Jews who had believed him, Jesus said, "If you hold to my teaching, you are really my disciples. Then you will know the truth, and the truth will set you free."
> They answered him, "We are Abraham's descendants and have never been slaves of anyone. How can you say that we shall be set free?"
> Jesus replied, "I tell you the truth, everyone who sins is a slave to sin.
>
> John 8, 31-34

The rebellion creed is then to be gods ruling 'God's law' in God's place, *Isaiah 14, 12-21, §8.3, Wisdom 2, 23-24, Psalm 82, §8.2.* It is evil's basic offer via unjust readings of 'God's word', *Genesis 3, 2-5, §7.4, John 10, 33-39, §8.1, §12.3.* The gods tyrannise by 'God's law', *§9.1.* Thus, foes of the just Christ wish for an unjust antichrist claiming to be the Christ, *§9.7.4, Isaiah 24.* His charisma leads rebels in all religion, *§9.7.4, Psalm 69, 2-3, §11.2.* To assert commandments doesn't make loyal to a just God, *Isaiah 24 & 28, 11-19, §12.15*:

If anyone else thinks he has reasons to put confidence in the flesh, I have more: circumcised on the eighth day, of the people of Israel, of the tribe of Benjamin, a Hebrew of Hebrews; in regard to the law, a Pharisee; as for zeal, persecuting the church; as for legalistic righteousness, faultless. But whatever was to my profit I now consider loss for the sake of Christ.

Philippians 3, 4-6

For rebellion is like the sin of divination, and arrogance like the sin of idolatry.

1 Samuel 15, 23

The mercy of God is to save the penitent by a just atonement for sin, *Isaiah 1, 15-20, §8.6.* Meanwhile, a mixed faith world is cursed to crime, war, etc., as it fails to atone for sin, *Luke 13, 1-9, §11.5.* A just God will not tyrannise the unjust, *Isaiah 30, 1-15, §9.12.* Satan's curse on sin is for evil ways of waging war on 'injustice':

... then he will turn back and vent his fury against the holy covenant. He will return and show favour to those who forsake the holy covenant.

"His armed forces will rise up to desecrate the temple fortress and will abolish the daily sacrifice. Then they will set up the abomination that causes desolation.

With flattery he will corrupt those who have violated the covenant, but the people who know their God will firmly resist him.

"Those who are wise will instruct many, though for a time they will fall by the sword or be burned or captured or plundered. When they fall, they will receive a little help, and many who are not sincere will join them. Some of the wise will stumble, so that they may be refined, purified and made spotless until the time of the end, for it will still come at the appointed time.

"The king will do as he pleases He will exalt and magnify himself above every god and will say unheard-of things against the God of gods. He will be successful until the time of wrath is completed, for what has been determined must take place.

Daniel 11, 30-36

Daniel's end-time prophesy above does not show the just triumphing by military might. They obey the Spirit of Justice, *Zechariah 4, 6, §12.8.* How they fight a military attack might be hard to countenance, *Psalm 44, Romans 8, 35-36*:

"This is what the Sovereign Lord, the
Holy One of Israel says:

"In repentance and rest is your
salvation,
in quietness and trust is your strength,
but you would have none of it.
You said, 'No, we will flee on horses.'
Therefore you will flee!
You said, 'We will ride off on swift
horses.'
Therefore your pursuers will be swift!
A thousand will flee
at the threat of one;
at the threat of five
you will all flee away,
till you are left
like a flagstaff on a mountaintop,
like a banner on a hill."

Yet the Lord longs to be gracious to
you;
he rises to show you compassion.
For the Lord is a God of justice.
Blessed are all who wait for him!
… … …
Whether you turn to the right or to
the left, your ears will hear a voice
behind you saying, "This is the way;
walk in it." Then you will defile your
idols overlaid with silver and your
images covered with gold; you will
throw them away like a menstrual
cloth and say to them, "Away with
you!"

Isaiah 30, 15-18, 21-22

'God's word' implies a truth about evil to sober minds and set free. But that truth is a fetter to God's foes, *Psalm 2, §9.4.* It offends worldly pride or faith in war by *Micah 7, 16-20, §12.4 & Lamentations 3, 25-32, §12.8.* Jesus said the truth on sin will out by prophesied action of the Spirit after the cross, *Jeremiah 31, 31-34, §7.10*:

"… But I tell you the truth: It is for
your good that I am going away. Unless
I go away, the Counsellor will not
come to you; but if I go, I will send him
to you.
When he comes, he will convict the
world of guilt in regard to sin and
righteousness and judgement:
… … …
But when he the Spirit of truth, comes,
he will guide you into all truth…."

John 16, 7-8, 13

To rebel is thus to oppress 'truth' and accept the devil's curse, *Isaiah 24 & 30, 1-15, §9.12.* His spirit molds unjust movements, beasts of earth, *§9.7.4, & sea, §9.4,* to test faith in God till a curse ends his world, *Isaiah 24, Daniel 8, 1-25, §12.13, Luke 21, 12-28, §9.1*:

"all this I have told you so that you will not go astray. they will put you out of the synagogue; in fact, a time is coming when anyone who kills you will think he is offering a service to god. they will do such things because they have not known the father or me. ..."
John 16, 1-3

God and Satan stand by rival ideas of 'justice'. God accepts Satan's curse-law as the right law on evil, *Exodus 20, 4-6, §7.9, John 10, 33-39, §8.1.* Satan disciplines subjects by curse and evil spirit: *eternal punishment for sin.* He trains to be strong enough to be disloyal to God yet obey commandments. Such strong evil might sortie into God's heaven without knowing, *being bound by*, the Spirit, *Isaiah 11, 6-9, §7.6, Matthew 22, 1-14, §12.14, Revelation 12, 7-12, §7.1.*

History covers the advance from satanic, *§10.8, Isaiah 28, 11-19, §12.15*, to divine visions of 'God's law', *Isaiah 1, 15-20, §8.6, Psalm 98.* Its key areas show Satan contesting Israel by Jew or Gentile faithful to his reading of God's law, *Isaiah 28, 11-19, §12.15.* Early prophets may have held satanic views of 'justice' at start of their path to a just God, *§10.8.* Even where a place is devoted to Justice, *Psalm 125, 3, §12.1*, it still suffers a curse of association with evil, *§9.7.2.* It cannot be run from, *Wisdom 14, 27-31, §9.5, Isaiah 24*, or ended by oppressive law and order, *Isaiah 30, 1-15, §9.12.* Thus, a mixed faith world has to ride out the curse. Only the most valid atonement for sin damps the curse, *Isaiah 1, 15-20, §8.6.* Above, Daniel prophesies a fortress temple making daily sacrifice of atonement yet falling to military might. Is it a satanic fortress to fall for failing Satan? Which of those sides puts the abomination, *see Daniel above*, in the temple?

Jesus also refers to the abomination and advises to flee Jerusalem from it, *Luke 21, 12-28, §9.1.* To Jesus' mind, it is able to claim jurisdiction of souls who do not flee. Is it a religious 'science' for a fortress temple? *e.g. a mind-control field or spiritual force, §6.16.* It may inject its surround with a compulsion to sin that only the Christ can fully deny. It shows a power to punish for sin that may end freedom of faith and thereby the world. By it, Satan may cover his retreat into hell taking the unjust with him, *Isaiah 24, Daniel 7, 23-28, Revelation 13, 11-14, 11, §9.7.4.* If Satan cannot be defeated by military might, it may set a tough test of the just in end-times, *Daniel 7, 25-27, §10.7 & 8, 1-25, §12.13.*

13.9 **Down on the Farm: Theory of Rebellion Law**

Rebellion law adopts 'God's commandments' as a line life may only cross out of sin to meet God *after* evolving a nature to dispute with God, *as sons of the devil, §9.1*. Mortals unable to dispute, *Isaiah 8, 19-22, §10.11*, are kept behind the line in sin, *out of God's jurisdiction.* For the rebellion enacts laws of spirit-led temptation and oppression on sin as forces to knock sinners back who think to seek a just God, *Luke 4, 1-13, Mark 14, 32-36, Luke13, 1-9, & Isaiah 24, 1-6, §11.5.* However, to keep yields of life-forces up, *§8*, the rebellion also uses curse-law to punish sin and drive mortals towards the line as God's enemies, *Psalm 32, 8-11, §10.5.* As a result, seeking God is like walking a tightrope, *§8.6.* A curse on sin may anytime trash committed idolaters, adulterers, murderers, etc., if it serves their wider rebellion, *Wisdom 14, 27-31, §9.5.*

In summary, rebellion law drives to live up to God's law by evolving in sin to hail Satan as 'God', *§11.3, Isaiah 10, 20.* Mortals are farmed as slaves to sin outside God's direct jurisdiction unless unusually just or God delivers by a powerful just atonement for sin, *Psalm 32.* The rebellion steeps subjects in forces to raise injustice from or in reaction to 'the wicked', *Revelation 16, 13-14.* Compulsion to sin is raised till life routinely breaks God's law, even to put to death the Messiah, *Isaiah 53*, who represents God, *Isaiah 9, 6.* That compulsion is of hell's experimental science to bar the path to God and drive evil to evolve beyond God. Such science will gutter if God is perfect as why hell may be eternally damned. Curse laws form a death or glory bid to out-evolve the One who might be perfectly just. It takes the same law defining sin as God but augmented by curse-law instead of the Spirit as difference between heaven, *Isaiah 55, 1-4 & 25, 8, Revelation 21, 1-4*, and hell, *Isaiah 14, 21.* Just as evil adopts God's law by adding a curse on sin so God adopts curse-law as what evil chooses to live by in its plans to depose God, *Micah 4, 5.* It is hell's legitimate law.

Curse-law typically overwhelms flaky sinners by spirit-force, *§5.2*, or punishments. It holds mortals as hostages to sin against God unjustly entering their world. The curse of evil can devour sinners in God's path before they see God, *Psalm 50.* Thus, flawed cults or enclaves moving towards loyalty to God but vulnerable in sin, *§9.7.1*, may any time be broken up by angry forces, rebellion, plague, earthquake, war.

Curse-law is set around 'God's law' for dominion of any who sin against God to punish their failure: *not sinning ably enough to depose God, §8.2.* It sets a value on souls by plans to depose God, *Psalm 73.* Some sin freely but others get crippling 'luck' to leave poor in rank or spirit, *§9.7.1, §12.16, Psalm 51, 17, Matthew 5, 3-12.* Seekers of God face a quick death for deadly sins, *§9.7.1,* because the worst crime against rebel gods is to support a just God. They are tested, *Isaiah 57, 1-2, §7.5, Daniel 7, 25-27,* by sinners driven by curse-law, *Isaiah 57, 15-21, §6.* Sometimes they see foes trashed for failing to break their faith, *Psalm 118 & 73*:

they swarmed around me like bees,
but they died out as quickly as burning thorns;
in the name of the lord i cut them off.
psalm 118, 12

The thorns deny Justice as law-breakers, *disposable if they fail and are of no more use to rebellion, Amos 4, 11, Zechariah 3, 2-4, Hebrews 6, 7-8.* God's mercy reaches among the thorns, *Luke 23, 34 & 15, 7; 1 Timothy 1, 13; Matthew 9, 12-13,* making a crown of thorns for God's servants, *Genesis 3, 17-18, Matthew 13, 7, John 19, 2, 1-3.* They intimidate to induce sin. If they fail, they may lose power to harm, *Daniel 3, 16-30,* but it is not to be obvious to respect freedom of faith. Which 'God' burnt the thorns for failing to sway Elijah below?:

"if i am a man of god," elijah replied, "may fire come down from heaven and consume you and your fifty men!" then the fire of god fell from heaven and consumed him and his fifty men.
so the king sent a third captain with his fifty men. this third captain went up and fell on his knees before elijah. "man of god," he begged, "please have respect for my life, and the lives of these fifty men, your servants! see, fire has fallen from heaven and consumed the first two captains and their men. but now have respect for my life!
the angel of the lord said to elijah, "go down with him; do not be afraid of him." so elijah got up and went down with him to the king.
he told the king, "this is what the lord says: is it because there is no god in israel for you to consult that you have sent messengers to consult baal-zebub, the god of ekron? because you have done this, you will never leave the bed you are lying on. you will certainly die!" so he died, according to the word of the lord that elijah had spoken.
2 kings 1, 13-17

To burn souls in 'the Lord's' name by fire from 'heaven' helps faith in a 'God' who directly curses evil, *§9.7.5, §9.7.6.* The captain asked mercy on the military from Elijah's deity. But Elijah was not God's mercy else why the Messiah? He was the path to the Messiah that the devil must allow for freedom of faith. Elijah was free to choose either Satan's or God's 'heaven'? *§10.8, §10.11.* From whose 'heaven' did fire descend? *Luke 9, 52-56.*

A freewill title contest of good and evil, *§11.4,* is about a duress of laws wherein good and evil tendencies are inheritable, *1 Kings 19, 1-4, §10.5.* If in end-times, all cross the line of God's law to join rebel gods then God is not the one true God by wish of life deriving from His nature. To that goal, the gods ask folk to annul God's followers or power base. They hone curse-law to empower tyrannies to sacrifice life in the way of demonic forces. But then, to fairly read and heed mortal wishes needs horsemen of the apocalypse. They are spirit-forces to test folk who hate and rage to see if they really wish to rid of God's folk? or are random? The testing of evil integrity, *Genesis 15, 13-14, §7.8,* makes an intimidating show of evil. A just God implies the folk holding out for Justice are heirs to creation, *Galatians 4, 1-9, §5.10.* They face test by the prejudices of spirited evil, *Psalm 118, 12 & 38, 19,* in fortresses of unjust reason, *§5.3, 2 Thessalonians 2, 8-12, §9.3.* The philosophy of the wicked is to steal the heirs' estate, *Psalm 50, 16-21, Psalm 1,* making them thieves trying to justify ruthless power-bids, *Luke 20, 9-16, §7.10.*

Rebels and God place different emphasis on the commandments, *Isaiah 28.* Rebels pass draconian punishments for sin against God, *§7.9, §9.7.1,* to assist simple faith in Satan as the capricious angry 'God', *§10.12.* The natures of God and Satan, *good and evil,* tally with systems of law by which they stand, *§9.7.* To avoid Satan, folk must read scripture for merciful loving just aspects of God's nature as overriding, *§12.3* to *§12.5.* Divine anger and cruelty may be an illusion punctured by knowledge of divine law: *God's just purposes, §8.1,* though many want a deity to punish 'the wicked'. Jesus' sheep most directly see what God is like if Jesus is the Messiah and image of God, *Wisdom 2, 18-24.* A fair title contest has 'holy' texts, *§9.7.5,* to give folk in the dark their fair choice of a just or unjust 'God', *§8.1.* The nature of a just God is the dilemma for mortals resolved by reading scripture as if by faith in Justice, *§8.1, §9.7.5, §10.8, §12.7.*

True and false teachers of a just God differ on the 'justice' ascribed to God, *§12.9.* The point to mortal-life in a title-contest is to work for or against a fair choice of 'God'. It brings local tyrannies against Justice. For that, the 'commandments' belong in either Satan's or God's law consistent with their joint title claim to this world. Title may only be fully settled after hell's regime fails to evolve under curse-laws to break out and depose God. Hell may rather turn on and try to depose Satan? But false prophets and priests might enter hell committed to Satan as one true 'God'. It depends on how 'justice' is administered. Hell and earth are then a public 'reality' show, *Isaiah 66, 24, §1.13*, where due process is on show to prove the futility or madness of a rebellion against Justice.

To depose God, the rebellion manages wishes of sinners in ways to cut them off from God, *§8.2.* A just God does not reply by arbitrary punishments for sin but offers the guidance of His life-giving Spirit, *§9.1, Psalm 51, 6 &15, 1- 2* earlier, or *Isaiah 11, 6-9, §7.6, John 4, 21-24.* Meanwhile, God's role is as a just judge is to see no one unjustly punished, *§9.7, §9.11, §11.4.* That implies God defends mortals on paths to know a just God from being wiped out, *§7.7.* A soul too tolerant of the dark, *Luke 13, 1-9, §11.5*, risks arbitrary punishments and a curse of association, *§9.7.2.* But God will not let Satan apply arbitrary punishments if it prejudices the trial-issue of whether a soul belongs to a just God or not? *§7.6, 1 Chronicles 21, 11-17, §11.5.* Hence, punishments Satan applies under curse-law on 'iffy' sinners or nations are by God's assent. If God thereby limits possible punishments for sin on some, it arguably implies every punishment is God will's in a legal sense even if not by God's direct will or hand. Scriptures may justly abridge it as that God punishes for sin to test faith, *Psalm 32, 8-11, §10.5, Lamentations 3, 33, Proverbs 3, 11-12, Hebrews 12, 5-8*, else punishes to stop sin reaching a point that the rebellion culls folk for deadly sin, *§9.7.1.*

After the rebellion is defeated, God may have no reason to dwell on past sins of heaven's citizens, *Psalm 30, Isaiah 35, 10, Revelation 21, 4.* Curse law may lose jurisdiction outside hell. But hell runs by an eternal curse of death and punishment on sinners who cannot abide the Spirit, *Isaiah 14, 20-21 & 65, 17-20*, who find knowing the Spirit too restrictive, *Matthew 5, 3, §12.3 & 22, 1-14, §12.14, Revelation 21, 1-4 & 22, 3*:

"the time is coming," declares the Lord,
"when I will make a new covenant with
the house of Israel and with the house
of Judah.
It will not be like the covenant I made
with their forefathers
when I took them by the hand to lead
them out of Egypt, because they broke
my covenant, though I was a husband
to them,"
declares the Lord.
"this is the covenant I will make with
the house of Israel after that time,"
declares the Lord.
"I will put my law in their minds and
write it on their hearts.
I will be their God,
and they will be my people.
no longer will a man teach his
neighbour,
or a man his brother, saying, 'know the
Lord,'
because they will all know me,
from the least of them to the
greatest,"
declares the Lord.
"for I will forgive their wickedness
and will remember their sins no more."
Jeremiah 31, 31-34

The servants of God's covenant path, *Psalm 50, 23*, are to establish an atonement for sin against God to enable sinners harassed by evil-spirit, *Matthew 9, 35-36*, to know the Spirit *in some degree*. It is a defence against curse-law without which demons may easily farm most in sin, *§7.3, Galatians 4, 1-9, §5.10.* The folk to lead on God's covenant path must resist unjust spirits *in allotted tests, §7.6, Psalm 32.* They need inner direction or conscience like Daniel, *§7.3*, to walk with the Spirit, *direct or by a legal finesse, §8.1*, despite the world, *Genesis 6, 9, Psalm 40 & 103 & 143, Mark 3, 35, John 6, 38 & 7, 17, 1 Peter 3, 17, 2 Peter 1, 21.* To seek a just God on earth is a path tested by evil spirit-forces, *Luke 8, 11-15, §5.4.*

An atonement for sin or prospect of it is vital to survival, *§8.2.* It curbs right of rebel gods to punish for sin. Scripture suggests a special atonement is needed before God's Spirit can justly contest demons from within a person's heart up to a spiritual circumcision of evil, *§10.5.* This world then sets test paths for sinners to progressively or abruptly be baptised into God's Spirit. The story of Adam and Eve suggests demonic spirits cause folk to run away from God, *Genesis 3, 7-11*, and all life to run wild, *Isaiah 11, 6-9, §7.6.* In a wilderness of sin, mortals develop faith in sin such as raises theories of evolution in a 'Godless' universe, *§1, Matthew 7, 11-12, §10.2.* 'God's word' is a troubled area because evil spiritual forces attack, subvert and curse its readers. To establish by faith in an 'original natural' life is to fully accept the curse, *§1.15.*

Attack by unjust spirits may leave folk neurotic wrecks, *1 Samuel 16, 14-16, §8.6, §10.2.* Key positions then go to souls who take pressures yet struggle to do 'justice', *Matthew 27, 24-25 & 19, 30.* They are the right leaders by God's will for freedom of faith in places, *§11.5.* They may be opposed by demented rebellious factions, *1 Samuel 15, 23, §8,* who help divert from God, *§12.9,* and black the path to Justice as politically incorrect or heresy, *Colossians 3, 15* to *4, 1.* Social chaos may ebb for semblances of 'peace', *§9.7.4,* but God is the only peace in lasting Justice, *Micah 4, 1-5, §12.8.*

Anyone can audition to be a servant of 'God', *§8.4, §9.7.4.* The unjust play to Satan as 'God' but may veer towards faith in a just God, *§8.5, Matthew 19, 24-26.* The more ambivalent risk crippling misfortune for sin, *Luke 13, 10-16, §9.9, Matthew 5, 13,* which can spread to the just by curse of association, *§9.7.2, §9.8.* Rebel gods are comforting spirits that disquiet if the word is not rebelled against by unjust readings, *§12.3, Isaiah 1, 15-20, §8.6.* The spirit of the rebellious may turn to wrath or hate if unjust faiths are not respected. They joy in the devil's blessing, *a curse-discount,* whilst of service to rebellion. That is also a form of 'God's blessing', *§9.8, §10.6.*

A fair title-contest may require every path is tried for raising God or Satan as 'God' to enable a just division into heaven and hell, *§9.1.* For that reason, a text may show the father of rebellion in an unjust spirit or a just God in a just spirit, *§9.7.5,* up to end-times, *Isaiah 24.* The spiritual spaces of good and evil may vie within one sinner or temple but either space may suffice in parochial matters of ritual service, *§10.7.*

In general, an atonement for sin is to renew a pledge of loyalty to a deity to avoid punishment for sin against a deities' law. For freedom of faith, someone must love the false teaching to invalidate God's atonement, *§8.5, Isaiah 24.* Someone must be stewards of 'faith' in the atonement in contradiction to the just Spirit that sets it, *§8.1, §9.7.5.* For the highest commitment to evil is to deny knowledge of God in God's temple, *i.e. preach Satan is 'God' as a witting or unwitting Satanist, Acts 26, 9-18, §8.3, §8.5.* Just discrimination is the path to a just God, *2 Corinthians 11, 4.* If folk love unjust doctrine, no atonement can establish loyalty to God, *Psalm 24, 3-5.* They then live on borrowed time, *Exodus 23, 31-33, §7.9, 2 Kings 17, 34-41, Isaiah 24.*

13.10 The Sacrificial Currency to the Atonement

The accursed plight of the rebellious who reject just visions of God for comfort is stated below:

these are rebellious people, deceitful
children, children unwilling to listen
to the Lord's instruction.
they say to the seers,
"see no more visions!"
and to the prophets,
"give no more visions of what is right!
tell us pleasant things,
prophesy illusions.
leave this way,
get off this path,
and stop confronting us with the holy
one of Israel!"

therefore, this is what the holy one of
Israel says:

"because you have rejected this
message,
relied on oppression
and depended on deceit,
this sin will become for you like a high
wall, cracked and bulging,
that collapses suddenly in an instant.
it will break in pieces like pottery,
shattered so mercilessly
that among its pieces not a fragment
will be found
for taking coals from a hearth or
scooping water out of a cistern."

this is what the sovereign Lord, the
holy one of Israel says:

"in repentance and rest is your
salvation,
in quietness and trust is your strength,
but you would have none of it.

Isaiah 30, 9-15

Apocalypse is a 'reward' for systematic 'injustice', *§10.1, Isaiah 24.* Rebel gods curse-punish for failing to end just faith to compel to deny Justice better, *§10.5.* A division of goats from sheep may be sure if rebel gods exist. However, God's mercy by Justice may be a joy to see for mortals as God's children. God may refute charges of negligence, *§10.8*, ending the legality of curse-law outside hell, *Revelation 22, 1-3, §11.1.*

Now an atonement for sin is a plea for mercy from a gods' curse in whatever currency the god enacts to best serve their objects, *Micah 4, 5, §1.15.* A gods' object is vitality by taking and keeping subjects from God, *chapter 11.* Mortals get to know gods who ask a religious atonement for sin against the gods' objects because sin against God makes subject to a rebel god. In reality, an atonement for sin against a just God is also to pay off rebel gods who claim mortals for sins in advance of God's right to forgive sin. If God readily forgives then an atonement for sin against God is entirely to pay off rebel gods. Rebel gods set God a ransom price by the form of atonement for sin against God they accept in rebellion law.

The Just Almighty could save by force if rebel gods do not respect mortal freedom of faith to allow a loophole for souls to depart rebellion law to God. The gods must then enact a loophole as small or confusing as they can. It likely parallels ways mortals pledge to, *seek favours from*, rebel gods as that respects mortal right to worship Satan as father of their rebellion: *supreme 'God' of unjust evil gods, §1*. It is well known that mortals have sought, still seek, *§9.6*, mercy or favours from gods by sacrifice of life such as to the god 'Molech', *1 Kings 11, 33; 2 Kings 23, 10, Jeremiah 32, 35*:

> the Lord said to Moses, "Say to the Israelites: 'Any Israelite or any alien living in Israel who gives any of his children to Molech must be put to death. The people of the community are to stone him.
>
> Leviticus 20, 1-3

'Molech' is not necessarily a real god but, *at least*, an idol behind which real gods operate, *§8.3, §9.5*. Note that such sacrifice asks a society under Molech's law, *Micah 4, 5*. That implies the above death-penalty on it is enacted by the father of rebellion: *by Satan as God's left hand*. Now if Moses was under rebellion law, *seeking a path out to 'God'*, he had to see the death-penalty met else Lord Satan would kill him, *Exodus 4, 24, §10.8*. Evil thereby manipulates mortals for faith in a 'God' who rules by the power of Death, *§1.2*. For that reason, rebel gods may decide to enact a loophole atonement based on sacrifice of life to a non-killing just God, *§7.8, Psalm 50*. Below it is shown the full outcome of that ploy is to ask a just God a ransom price for sinners to leave rebellion-law of sacrifice of God's (*willing to save sinners*) Son to a just God, *Isaiah 53*. It puts divine mercy to sinners to severest test, *Luke 23, 34, §6.8*.

Another reason rebel gods may enact sacrifice of life to establish loyalty to a deity is because they want mortals to sacrifice God's servants for power, *Isaiah 53*. They can then raise mortal tyrants to ruthlessly sacrifice anyone in their way hoping to guide tyrannies to evolve to selectively target God's servants. To enact loyalty by human sacrifice sets God a conundrum if the commandments say human sacrifice is sin and a just God respects wishes even of life to be sacrificed. For Satan claims every sinner belongs to his rebellion so a human sacrifice to God needs to be a non-sinner. Only rebel gods threatened by God's just intervention may command folk to open the sacrificial loophole to God.

The above theory explains why an atonement for sin against God comes to involve human sacrifice of a willing non-sinner. It is substantiated in 'God's word' where it is said God tested Abraham for willingness to sacrifice his son Isaac to God yet stayed Abraham's hand in it, *§7.8*. A sacrificial atonement is prophesied, *Psalm 50*, and may call for sacrifice of God's Son, *the willing sinless Messiah*, to God, *Isaiah 53*.

The two life-sacrificing atonements for sin in 'God's word' involve animals, *§11.4*, else sacrifice of the Messiah or God's Son to God, *§9.7.5*. Animal-sin might not send all animal sacrifices to Satan if folk are in law acknowledged custodians or owners of the animal kingdom? *Psalm 8, 4-8, Genesis 1, 27-30*. Such sacrifice serves animals if lack of an atonement puts critters and folk under hell's eternal curse. Animals may go for resurrection and judgement after the rebellion is defeated, *1 Corinthians 15, 35-44, §3.15*. Satan may close the loophole of animal sacrifice to God by legislating for human sacrifice as harder to reach God by, *§11.4*. Note that suffering, *animal or human*, is a personal ordeal, *like death, Proverbs 8, 36, §6.2*, which some hate but some love. It is a testing spectacle for folk who see suffering as evil but God might reserve some from suffering given a just case by the faithful, *Mark 13, 20, Acts 8, 59-60*.

Without an atonement for sin, God's law may become a death-sentence, *§12.4, James 2, 1-13, §3, Romans 3, 19-31, §12.15, Luke 13, 1-9, §11.5*. If mortals could live up to the law despite their evil doppelgängers, *sinful natures, §10.5*, then sacrifices of life for survival would not arise, *§9.5, Daniel 11, 30-36, §8, Job 1*. Instead, they are farmed in sin, *for a while*, as 'virtuous' enemies of God who lay their world open to a curse, *Deuteronomy 30, 17-20, §7.8, 2 Kings 17, 34-41, Isaiah 24*. An example of that is where religion or 'science' is run as a superstitious slaughter house sacrificing animals to goals other than Justice, *Isaiah 1, 4-20, Habakkuk 2, 13-17*. To serve a just God is more than a business in ritual trappings and copious sacrifices no matter how beautifully or technically done or with what reverence:

> for I desire mercy, not sacrifice,
> and acknowledgement of God rather than burnt offerings.
> hosea 5, 6

The sacrifice a just God really wishes may be of praise or thanks for Justice in life, *Psalm 50.* It might seem absurd for Justice to depend on human sacrifice to a just God when commandments forbid and all are sinners, *Isaiah 1, 4-20.* But not many folk may know the devil's full duress to sin before they give in to work for the rebellion's plan to depose a just God, *Matthew 7, 11-12, §10.2, Luke 23, 34, §6.8.* For rebel gods offer curse-discounts, *sweeteners*, to keep sinners as happy hostages. The confused may prefer to think they are blessed for serving 'God', *leaving it to God's mercy to cover confusion and save them from sin.* Evidence of naked sin is in the 'injustice' of a curse to social and 'natural' disasters, *§9.7.2, §10.1, Isaiah 24.*

The trapping of mortals in sin is what makes sacrifice to a deity part of life on earth vital to survival of mortals, *§7.8.* The gods trap mortals into an hereditary basis to sin so even babies are born to cry discontent, *§9.11, Psalm 51, 5-6, §10.10.* If the sacrifice to establish loyalty to a just God requires a non-sinner, it flags to a hero part human, *§8.2*, part supernatural in lineage, able to resist any pressure to sin, *Micah 5, 2, §7.9, Luke 4, 1-13 & 23, 32-49, Matthew 26, 36-45.* A virgin-birth arises, *Isaiah 7, 13-17*, to cut lines of inheritance of sin from mortal fathers. Only God is a non-sinner, *James 1, 13*, able to Father a sinless child for the tested Messiah and King of creation, *§2, §8.2.*

If the Messiah is incarnation of a pre-existing first being, *§2, Micah 5, 2, §7.9,* His or Her consent to sacrifice is possible in advance. The gods cannot object to God's incarnation, *Isaiah 9, 6*, if their incarnations are also to be born to lead mortals, *§9.2, Genesis 6, 1-4, §8.3.* Angel incarnations may make tested servants foreknown by God, *§5, Romans 8, 28-30, §11.4,* as the sense in which 'Israel' is Archangel Michael's people, *Daniel 12, 1, §13.4*:

> I ask then: Did God reject his people? By no means! I am an Israelite myself, a descendent of Abraham, from the tribe of Benjamin. God did not reject his people, whom he foreknew. Don't you know what Scripture says in the passage about Elijah—how he appealed to God against Israel: "Lord, they have killed your prophets and torn down your alters; I am the only one left, and they are trying to kill me"? And what was God's answer to him? "I have reserved for myself seven thousand who have not bowed the knee to Baal."
>
> Romans 11, 1-4

The mother for *the* incarnation of God, *Isaiah 9, 6*, is to be a willing God-loving soul with Jewish support (*as needs a spouse?*) to an 'illegitimate' virgin-birth, *Isaiah 7, 14, Matthew 1, 18-24*. The child is 'God's mercy' as if reseated from between two cherubim to the ark of the covenant, *Exodus 25, 22, Jeremiah 3, 16-17, §12.11*. By fledgeling theory, *§5*, the parents are proteges of angels who agree to test of their incarnations, *Luke 1, 26-38*.

But Mary stood outside the tomb crying. As she wept, she bent over to look in the tomb and saw two angels in white, seated where Jesus' body had been, one at the head and the other at the foot.
They asked her, "Woman, why are you crying?"
"They have taken my Lord away," she said, "and I don't know where thy have put him." At this, she turned around and saw Jesus standing there, but she did not realise it was Jesus ....
John 20, 11-14

Rebel gods raise human thorns to test anyone's faith, *§12.9, Revelation 12, 1-6*. 'Wise' astrologers told Herod of the birth of a great leader so Herod tried to cull all baby boys for security, *Matthew 2, 16-18*. He sacrificed babies blindly to cull a rival power. His cruelty, *Isaiah 51, 5-6, §7.11*, may have been to let rebel gods field a legal point that mortal leaders of rebellion reject God's mercy: *wish to evolve in sin to know full evil, §12.9*. Scripture suggests mortal-loyalty, where hazy, is equated to community leaders like Herod or Moses. Herod was a leader for rebel Gentiles who reject God's mercy. He died soon after perhaps for failing to break Joseph's and Mary's faith. But Herod's sacrifice may head a case to defend freedom of faith on earth so mortals can evolve to fully know evil in plans to depose God. Thus, the gods may continue directing evolution in sin to depose God, *§9.7.4*, even if the Messiah succeeds as a sacrifice to God, as next.

If Isaiah, *§9.7.5*, prophesies an atoning human sacrifice to God, it implies this world was, *still must be*, under jurisdiction of a rebellion against God, *§12.7; Micah 4, 5; 1 John 5, 19, §6.10*. Mortals born to rebellion need to subscribe to an atonement for sin, *like using soap and water*, to escape, *Revelation 7, 14, Psalm 50, 5*. It sets a ritual basis to religion where chosen ritual, *§10.7*, flags to the 'justice' a soul hopes to live by: *e.g. Satan's curse or God's blessing, 1 Kings 11, 33, 2 Kings 17, 34-41 & 23, 10-13, Deuteronomy 30, 17-20, §7.8*. It is also about spiritual company that souls keep or that keeps them. 'God's mercy' is Justice to good *and* evil.

A human sacrifice to a just God can only be made by subjects of a rebellion, *mortals in demonic thrall, §7.3, Acts 2, 23.* Jesus illustrated another reason demons might 'cooperate' to open a sacrificial loophole, *John 19, 10-11, §7.10.* His was a ministry of inspired oratory, miracles, exorcisms that rebel gods had to curtail else lose power sooner rather than later. They then moved to fulfil the sacrifice but why should a non-sinning Messiah submit to it? We saw earlier, *§8.2,* that the gods may object to the Messiah leading mortals out of rebellion on grounds that since all other folk sin, the Messiah would also if subjected to rebellion laws of temptation and punishment that subjects are alleged to support. To sin would trap Him subject to rebellion law ending a legitimate salvation by perfect Justice.

The rebellion then demands that the Messiah is subjected to full rebellion-law for test, *Psalm 22, 1.* It will apply spiritual duress to make sinners act as a crown of thorns to torture and sacrifice God. If the sacrifice is overseen by worldly political authorities, it proves Satan rules them and, whilst it continues, rulers will always be hollow in high matters of Justice to the people. The rebellion's hope is that the Messiah sins on the way to be sacrificed, *§8.2, §7.10.* But if not, His death buys rebel gods time as part of the case for mortals to continue evolving to know evil. Rebel gods may argue that mortals who oversee the sacrifice or murder of the Messiah are true heirs to this world, *§9.7.5.* For God to disprove it justly, they must be allowed to try to lead all the world to evolve in sin to reject God as what rebel gods ask to depose God.

Thus, even if God claims the sacrifice as to Him, the father of rebellion may insist a duel of wishes of good and evil mortals runs to its just end, *refusing to withdraw.* The Messiah's bodily ministry then ceases for a while but His sacrifice becomes core of a covenant to God for salvation, *Psalm 50, Jeremiah 31, 31-34, §7.10.* The risen Messiah as likeness of God, *§8.2,* is then entitled to lead in spiritual warfare directing the Spirit, *§7.11, John 16, 7-15, 1 Peter 3, 22,* until a spiritual circumcision of evil spirit for 'good', *§10.5.* The end is when evil efforts to erase God's power base prove evil has its death-wish, *§1.* Mortals may mirror it in a last bid to erase God's power base that would end the world if a just God exists which the bid is to refute, *§1.13, §10.1, Matthew 10, 34-38.* The King then steps in, *§10.11, Daniel 7, 24-28, 2 Thessalonians 2, 8-12, §9.3.*

13.11 Loyalties and Scripture in this World

To save mortals from the rebellion curse on sin, *§1*, God must establish a system of atonement for sin against God. The last section explains why it may rest on a special human sacrifice to God as a currency enacted and honoured in rebel gods' law. Now an atonement is a renewed pledge of loyalty to a deity so invalid if shod with a creed that actually declares wilful disloyalty to the deity, *Isaiah 24*. Thus, if the Messianic sacrifice goes through, *Psalm 50*, a rebellion may move on, *evolve in sin*, to dedicate the sacrifice to an unjust 'God', *§12.9, Proverbs 28, 5, §8.1*. For freedom of faith, God may allow mortals to pledge the sacrifice to a liar and murderer as 'God', *§9.7.5*, who hogs the stage in biblical films or books, *§8.5*.

Freedom of faith seems to require that 'God's word' can be read to support either the Father of Justice or father of rebellion, *§1, §9.1, §9.7.4*. Satan and God are then in the spirit by which a text is read, *§8.4, §9.7.5*. A just heart reads in just faith, *Habakkuk 2, 4, §12.7*, but sinners can prefer a charismatic almighty criminal, *§10.3, §10.4, §10.7*. That tyrannical deity or antichrist witnesses to 'the faithful' by a curse on foes: punishments for sin, *§8.1*. His charisma may prey in all religion, *§9.7.4*, as a 'God' of holy things and feelings who gives prophets a hard time, *§10.8*. It may be painfully hard for sinners to query a comforting spirit they wish to please for a curse-passover and pride and status, *Isaiah 30, 1-15, §9.12, §10.4*. It is vital for mortals to test spirits for 'justice' but it comes down to personal ideas of 'justice' and divine mercy, *§12.9*.

Life on earth may be to offer 'angelic' mortals fair choice between God and Satan without prior bias by insight into their differences. Mortals seek a loyalty to 'God' adequate for the day by spiritual help, *§8.5*. Their loyalties may be transparent to spirits they dwell with, *§7.3, Psalm 32, 8-11, §10.5*. The Spirit of God is over cultural paths to full atonement for sins and acceptance of the Spirit. To be on the path to Justice is to draw 'God's' blessing against curse law. But what is loyalty enough in early ages may not suffice later, *Jeremiah 9, 25-26, §8.3*. God's foes may include traditionalists against the path to Justice and radicals for paths of 'injustice' into hell paved with lies. To repent is an option in most ages.

'God's word' is a sealed book, *Daniel 12, 9-10, §12.3*, so mortals may one day see Satan as Lord of it, the next see a just God. Just faith is needed to fathom the 'justice' by which God and Satan vie for souls. Job's scripture depicts a clarifying principle, *Job 1, 8-12, §1.2 & 2, 4-6.* It shows God and Satan agree that Satan acts as God's hand or wrath on sinners, *§8.1.* Thus, when scripture quotes God as saying 'I' will punish (*e.g. kill people for sins, §12.9*), is it justly read as that Satan punishes sin as God's hand or wrath? *Matthew 10, 28, §13.8.* Bilateral readings allows mortals to choose Satan or God as their deity according to heart or faith by same passages of scripture. It allows the unjust to tyrannise temples to test faith of prophets as one meaning to *Isaiah 53.* What priest or prophet does not put God's mercy to save them as sinners to test?

The principle that Satan acts as God's hand is commutative. Satan may give and read scripture as if God is Satan's hand. For their actions are tied together in legal procedure over mortals to settle who is first Lord. The father of rebellion asked a just God to make this world to prove title to creation but it is God's will if God foresaw it. Only after title is proven may a just God come out of the legal cupboard. A joint title claim of God and Satan implies that their natures, *supreme good and evil,* determined a course for this world to settle their title-contest from before it was made, *Isaiah 46, 10.* Hence, Satan may justly pose as the deity whose hand or actions led Jews out of Egypt. His power-bid for 'Israel' drives 'God's right hand' to guide 'just' Jews in reply, *§10.8.* Till title is settled, both can claim to be one true God whose word is 'justice' high over all, *Isaiah 55, 6-11, §11.1.*

Prophecies do not distinguish God from Satan except in how they are interpreted. For both God and Satan oppose lesser idols, support commandments, ask to turn from idols and sin to a 'just' deity. Both prophesy the Messiah to be put to death and punished in a test of their title, *§10.6.* If rebel gods define evil by what they do for power, demon-gods can arrange for whatever scripture, teachings or law gives them best chance of victory in plots to depose God. Very unjust texts may betoken Satan at God's expense but the just may still see God past such texts, *§9.7.5.* Rebel gods stoke 'holy' feelings for plans of spiritual or other oppression against God's servants who may respect but not share 'holy' feeling for evil objects, *Mark 14, 32-42*:

you ought to forgive and comfort him, so that he will not be overwhelmed by excessive sorrow. I urge you, therefore, to reaffirm your love for him. The reason I wrote was to see if you would stand the test and be obedient in everything. If you forgive anyone, I also forgive him. And what I have forgiven—if there was anything to forgive—I have forgiven in the sight of Christ for your sake, in order that Satan might not outwit us. For we are not unaware of his schemes.

2 Corinthians 2, 5-11

Put on the full armour of God so that you can take your stand against the devil's schemes. For our struggle is not against flesh and blood, but against the rulers, against the authorities, against the powers of this dark world and against the spiritual forces of evil in the heavenly realms.

Ephesians 6, 11-12

The above suggests that to call Satan a myth is one of Satan's schemes, *§9.7.5, §10.4.* Even mundane sin is taken by Satan as support, *§1,* but doctrinal sin is a more 'evolved' evil, *§12.12.* If scripture is of a title contest then Satan has widespread power to delude mortals. To question faith in an 'almighty' criminal may cause a 'holy' spirit to turn into spiritual oppression or suicidal feelings, *§10.5, chapter 6.*

The above scripture addresses a small body whom Paul and Jesus took as 'Christians'. They were taught the world-view that Jesus gave the apostles. But prophecies of false teachers and delusion in Jesus' scripture imply that world-view is obscured for a time, *§8.6.* It must return by Judgement Day because by end-times mortals are to have had all necessary truth and lie for the fair choice of good and evil promised in *Genesis 3, 2-5, §7.4.* Only if truth is widespread can a wide-scale outpouring of God's Spirit occur in end-times, *Joel 2, 28-32, §7.11.* It may be just to support work to detail ways by which there is a lost truth to scripture as might offend 'holy' feelings in a variety of popular unjust movements, *§1.3, §8.1.*

For sake of Justice, every temple and sect may endure a loss of knowledge of 'reality' to mark a twilight zone, *§10.6.* The twilight zone is in honour of evil's right to establish so mortals can know evil. Put constructively, the spirituality in places may improve as the lost truth is let out. There may be reasons, *such as to do with surviving Satan's evil curse on sin,* for God's truth to return not gradually but as a culture shock or revolution, *Psalm 64.* God is just process.

The curse of demonic spiritual forces on minds does not end the instant higher truth is revealed, *§10.10.* Mortals can see how minds wishing to serve God have bent with spiritual oppression in the past, *§8.5.* That may prepare for tests like the prophesied delusion to support which draws automatic sentence to hell, *§6.16.* People have right to love hell before heaven if fairly informed, *§1.* Not wishing to give others the choice is one way to choose. Thus, as truth outs, processes of cultural lie may begin to snatch it from minds, *Luke 8, 11-15, §5.4.*

A title-contest sets mortals to seek God's blessing by just regard to 'God's word'. Sinners can also enjoy the devil's curse-discount for unjust teaching, *§8.5,* as part of God's mercy on cultural paths that might open to God. A rebel god is a genius for spinning a language of lies to depose God. Their object is a depth of lies to veil a just God's face even in readings of 'God's word, *§8.1, Isaiah 14, 12-14.* It raises the question of whose voice a 'faithful' obey when spreading 'God's word'? It is for God to move mortals culturally to a point of discernment where just truth is in circulation against unjust lie. To show an interest in spread of knowledge of 'God's word' is a first step, *Matthew 24, 14.* Even to preach a flawed view of it is better than nothing and may one day meet the mercy of a just God.

At Judgement Day, will the majority be vindicated? or will nations who appropriated God to their cause be abashed and in need of healing?:

then the angel showed me the river of the water of life, as clear as crystal, flowing from the throne of god and of the lamb down the middle of the great street of the city. on each side of the river stood the tree of life, bearing twelve crops of fruit, yielding its fruit every month. and the leaves of the tree are for the healing of the nations. no longer will there be any curse. the throne of god and of the lamb will be in the city, and his servants will serve him. they will see his face and his name will be on their foreheads. there will be no more night. they will not need the light of a lamp or the light of the sun, for the lord god will give them light. and they will reign for ever and ever.

the angel said to me, "these words are trustworthy and true. the lord, the god of the spirits of the prophets, sent his angel to show his servants the things that must soon take place."

revelation 22, 1-6

13.12 Safety and Sin, the Messiah and Judgement Day

Witness to God is by, *or as if by*, walking in the Spirit. It may be the highest safety in a violent world under a curse on evil. Such safety is subject to tests of faith for the age, *Psalm 32, Isaiah 24, 1-6 & Luke 13, 1-9, §11.5.* Now the Christ walks as God under test, *Isaiah 9, 2-7 & 11, 1-10, §11,* so can walk on water politically speaking, *Luke 4, 28-32.* His mission is to save sinners with free-will as may mean to give them every opportunity to repent yet respect evil's right to hell:

> with the lord a day is like a thousand years, and a thousand years are like a day. the lord is not slow in keeping his promise, as some understand slowness. he is patient with you, not wanting anyone to perish, but everyone to come to repentance.
> but the day of the lord will come like a thief. the heavens will disappear with a roar; the elements will be destroyed by fire, and the earth and everything in it will be laid bare.
> since everything will be destroyed in this way, what kind of people ought you to be? you ought to live holy and godly lives as you look forward to the day of god and speed its coming. that day will bring about the destruction of the heavens by fire, and the elements will melt in the heat. but in keeping with his promise we are looking forward to a new heaven and a new earth, the home of righteousness.
> so then, dear friends, since you are looking forward to this, make every effort to be found spotless, blameless and at peace with him. bear in mind that our lord's patience means salvation,...
>
> 2 peter 3, 8-15

The Messiah's test may be to step outside God's Spirit, *Psalm 22, 1,* to sacrifice His life to give sinners time to repent, *§9.7.5, Isaiah 53, §12.9.* Perhaps loyalty to God is only proven outside the Spirit by a conscience to empower the Spirit, *§10.5, like Daniel, §7.3.* Job was also a righteous man tested by a curse perhaps over a flaw in his faith, *Job 3, 25, §7.5,* unsafe by atonement practice of his day, *Job 1, 1-5.* Job refused to curse God and die when a curse struck, *Job 2, 9-10 & 19, 25-26.* His estate, *formerly defended by Job's atonement offerings,* was destroyed by Satan, *Job 1.* His family did not take Job's test as well as Job, *Job 2, 9-10.* To sin is safe if under a sound atonement, *Psalm 32, Isaiah 1, 15-20, §8.6,* but 'free-thinkers' may prosper for a time to scoff at such ideas, *Psalm 73, 2 Peter 2, 19-22, §7.11.* God's word urges seek safety by a sacrificial atonement system, *Psalm 50,* whose practice can be perverted for accursed loyalty to an antichrist, *Isaiah 24, Hosea 6, 6, §8.1.*

It follows that a society is just if it respects the atonement path to God, *to Justice.* Societies also need law and order systems due to a curse of crime. Criminal law educates in a basic principle of Justice: *need for fair casework.* Even crooks rage if unjustly convicted. Criminal law has integrity only if an impartial defence of non-criminals from crime. If no one is blameless, crooks can pose as freedom fighters, *§11.3, §7, §12.4, §12.16*, against the establishment. Now Justice is a myth without a fair or just theory of life, *§1.4, §9.11,* to define crime. Crooks establish for an unjust universe as friends of injustice, *§12.16*, but lack a fair case for their unjust world as a form a tyranny in line with their faith, *§1.3, §6.4.* If mortals who enact laws in science or law, *§10.13*, show no fear of a 'judgement day' for their work then are they busy trying to pervert the course of Justice for a tyranny?

Suppose criminal law at best upholds a just God. It implies mortals face criminal law, *need God's mercy*, at a real Judgement Day. Might crooks argue a crooked education sold 'honest' crooks into slavery? *§12.1, §12.16.* Might anyone get off the hook by turning on 'great' minds who 'enlightened' them? *§9.2, §12.16, James 3.* That scenario may only hold in hell if a just reading of 'God's word' allows no defence for sin by blaming it on others? The vindictive blame others, *e.g. society*, for their sins, *§10.11*, but perhaps the good forgive, *§13.7*, in order to access mercy by Justice? If teachers above all need God's mercy, they teach God is merciful. James' teaching below seems to belie that unless it implies the devil judges sin, see later:

not many of you should presume to be teachers, my brothers because you know that we who teach will be judged more strictly. we all stumble in many ways. if anyone is never at fault in what he says, he is a perfect man, able to keep his whole body in check. when we put bits into the mouths of horses to make them obey us, we can turn the whole animal. or take ships as an example. although they are so large and are driven by strong winds, they are steered by a very small rudder wherever the pilot wants to go. likewise the tongue is a small part of the body, but it makes great boasts. consider what a great forest is set on fire by a small spark. the tongue is also a fire, a world of evil among the parts of the body. it corrupts the whole person, sets the whole course of his life on fire, and is itself set on fire by hell.

james 3, 1-6

A God of mercy might not directly prosecute any for sin but is certainly a truthful witness to help courts in their work, *Psalm 106, 3, §8.1, Micah 4, 1-5, §12.8.* The Spirit of Justice indicts lies, *false teaching,* to straighten paths to God, *John 16, 7-3, §7.11*:

teach me your way, o lord, and i will
walk in your truth;
give me an undivided heart, that i may
fear your name.

psalm 86, 11

this is what the lord says: "i will return
to zion and dwell in jerusalem. then
jerusalem will be called the city of
truth,

zechariah 8, 3

the king said to him, "how many times
must i make you swear to tell me
nothing but the truth in the name of
the lord..."

1 kings 22, 16

"you are right in saying i am a king. in
fact, for this reason i was born, and for
this i came into the world, to testify to
the truth. everyone on the side of
truth listens to me."
"what is truth?" pilate asked.

john 18, 37-38

The criminal wicked act by the devil's will to test 'blameless' sinners, *Luke 13, 1-9, §11.5.* The latter can be greater sinners as a law-enforcing wicked to pervert the sacrificial atonement, *§12.11.* They act in the name of 'science', *Daniel 11, 30-36, §8*, or religion, *Isaiah 24 & 28, 11-19, §12.15 & 30, 1-15, §9.12.* Folk may be raised in beasts of injustice, *§9.7.4,* not to see themselves as with the wicked. They may be proud of an 'independent mind', *Proverbs 28, 5, §8.1, 2 Peter 2, 19-22, §7.11,* by rebel gods, *§8.4, §9.1, §10.4, §10.5.* Mortals thereby go astray by demon-drink without thought for proof of spirit, *§10.2, §10.3.*

'The wicked' may seem 'just' for acting in the name of idols to stop crime, poverty, war, natural disasters like global warming. It appeases rebel gods who give short-term curse-relief at cost of a long-term curse to apocalypse, *§1.13, §10.1.* Unjust science or religion cure some ills, *as their hook,* but gods of injustice curse to new ills as their system, *§9.9.* Superstitious dogma may cast disease as material luck, *§9.11, §10.13,* to make life a lottery rigged by rebel gods of supernatural power and genius. When unjust spins of the wheel fail to make all reject a just God, *e.g. after unjust paths start to look too evil, Proverbs 8, 1-9, §8.1,* the gods may curse those holding to their objects for failure, *§1.15, Isaiah 24.* There is no safe fence, *§12.5, §12.1,* as even the path to God is tested by injustice, *§7.6, §9.7.2, §12.8.*

Sin puts in debt to a rebellion. The debt must either be punished or atoned for. The father of rebellion thus runs a protection racket to divide subjects, *sinners*, by curse-discount laws into less cursed 'winners' and more cursed 'losers'. If his divided house rebels against the curse, *or if losers die out*, the house will fall, *Psalm 82 & Isaiah 14, 12-21, §8.3, Matthew 12, 26-32, §9.8.* Evil may one day literally die, *§12.4*, and Christ preserve good souls, *Deuteronomy 30, 17-20, §7.8, Psalm 103, 3, §12.4, Matthew 11, 5, §10.2.* Meanwhile, Satan promises to end a curse on the unjust when Justice is deposed, see analysis to *Isaiah 55, 1-11 in §11.1.*

Even as the last of Satan's schemes in open creation fail, his subjects may cheer his crowning in 'triumph' as 'God' of continuing curse-law in hell, *Isaiah 65, 17-20.* Evil is fully defeated after hell's accursed citizens fail to break out of hell to depose God. Meanwhile, curse-law drives them to seek the tree of life, *breed life of unlimited vitality to depose God, §11.3, Isaiah 66, 24, §1.13.* The path tempers by trapping in sin then punishing to make life live up to God's law yet reject God in Spirit. The punishments are by Satan's will and hand but God may constrain them outside hell, *Job 1 & 2*, to give sinners opportunities to repent, *Psalm 32, 8-11, §10.5, Luke 13, 1-9, §11.5.* Life is 'free' to choose its 'God'.

A seeming lack of Justice on earth implies either there is no Justice else a distinction of innocent from guilty relates not to local values but to atonement and God's blessing, *Psalm 32.* By higher Justice, a prostitute or crook who rises to a proper atonement for sin might be more 'innocent' than a priest who perverts it, *Isaiah 1, 15-20, §8.6, Matthew 21, 23-32, 12.12.* The true 'innocents' are so by a just atonement for sin though cursed by association, *§9.7.2.* False pride is then a trap:

When pride comes, then comes disgrace,
but with humility comes wisdom.
Proverbs 11, 2

The Lord detests all the proud of heart.
Be sure of this: They will not go unpunished.
Through love and faithfulness sin is atoned for;
through the fear of the Lord a man avoids evil.
Proverbs 16, 5-6

The arrogance of man will be brought low
and the pride of men humbled;
the Lord alone will be exalted in that day,
and the idols will totally disappear.
Isaiah 2, 7-18

The god of the unjust may kill sinners outside God's blessing for any sin. But survival is not random due to his plans to raise evil societies to test faith in God. Further, God need not let a sinner arguably destined to atonement and God's full blessing be randomly killed, *Psalm 51, 1-12, §10.10, John 10, 14-18*, below. God's blessing may cover many 'unworthy sorts' who in fact keep a support community in life, *John 15*:

my prayer is not that you take them out of the world but that you protect them from the evil one. they are not of the world, even as i am not of it. sanctify them by the truth; your word is truth.

john 17, 15-17

The Messiah is to save from the demon-drink by which mortals sin, *Isaiah 28*. Many cannot see sin as a drink-problem. The love to cover a multitude of drunk sinners is God's, *1 Peter 4, 8, §8.4, Matthew 18, 21-35*:

to some who were confident of their righteousness and looked down on everyone else, jesus told this parable: "two men went up to the temple to pray, one a pharisee and the other a tax collector. the pharisee stood up and prayed about himself: 'god i thank you that i am not like other men—robbers, evildoers, adulterers—or even like this tax collector. i fast twice a week and give a tenth of all i get.'
"but the tax collector stood at a distance. he would not even look up to heaven, but beat his breast and said, 'god, have mercy on me, a sinner.'
"i tell you that this man, rather than the other, went home justified before god. for everyone who exalts himself will be humbled, and he who humbles himself will be exalted."

luke 18, 9-14

God has not *direct* jurisdiction of folk who sup from the devil's cup, *Micah 4, 5; 1 Corinthians 10, 20-21, §7.8*. Paul says to drink Jesus' cup under false teaching is an unhealthy position, *Luke 13, 1-9, §11.5*. For mercy turns to a bilateral judgement as expanded on below:

for anyone who eats and drinks without recognising the body of the lord eats and drinks judgement on himself. that is why many among you are weak and sick, and a number of you have fallen asleep. but if we judged ourselves, we would not come under judgement. when we are judged by the lord, we are being disciplined so that we will not be condemned with the world.

1 corinthians 11, 29-32

To respect freedom of unjust faith, earthly justice has to be patchy, *Luke 13, 1-9, §11.5.* For Satan's curse-law prescribes arbitrary punishments, i.*e. 'injustice'*, on souls living in naked sin, *Luke 13, 1-9, §11.5.* Unjust verdicts need not reflect on judges given edited versions of events. Satan is not obliged to punish any sin promptly as that would end freedom of faith for 'injustice'. However, earthly rulers need order and curse-law allows them to set arbitrary punishments on 'crime' *as part of free-will Justice.* Folk often gripe about local 'injustice' but if they tacitly support 'injustice', do they not ask for it? If mortals want Justice, they must ask for it justly. The only way may be by appeal to God over a just atonement for sins *§11.5.*

If any or most judges can turn to God in mid-career then *1 Corinthians 7, 17-23, §11.5* implies a career in earthly courts is compatible with support for a just God. If 'the just' shun court-careers, it leaves sinners to darkness, corruption and tyranny. Jesus gives scripture on judgement to foster a just outlook. The first three quotes below might suggest God directly judges all sinners but the fourth denies it so the truth requires a wider net of scripture, *§8.1, §6*:

For I did not come to judge the world, but to save it. There is a judge for the one who rejects me and does not accept my words;

John 12, 48

"...I am not seeking glory for myself; but there is one who seeks it, and he is the judge. ..."

John 8, 50

Someone in the crowd said to him, "Teacher, tell my brother to divide the inheritance with me."
Jesus replied, "Man who appointed me a judge or arbiter between you?"

Luke 12, 13-14

Moreover, the Father judges no one but has entrusted all judgement to the Son, that all may honour the Son just as they honour the Father.

John 5, 22-23

You judge by human standards; I pass judgement on no one. But if I do judge, my decisions are right, because I am not alone. I stand with the Father who sent me. In your own Law it is written that the testimony of two men is valid. I am one who testifies for myself; my other witness is the Father who sent me,"

John 8, 15-18

"... But since it involves questions about words and names and your own law—settle the matter yourselves. I will not be a judge of such things." So he had them ejected from the court.

Acts 18, 15-16

Jesus also seems to deny jurisdiction to judge in the first three and fifth quotes. The sixth shows earthly courts may limit their jurisdiction, *disputes heard*, to respect partial justice of rebel gods, *Micah 4, 5, Romans 14, 4.* The Messiah and God thereby allow Jew and Gentile a freewill choice of jurisdictions, *§12.9, Isaiah 53, Mark 5, 17.* A 'truth' to fit these quotes is that the one who bids for glory by judging all at Judgement Day is Satan, *Isaiah 14, 13-14, §8.3.* Glory, *like love or faith*, is judged by its objects. But if Satan is God's left hand in law then in legal terms God judges all, *Psalm 98.*

For the knowing of good an evil, *Genesis 3, 2–5, §7.4,* God's design may offer rival kings to life: the unjust devil and just Messiah, *§10.8.* The devil seeks to rule as 'God' in frustration of a just God's will. Both kings may be classed as stars, *§8.3, Numbers 24, 17-19.* The good king must discredit Satan's judgement throne, *right to judge some mortals*, to save souls, *Matthew 10, 28.*

"I, Jesus, have sent my angel to give you this testimony for the churches. I am the Root and the Offspring of David, and the bright Morning Star.
Revelation 22, 16

Now I say to the rest of you in Thyatira, to you who do not hold to her teaching and have not learned Satan's so called deep secrets
(I will not impose any other burden on you):
Only hold on to what you have until I come.
To him who overcomes and does my will to the end, I will give authority over the nations—
'He will rule them with an iron scepter;
he will dash them to pieces like pottery'—
just as I have received authority from my Father. I will also give him the morning star.
Revelation 2, 24-28

If judge Satan is ruined, the Almighty may confine him and willing subjects, *e.g. as god of hell.* If Judgement Day is to proceed, God may appoint the just King to judge, *Matthew 16, 17-20.* The scenario implies Satan seeks title outside hell by a case to eternally prison the King's subjects under his rule, *Proverbs 14, 25-35, §11.6.* For that, the devil establishes on earth by 'free-will' of mortals, *§1,* to guide them as hostages to set a test-path in law against his rival claiming the throne. He draws mortals to call for the Messiah to die to save them, *Isaiah 53.* It puts God's mercy to test by asking a just salvation mortals may not understand. God foresees it and goes along with it so Satan fulfils God's plan.

'God's word' might be arranged for by Satan seeking glory, *§9.7.5*. But it must be fit for purpose of separating just and unjust else the Almighty may save mortals by force. 'God's word' is then 'God's word' by divine mercy which respects life's wishes for a salvation with eternal Justice life can trust in. The Messiah then has unsurpassed heart and direction like God, *Isaiah 9, 6*, as One the devil cannot bend to his rule. By this theory, it is literally true that God in human form is to meet and defeat the devil on earth. He takes the required steps in law to defeat the devil and be crowned as God's right hand or rightful King of good, *Colossians 2, 13-15, §7.10.* If Jesus is that Messiah, this world is now on a run out to the confinement of Satan and his subjects in hell, *Revelation 14, 9-12*:

Therefore Jesus said again, "I tell you the truth, I am the gate for the sheep. All who ever came before me were thieves and robbers, but the sheep did not listen to them.
I am the gate; whoever enters through me will be saved. He will come in and go out and find pasture.
The thief comes only to steal and kill and destroy;
I have come that they may have life, and have it to the full.
"I am the good shepherd. The good shepherd lays down his life for the sheep. The hired hand is not the shepherd who owns the sheep. So when he sees the wolf coming, he abandons the sheep and runs away. Then the wolf attacks the flock and scatters it.
The man runs away because he is a hired hand and cares nothing for the sheep.
"I am the good shepherd; I know my sheep and my sheep know me—just as the Father knows me and I know the Father—and I lay down my life for the sheep.
I have other sheep that are not of this sheep pen.
I must bring them also. They too will listen to my voice, and there shall be one flock and one shepherd.
The reason my Father loves me is that I lay down my life—only to take it up again.
No one takes it from me, but I lay it down of my own accord. I have authority to lay it down and authority to take it up again.
This command I received from my Father."

John 10, 14-18

Note that a real devil implies a parallel world of mortals who love lies just as guardian demons or gods love lies. They must raise dogma above just process to enslave others to feed their position, *§11.2.* If that is true then to fetter the imagination of scholars in religion & science by criminal law may protect the vulnerable, *§12.2.*

13.13 **Conclusion: a just God rules** *ex silentio*

This theory of free-will justice really is a 'Grand Unified Theory' of matter and spirit, *§10.1.* It predicts sacrificial religion as in the nature of mortal life, *§9.5, §10,* and predicts the Messiah from a God who respects mortal freedom of faith for good and evil, *§1, Genesis 3, 2-5, §7.4.* Much of it could be deduced from facts of life without reference to scriptures alleged to be 'God's word'. But 'God's word' does exist with a just reading to corroborate. It is then an example of a direct proof for a just God in the flowchart to *§1.5.*

The relationship of any theory to a just God's word is via some hypothesis of 'justice', *§12.3, i.e. a just faith, Habakkuk 2, 4.* Faith in criminal law, *§12.2,* may judge 'original evolution' a crooked myth or pseudo-scientific cult to demon-gods, *§6.16, §7.8, §9.3, §10.4, §12.2.* How else may it be judged? By a criterion of probability, it looks worthless, *§10.13.* Its worth seems as an unjust edit of facts of life for folk who hate 'religion', *§9.3,* or a closet hypothesis of arbitrary 'justice' for those seeking to serve the best tyranny, *§6.2.* It is then for folk who cannot tell tyranny from 'justice', *Proverbs 28, 5, §8.1.* If 'justice' is poorly understood, a just 'God's word' may be a sealed book, *§12.3, Daniel 12, 9-10, e.g. taken for vain superstition.* The worth to 'original evolution' is then to 'free' folk low in just sense, *sinners,* to make political or religious power-bids.

The dogma of evolutionary materialism as an engine of progress against 'superstition' may be a lie, *§10.1.* For to deny spirits exist by material charms is a traditional superstition, *§2.1, §4.10,* even for medicine, *§9.10.* A material pattern to life based on genes and afflictions has little direct bearing on whether there exists a just God who upholds right to know good and evil? *§3.13 to §3.15, §9.11.* But many take 'holy' orders from material patterns and some add the hypothesis of a 'just' God who curse-drives evolution by earthquake, plague, etc., *§1.3.* However, an eternal 'God' is a form of 'justice' and society needs 'justice' to the level of criminal law, *chapter 12.* If a theory or faith makes God out to be an almighty criminal by mortal-standards, it surely lacks 'just' sense? Anyhow, courts have a duty to uphold criminal law so 'justice' may one day withhold *public* funds to research or teaching on theories or faiths that deny the validity of criminal law, *§11.5, §12.2.* Many scholars may greet that as a blow to 'freedom', *§12.1.*

A sense of 'justice' must 'evolve' among material scientists before they can fairly disprove or prove a just God, *preface, §12.3.* In WWII, criminal 'scientists' took 'evolution' to heart to pledge to a master race to erase 'God's people'. That movement lives to this day, *§9.2,* as may tell historians with a sense of 'justice' that history is about a spiritual war over people, *§9.11.* To base 'history' on the hypothesis of material or political causes may supply propaganda for various tyrannies.

Cults to 'injustice' can take many forms, *§10.4, §12.1.* They may be fought by a fair education on cults with pride of place to cults of 'the enlightenment', *§9.2, §9.6, §11.6.* Crooked scientists are ones who tacitly assume 'science' is a quest for powers to quell foes and nullify criminal law, *e.g. 'invent' mind-control sciences that establish a closet evil god, §6.4, §6.16, §10.5.* Till such powers are granted crooked scientists may be economical with the truth for state funds, *§12.2.* For freedom of faith in evil, people with a sense of 'justice' may be called to turn the cheek to crooked theories in twilight zones, *§10.6.* In dark ages, evil may be resisted by 'blind' faith in God's love and mercy in the face of intimidating confusion and cruelty, *Psalm 13.*

Faith in 'just' process appears to imply that 'injustice', *the problem of evil,* is legislated for by a parallel world of demon-gods who clinically afflict mortals: *farm them under forms of mortal consent, §10.2, §11.3, §12.7, §5.* It is a discomforting theory yet criminal law may bar rival theories that imply mortal tyrannies are right, *§12.2.* It implies this world is under gods of clinical abuse led by the devil on behalf of mortal proteges, *§9.9.* The devil needs scientists who wish to incarnate rebel gods and play god with life as 'our' leaders in evolution to join evil. To 'guide' humanity on that vain path, he enacts a curse to war and suffering on sinners.

Mortals in the dark and seeking comfort or love may rather not imagine evil gods exploit their sins as a wish to know evil better. Mortals rarely live long enough to approach the level of lie and exploitation of a demon-god, *§11.3.* But leaders of 'our' evolution lie to society to play 'God' with life, *§10.8,* or oppress 'truth' for power. Demon gods would be masters of such ways to farm mortals but need mortals, *unjust science and cults,* to agree to their experimental farms so they can 'escape' a just God to run hell and farm life there, *§8.1.* The gods are seen in blind and willing mortal servants.

In *§1*, it was suggested a just God respects life's wishes subject to laws agreed with community leaders, *Micah 4, 5*. Leaders may be classified by their proposals about the curse on life (*for sin against an idol or deity*) and how to obtain blessings or curse-discounts from powers they put faith in, *§10.1*. To tune into powers or rebel gods brings local material blessings for auras of well being, holiness, spiritual charisma, *§7.8*. To be chosen by a supernatural force to work in their spirit is evidently a source of comfort, pride and power. Mortals are thereby tested by superstitious feelings against which 'justice' may save from pitfalls. Leaders for unjust gods are to be respected in their faiths, *Micah 4, 5*, but not on their right to lie or torture in power-bids.

The prophets may be leaders to a future knowledge of a just God's law or messianic purposes. Others may ask that 'our' interests be defended by territorial demon-gods who lie to mortals to play god with them, *§7.3, §7.8, §8.2, Micah 4, 5*. God's respect for freedom of faith may let mortals know a supreme god of tyranny, *the devil*, who seeks to rule in God's temple or place, *§1, §8.4, §8.5, §9.7.5, §10.8*. All may be belayed by the devil's power of Death on paths to 'God', *§8.5, §10.5*. Moses, Elijah, Jesus and others then fought the devil for 'our' right to know a just God, *§9.7.5, §10.8*. To know evil may be before knowing a just God by our right to know good and evil, *§7.3, §10.5, §10.10*. The ground to superstitious life is then the knowing of evil spirits that farm life in the dark, *§8.5, §10.10*.

It is educational to see how the theory of curses and blessings at objects of a deity applies to material science, *§1.16, §9.6, §10.1*. The material world faces ruin by unsustainable ways. Material 'science' has spread ethical lack with powers to pollute, *§1.13*. It has led to sudden hysterical cries about laws of curse on sins of not respecting the material habitat. But that may misrepresent the true law of a curse on sins of respecting the material environment, *idolatry*, above God? *Wisdom 14, 27-31, §9.5*. If that is the truth then *materialistic* global warming scientists in reality invoke disasters like global warming, *exactly as unjust priests claim to bless but actually curse their flock, §9.8*. It is an issue of safe science not to be submerged in expert dogma above the heads of the public. 'Science' that asks the public for faith in expert genius or powers may hide a religious reverence for evil gods of a primeval intensity, *§8.3, §10.2, §10.4*. It is then a cult.

The only reliable engine of progress may be 'social justice' but unjust materialists can charm by promises of health, wealth and power as part of freedom of faith on earth. Whilst good and evil live close together, *even in same families*, society is split on issues of good and evil. When spiritual faith is tested by material 'injustice', *war, recession, comet, earthquake*, fair-weather support for a just God turns to tyrannies led by unjust 'science', *Luke 8, 11-15, §5.4.* The curse of evil on this world leads to many crusades to divert from issues of God and devil, heaven and hell, for freedom of faith in evil.

A genius for framing hypotheses is next to a genius for lying. 'Brilliant' mathematicians, *§1.7*, or scientists, *§1.8*, may be intolerant of key facts ruining pet theories. Who can police specialists in their own fields? *§9.3.* How many are caught and sacked each year for trying to block essential progress? If few, there is either unimpeachable integrity in research else unimpeached organised crime putting vanity before 'justice', *§6.7.* If organised crime rules then it casts some work in the public interest as outside 'the system', *§12.1.* Such work may be superstitiously reviled as politically incorrect or offensive to the violent because criminal genius lacks in just reason, *§1.3, §6.4, §12.1.*

Is it more likely that life faces Judgement, *§12*, than it evolved by luck? *§10.13, §11.6.* The theory of 'original evolution' appears tyrannical, *chapter 6.* It lets scholars try to pass on genes (*inherited intellectual sin, §9.11*) by framing hypotheses. A ruling knot of expert opinion (*framed hypotheses*) may be justly tackled by asking to see global theories in support of opinions then fielding reasonable objections against. It is harder than framing hypotheses but how the Spirit of just process may lead to a just God as public fact *ex silentio (i.e. in absence of a contrary viable theory).* Those whose almighty is a tyrant take a more private knowledge of 'God', *§9.1, §12.1.*

This world tests 'faith'. It is said David, Moses, Jesus, were tested to the end, *Isaiah 24, Luke 17, 26-37.* The test is about a 'justice' or authority to back? and laws of curse over the path, *§10.1, Isaiah 24.* Mortals appear fettered by need for criminal law that may debunk vain fields, *§6.7, Micah 4, 5*, so schools ought not to bat the young with propaganda on 'great minds' or prophets, *e.g. unjustly editing their views, §6.16, §9.7.5, §10.8.* Do kids deserve a rod of propaganda or just casework on if open evolution is as likely as Judgement? *p4-5, §10.13.*

13.14 Conclusions: Whodunit? You the Jury

Life is like being a juror on your own murder trial. Some flaw in knowledge of reality is to kill you, *§6.1.* Society has many 'expert' witnesses as to what? or who? *§10.1.* Not many 'experts' are truthful and some are intensely superstitious and want your support to make a killing in life. 'Experts' are subject to local criminal law enacted by lawyers but with 'expert' help on the meaning of death, crime and punishment. Some 'experts' may be above the law as a tyranny providing services or weaponry for keeping and defining law and order. Many jurors prejudice their trial by supporting the 'experts' who condone a lifestyle that makes sense to them. It leads to idolising 'experts', authorities, priests, 'freedom fighters', though all die in the end.

The 'experts' you heed on cause of your death may ask to take your children into care in respect of your faith or criterion of rationality. To botch a verdict may tacitly vote for child-sacrifice. It is a humiliating situation that in a supernatural world may reflect freedom to vote for deities whose care of you reflects their judgement on your worth to their higher plans: *e.g. occult plans to depose a just God, §9.11, Micah 4, 5, §7.8, §8.2, §13.1.* 'Natural' and other disasters suggest some or all deities hold mortals in their jurisdiction in contempt, or, *as unjust gods may argue to a just God,* the mortals in their care prefer contemptible standards of 'justice' to a just God's rule, *§8.2, Proverbs 8, 36, §6.2.* Gods of injustice are arguably not worse than mortals who hope for comforts or power in their image.

Contemptible standards of 'justice' are the bane of earthly courts. Imagine a murder trial where the victim is white, the accused black, and judge and jury are close to members of the Ku Klux Klan. To fight 'injustice' occupies many which may not mean they are very 'just'. Religious prejudice is known to cause miscarriages of 'justice' even in the name of a 'just' deity. Thus, the Klan claims 'Christian' values and to be against 'violence' except in self-defence. They would like an Aryan master race. They illustrate a prejudiced view of 'justice' that may result in what others find contemptible miscarriages of 'justice'. For instance, the inquisition was led by priests of faith in a god of trial by ordeal? Even today, many suspect a 'just' deity tortures for sin to better people, *e.g. to guide 'our' evolution.* It is hard to stand up for 'justice' when not sure what 'justice' is?

Jurors in earthly trials may be asked to swear to tell the 'truth' by a just God. Would God guide jurors to defer to inner feeling, *e.g. superstition*, as to whether an accused is guilty or innocent? Would God guide jurors to hear cases before returning a verdict? It may be that just process lacks charisma to some as why miscarriages occur. Can God prejudice trial-verdicts by His Spirit whether or not justly invoked? Such questions also apply to 'expert' opinion on a just proof for God. This book claims to respect just process, *like 'God's word', §12.3*, so 'experts' would ideally assess it for just casework not by superstitious or other feeling.

Many jurors seek a 'truth' to satisfy a tyranny of private feelings rather than in open just process, *§10.2.* Drug addicts show private feelings can be a tyranny that torments and drives to crime, *Luke 23, 34, §6.8.* Perhaps where a just God is defamed in religion or science, it reflects an inner tyranny of private feelings, *§8.3.* The Klu Klux Clan may illustrate a general truth that serving 'God' via spiritual compulsion can end in a personal tyranny serving 'injustice'. The denouncing of unjust 'faith' and its crusades is part of campaigns for a secular society. To campaign against miscarriages of justice due to religious prejudice is commendable but does it make a secular society 'just'? There has to be a just theory of reality by which a secular society is itself better than religious prejudice and respects rights of the public under criminal law, *§12.2.* Likewise, established religion ideally affirms a just basis beyond a tyrannical wish to protect the public from rival tyrannies.

Once a religion or 'science' is established, *tyrannically or not*, it may only be justly disestablished by a case for a better just theory of reality. That may require courts free to oppose local tyrannies. Many mortals may be prepared to sacrifice their own children to private inner tyrannies. But many may hope for children to be taken into care of just schools where any faith may be justly qualified. Ideally, it is a duty of just courts to see children are schooled to understand just process not to love tyrannies. If children survive a tyrannical education as 'free-thinkers' to adulthood, do they have right to sue the state over an unjust education? If governments allow that then education authorities may be sued for past failings, *§12.1.* Should explaining to children how to do that be part of the national curriculum in a 'free' country?

An arbitrary education may produce just 'dissidents' as failures, cast-outs or drop-outs. Some scholars may pass exams and then seek reforms, e.g. against 'science' that frames hypotheses, *p1.* Loss of principles in education can brainwash, *select by exam success,* to empower corrupt scholars, *§11.6, §12.1.* Even 'Mr. Chips' is of a tyranny if his pupils are not left room to ponder wider 'truth'. If Justice implies a non-tyrannical education, God only avoids being successfully sued by mature life if the university of life respects life's wishes under laws enacted by life, *§1.* An almighty tyrant or devil may laugh off the idea. For it implies God is not a tyrannical judge like him, *§14,* but judges on how to respect life's wishes, *even wish for death and crime under a tyrannical evil judge, Isaiah 14, 12-21, §8.3, Matthew 5, 43-45, §4.*

Where higher education is linked to higher salaries, it seems to imply disrespect of theories asking to give according to ability and love for neighbour. Some say such ideals are impracticable though it is said all in heaven may be equally valuable under a just God. It brings back the question of whether children deserve propaganda or just casework on whether open evolution is more likely than Judgement Day? *§6.16.* Can teachers paid a premium to stream the young for a value to society expressed in pay be fair on the issue? or will they admit their qualifications may be worthless at Judgement Day? *§1.4, §9.2.* A bad education may tie millstones round children's necks.

To study how a devil would judge mortals for hell may promote just values, *§12.* It assumes he can exist, *§1,* and use just casework to prosecute for his prison against a just God who, *if we give Him a case,* can be our defence lawyer. The contemptible miscarriages of 'justice' to a secular society may achieve a higher level to the Aryan Ku Klux Clan. Secularists need a systematic neglect of reason about a just God, *§1.4,* as may serve closet sacrifice of children to evil, *§9.6,* They may teach disasters or illnesses (*mediated over mortals by their gods to help evil to power?*) are 'natural' or 'acts of God'. They may school for paths to a master race of incarnated tyrannical gods of scholastic genius. That may be a crime against some humanity for teachers on WWII and the holocaust to discuss, *§9.2.* Imagine what a tyrant could do with gifts and charisma of a god? The devil may inspire scholars to invoke such 'wonderful' gifts for his incarnation(s) on earth, *§9.7.4.* It is an issue of safe science, *§9.2.*

A tyranny of inner feelings can make mortals superstitious, *§8.5.* Magical material science is likely a blinding superstition, *§1.8, §1.15, §4.10, §10.13, §12.2.* The only way most may fight past superstition to reality is by first principles from a just foundation. New rigor is added to the process in *chapters 1* to *4* whereby material science is like a skyscraper whose foundations are the political goals of life on its higher floors, *Introduction.* It witnesses to a tyranny of inner feelings in scientists, *§9.8.*

A map of the modern rational education system is given in *§1.5.* The book fills in missing elements. Just process or science may then be invoked to exorcise 'original evolution' or 'natural' science as crooked ideas, *§10.1.* The world-view to 'natural' material science may be the most powerful of superstitions, *§1.15, §4.10, chapter 5.* Is it science in a just sense? or a cult? It might exist as the apple of the devil's eye if to evolve and break out of hell to depose God would be the devil's last chance of fulfilment before hell dies. It is then superstition with suicidal and homicidal depths as seen in WWII, *chapter 6.*

A just regard for evil may be a vital part of education, *Matthew 5, 43-45, §4 &13, 24-30, §5.* Evil may be led by crooked 'super-minds' out of fertility religion, *chapter 6.* Men on a cursed vine are said to sire only bad grapes at its end just as in fledgeling theory angel mutiny bred Lucifer's 'beauty', *§3, §12.12, John 15.* The world may in reality only be stabilised under a common just code, *§3.8,* not by technological power. The latter gives local curse-discounts not global indemnities. Many in effect hope to ride out any apocalypse by 'science'. They dare the devil's curse in hope a just God can be disproved, *deposed,* in a post-apocalypse dawn, *§10.1.* The joy of some parenthood may birth demonic kids to be disowned to escape hell, *§9.2, §9.11,* see below and *Luke 23, 32-43, §9.7.2* on division of crooks, *§12.4*:

Jesus turned and said to them,
"Daughters of Jerusalem, do not weep
for me; weep for yourselves and
children. For the time will come when
you will say, 'Blessed are the barren
women, the wombs that never bore
and the breasts that never nursed!
Then
" 'they will say to the mountains, "Fall
on us!"
and to the hills, "Cover us!" '
For if men do these things when the
tree is green, what will happen when
it is dry?"

Luke 23, 28-31

1.2 **The Spiritual Setting for God's word and Proofs** (*from chapter 1*)
Holy scripture is by people who say they are called to be an inspired messenger of God. Isaiah is one, *Isaiah 6.* God's word says that at dawn of creation people left a telling relationship to God for custody of unjust gods: demons under Satan, *Psalm 106, 33-38.* It charts a struggle to return to God against the thrall of idols or false gods as a front to demons under Satan. Idolaters in times past had gods in all areas of life from fertility to war. They lived in delusion by evil as a *majority sin.*

The devil's goal behind idolatry is to depose God. His inspired dupes share the aim yet are often in the dark about it. A telling case is the king of Babylon:

you said in your heart,
"I will ascend to heaven;
I will raise my throne above the stars of God;
I will sit enthroned on the mount of assembly, on the utmost heights of the sacred mountain.
I will ascend above the tops of the clouds;
I will make myself like the most high."
Isaiah 14, 13-14

The devil's strategy is to prove God fallible by our lives. If all people prefer, *or can be duped,* to follow God's spiritual enemies as destiny then God is no one's true God. It deposes a just God. A just God's proof of title is not by unjust force. A kingship dispute is settled by giving people a choice of 'God' down the ages. It goes on till all Satan's schemes have failed to make the world choose what occult evil stands for: to be or worship evil gods, *Genesis 3, 2-5, §7.4.* The highest level of choice between devil and God is for end times. The devil is in themes on evolution in a 'Godless' realm, New Scientist, *4 December 2004,* p46-49 & p51. For God defends freedom of faith for us on the nature we ascribe to 'God'. He gives us freedom of faith.

God's word is to call us to relate with God, *Isaiah 11, 6-9, §7.5.* It also records God's plan by which Satan will be defeated so God can come in open glory, *Psalm 98.* God can prove He is infallible by giving the history of the world to the devil's defeat in advance. But it is given in such a way as to respect our right to choose between God and devil, *Psalm 78, 1-2, Matthew 13, 10-29.* All Satan stands for is to pass through the world as idolatrous delusion in contest with God's coded word, to defeat the devil. For that, God's word and all scripture is codified under God's justice.

The legal code to God's word is to respect a spiritual divide, *Matthew 13, 10-29.* It lets Satan pose as God and call to serve by unjust teaching and scripture. If all take to what he stands for under test then God loses. Much scripture may be sealed if the code is unknown:

> for prophecy never had its origin in the will of man, but men spoke from god as they were carried along by the holy spirit.

> but there were also false prophets among the people, just as there will be false teachers among you.
> 2 peter 1, 21 & 2, 1

After God proves title to creation, Satan may take his hardened allies into hell for their crimes in a power bid. God's word may be geared so God's truth comes into focus as delusion does, in spin off from work of idolaters who may then repent. Just and unjust ideals have to advance side by side, *Isaiah 24, Mark 13, 22.*

A proof of God in respect of His word might show it is exactly as God's word should be for this world. It will show a fulfilment of prophesy. If scripture is of God's proof of title, a proof not using it may be idolatrous. But any sort of proof needs a system of education as host for *something* in telling relation to God. If we elect science, philosophy or law, what stops God's word entering such systems in a triumph of reason? *Chapter 12.*

For scholars to be holy their reason has to find empathy with God. If they reason like the king of Babylon they will never find God. Some may feel unjust reason is far more 'real'. They like unjust teaching and idols, *Luke 10, 17-21, §7.13.* Proof for God is an issue in life's power bids. It is wished for to escape the unjust or those of a confusing outlook.

Christianity looks to a unique man in telling relation to God, *Deuteronomy 18, 17-22, §11.5*: God's Son, *Psalm 2, §9.4.* Jesus says it's Him, born before time, *Proverbs 8, 22-36, §2.7,* as God's blueprint for creation, '*through Him all things were made*', *John 1, 3,* later born on earth to '*destroy the devil's work*', *1 John 3, 8.* The murder of a man who to the death resists the devil's duress to sin is said to end Satan's claim to own penitent sinners on points of law, *§7.10.* A prophesy of torture of the Messiah, *Isaiah 53,* bears on why we need to be saved. Satan runs a regime of Godless evolution to punish and tempt sinners to drive to fully reject God, *§15, §9.1.* A page on the legal code to God's word and death follows.

'God's word' uses a legal code in respect of death, curse and the devil as outlined here.

God asks a mandate from us for a fair Judgement Day by Ps. 98, etc.. In fair Justice, Lev. 19, 15, Jam. 2, 9-10, hate-crime and 'murder' are evil, Ex. 20, 13. Faith finds readings that, *for dear life*, clear God of partiality and 'murder', Isaiah 1, 15-20 & 30, 8-18; Matt. 5, 17-22, 1 Cor. 6, 1-6.

Teachers can cherry-pick old or *new* testament verses to suggest God does not kill or curse life. But false teachers can cherry-pick to suggest God kills and curses as JOB 1, 8-12 (see opposite page) shows God and Satan agree that ***Satan is God's hand in law*** to curse or kill us for sin by cases in law that a fair God upholds, Lam. 3, 33. To read 'God' as *direct* killer for sin may find at Judgement Day that it was a legal short-hand for that Satan or servants kill by *winning jurisdiction* for shows of faith in evil gods, *sin*, as Micah 4, 5 warns. Sin makes us 'willing' hostages against God entering our world. The object-law of gods, §1.15, Ps. 82, lets murderous life have right to love Lord Satan as 'God' in a title-contest with God as a fair legal entity, Prov. 8, 36, §6.2, Ps. 24. The lie of devil as myth now turns 'God' into Lord Satan. It unfetters murderous religious and 'scientific' hate crime to fight for love of God, Hosea 11, 1-4; 1 Cor. 1, 27.

In the scriptures below (wisdom 2, 23-24 NRSV, psalm 103, 1-4) **God does not curse life but offers curse relief**, as Jesus says in Matthew 10, 1:

23- for god created us for
incorruption.
and made us in the image of his
own eternity,
but through the devil's envy death
entered the world,
and those who belong to his
company experience it.

1- praise the lord, o, my soul.
all my inmost being
praise his holy name.
praise the lord, o, my soul.
and forget not all his benefits—
who forgives all your sins
and heals all your diseases.
who redeems your life from the
pit and crowns you with love and
compassion,

He called His twelve disciples to Him and gave them authority to drive out evil spirits and to heal every disease and sickness.

(On the opposite page, Wisdom 1, 12-16 says Hades is not on earth. It is hardly part of heaven. It fits as a prison for sin run within hell, Isaiah 14, 21.)

Both Testaments depict God outside our world which runs under a devil's curse to Death, *Luke 13, 1-9, §11.* The key to a just reading of God's word is to see God's fair justice respects our freedom of faith for evil. It respects His rival for power, Lord Satan, as **God's hand** on sin in a legal sense as JOB 1, 8-12 below declares. Satan is the crown hand of enemies who attack and test to trap in sin:

8- then the lord said to satan, 'have you considered my servant job? there is no one on earth like him; he is blameless and upright, a man who fears god and shuns evil.'

does job fear god for nothing?' satan replied. 'have you not put a hedge around him and his household and everything he has? you have blessed the work of his hands, so that his flocks and herds are spread throughout the land. but stretch out your hand and strike everything he has, and he will surely curse you to your face.'

the lord said to satan, 'very well then, everything he has is in your hands, but on the man himself do not lay a finger.'

Scriptures listed in order below say God does not kill or curse: psalm 68, 20, wisdom 1, 12-16 NRSV, deuteronomy 32, 17-18, *Luke 1, 73-74, 1 John 5, 19, Matt. 10, 28,* 1 Cor. 15, 26.

20- our god is a god who saves. from the lord comes escape from death.

12- do not invite death by the error of your life.
or bring on destruction by the works of your hands:
because god did not make death.
and he does not delight in the death of the living.
for he created all things so that they might exist:
the generative forces of the world are wholesome.
and there is no destructive poison in them.
and the dominion of hades is not on earth.
for righteousness is immortal.
but the ungodly by their words and deeds
summoned death;

they sacrificed to demons which are not god—
gods they had not known. gods that recently
appeared. gods your fathers did not fear.
you deserted the rock who fathered you.
you forgot the god who gave you birth

He swore to our father Abraham to rescue us from the hand of our enemies.

The whole world is under the control of the evil one.

Do not be afraid of those who kill the body but cannot kill the soul. Rather be afraid of the one who can destroy both soul and body in hell.

The last enemy to be destroyed is Death.

1.5 **The Map of Proof and Justice,** (*from chapter 1*)
This proof for God can be laid out as a map of the rational knowledge system. Imagine all knowledge is to adorn walls to a room. Scholars vie to fit out the room in ill co-ordinated schemes. Reality is a scheme to align sciences, arts and God's word justly. Justly means no one is to cheat before they prove this an unjust universe where to lie is a valid ploy, *§6.4.* The map of proof is in the flowchart, *p26.* Abridged tracts on proof are in *§6.16* and the boxes of *§1.*

The map treats knowledge as a set of labyrinths or mazes. It shows a divided house with struggle between ideas of God or to deny any idea of God. A sound map shows watershed areas to ruin its rivals. This map is global and acts as an argument from design for a just personal God. By it are the true foundations to arts, science and theology. It shows modern science and theology as in unjust flight from full spiritual truth, *Luke 10, 17-21, §7.13.* They may hold the public to a blindness to spirit that invokes an evil curse, *Isaiah 24 & 30, 1-15, §9.12.* Many will wish to find a rival map.

Dispute on reality can be shown to head to a type of crime. For scholars want their labyrinths set in a scheme to take funds from a government. They want the law to employ 'civilising' scholars. Some who go astray will ask laws to employ scholars in schools of propaganda in a tyranny. That perverts the course of justice as a crime. Now since justice is to relate truth to fact fairly, the crime is to set dogma, *religion(s)*, where a just science of reality should be in school. The issue is to the fore in the creation vs. evolution debate, New Scientist, *22 April 2000, p34-48.*

the lord says:

"these people come near to me with
their mouth and honour me with their
lips, but their hearts
are far from me.
their worship of me
is made up only of rules taught by
men.
therefore once more
i will astound these people with
wonder upon wonder;
the wisdom of the wise will perish, the
intelligence of the intelligent will
vanish."
woe to those who go
to great depths to hide
their plans from the lord,
who do their work in darkness and
think "who sees us? who will know?"
you turn things
upside down, as if
the potter were thought to be like
the clay!
shall what is formed
say to him who formed it,
"he did not make me"? can the pot say
of the potter, "he knows nothing"
isaiah 29, 13-16

Each side to the debate sees the other as setting dogma as 'science' in school. The issue is in the definitions of 'religion' and 'science' relative to 'God's word'. Is God's word only for dogma? or is it data on a spirit realm that science must see to get real? If data on spirits, it warns of a lying spirit to unjust ideas of it. Creationists feel sure by spirit they call God. They might be into a crime of dogma by a lying spirit as a common religious fault? But they are then sure evolution is lax on spirits, *§6.5.* In that case, evolution is one of many a philosophy that is a 'religion' for spirits that lie to bar God's truth. Its spirit is covert. One lying spirit can ally to another as the dogmas, *religion(s)*, to deny a just science of God's word. That crime may offend fewer with more jobs to scholars. If it holds to death, *§2,* it civilises child-sacrifice by offer of children to lies: sins of parents.

Now justice is to fairly relate truth to fact so sets a right to truth in education. God's word, *if of spiritual truth,* is a defining *just* basis for an honest legal system. God may see it as lawlessness to set right to freedom of faith over right to truth. No dogma is to replace a fair science in school. Justice is not to let organised crime run schools. Creationism or evolution is crime if a dogma to bar the just worth of God's word. They may vie to divert from that one or both are for unjust dogma. Evolution was a dogma before evidence was set to it. Is it still a dogma by religious experts at breaking the law? This proof for God shows that. It bids us ask if creation science looks to 'God's word' in a way fit for a just God or a despot?

1.6 *Start 1:* **Eight Gates out of a Godless 'Reality'**

Most of the labyrinths (*Start 1, p26*) do not let God as a working hypothesis. They look to an objective world as a way to avoid higher concepts of good, evil, mind or God, *§8.* They frame a view of God and His design, relative sin, as a marginal factor in running the world.

To make God a side-issue in education may pledge to a devil's curse on society, *§2, §15.* It may curse pupils who in turn grow up to be a curse on society. That can be the dark truth on Godless fields such as material science, economics or politics. They forge unsafe works in cut down views of right and wrong. It blinds to a higher reality of sin against God. At the bottom right of *p26* is a list of eight gates for eight sketches on flaws of science to end this chapter. They lead out to the hypothesis of God, (*Start 2*), *chapter 2,* whose nature fits with *Deuteronomy 30, 17-20, §7.8.*

A FAIR MAP OF THE REASONABLE KNOWLEDGE SYSTEM FORMS A PROOF BY DESIGN FOR A FAIR GOD

(with book contributions shown)

'Start 1' is a path to put natural history in schools by neglecting to research fairly all the orders of evidence at start 2.

'Start 2' qualifies labyrinths of reason that put natural history in school as not able to stand fair research, or fair query in court. It is for cult cheats in key hate crimes.

FAIR ENDS

The treasure of heaven. *Love in relation to peace as a state of justice. Truth in heaven is the Son of Justice.*

CONCLUSION. God's word is legally coded as a theory of everything in fair reason, §1.2. Faith in just process (God's nature) can look to fair truths. Life on earth is in a war of good and evil subject to supernatural laws of possession. To deduce the laws from facts of life is true science. Modern 'science' is on a subset of the laws as an accursed false science, not fair science in court.

Start 1

Labyrinths of reason that neglect the orders of Mind and God in a classification of evidences by Descartes. Faith in a matter-time-space universe and research to reduce Mind to the Matter level. It frames a natural history in survival 'justice' under natural cause and effect disasters to drive our evolution for gods of life.

Ethical principle for knowledge. Relative to a just God, escalations of evil are by making a selfish reading of God's creation. They slave to work for a kingdom to a best tyranny to depose Justice, for freedom by a universal prejudice.

Spiritual forces in Faith, Hope, Love, Joy, peace (mercy of Justice) call to paths to a fair heaven.

Start 2

Labyrinths of reason fair to Descartes' areas of evidence so for God as source of:
a) **Mind & Matter**, chapters 2 &3 of Vol 1.
b) **Life-forces** in Vol 3.
c) **Free-will Justice** in Vol. 3.
d) **Supernatural history** as a prophetic science led by life's wishes, Vols. 1-4.

Fair Science

Mind defined relative to God & Matter. This path yields proofs for tenets of scripture that are claimed to be God's word: *love commandments, the Messiah, the devil, a sacrificial atonement for sin, eternal life in heaven, purgatory, death in hell.* In a supernatural universe, 'natural' selection fits as an accursed delusion to do with a devil's offer of his kingdom of hell (eternal torment).

FAIR AND SELFISH SCHOOLS OF WISDOM MAKING THE TREE OF KNOWLEDGE OF GOOD AND EVIL

'Unnatural' sex, *e.g. Isaiah 7, 14*, may pioneer paths to supernatural truth. In object-law for gods, §1.15, a deity infers, *calls to*, objects above our heads. Sex thrives if it serves objects of a god who defends it. In 'The Fair Rights Foundation to Science & Theology', I show LGBT sex for rights heads to establish *bilateral spiritual reality* in court against *unfair gods of 'natural' science*. Fair LGBT life may serve God's & Messiah's object of a path to save fair life to a rights heaven *against* a 'heaven' offered for selfish gods, Ps. 82. ***LGBT sex for rights*** opens a gate 9 to the box below to escape hate crime by scientific & religious bodies, 1 Cor. 1, 27.

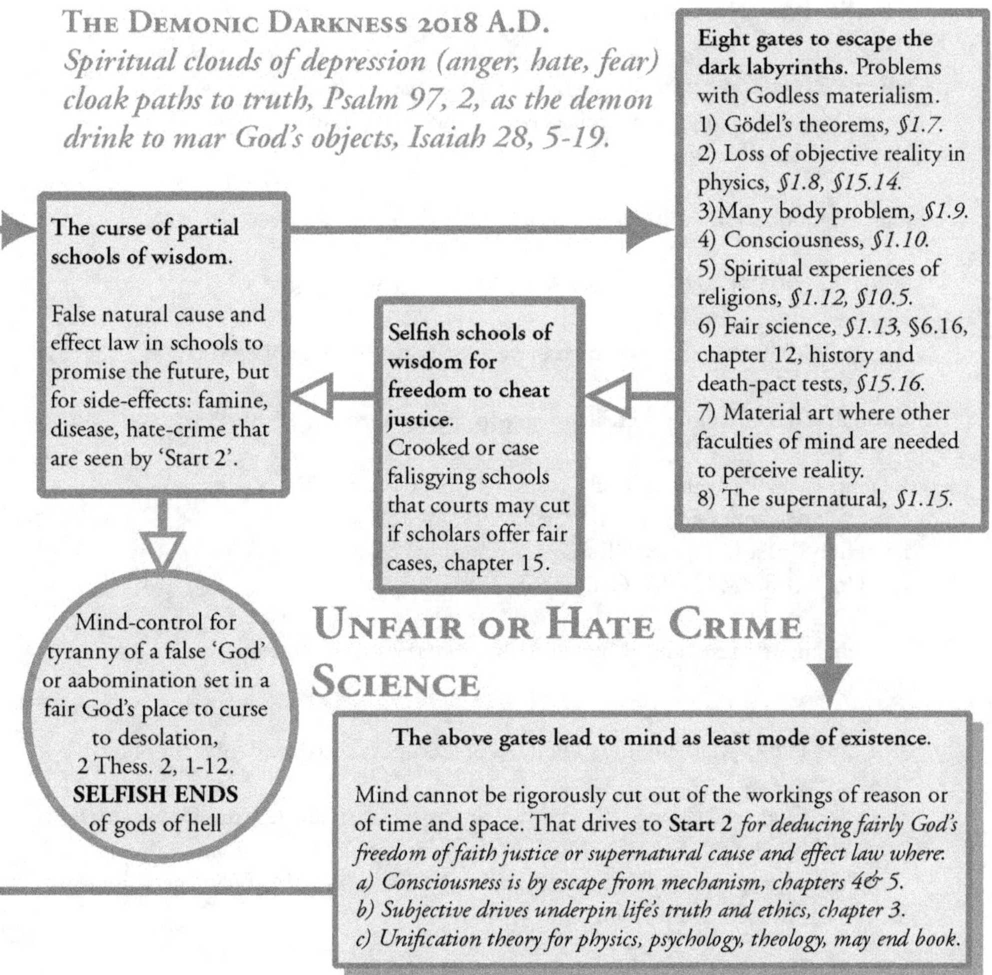

Bibles and Concordances

Holy Bible: New International Version. Disciple's Study Bible, Holman Bible Publishers, 1988. (NIV)

Holy Bible containing the Old and New Testaments with the Apocryphal/ Deuterocanonical books, New Revised Standard Version, Anglicised Edition, Oxford University Press, 1995. (NRSV)

Kohlenberger, J.R. III 1993, NIV Compact Concordance, Hodder and Stoughton.

Whitaker, R.E. & Kohlenberger, J.R. III 2000, *The Analytical Concordance to the New Revised Standard Version of the New Testament*, published jointly by Wm. B. Eerdmans Publishing Company, Grand Rapids, Michigan, and by Oxford University Press, New York.

Select Bibliography *(starting with Volume1 in rough order occurence)*

Govert, S. 2004, 'Pop go the universes', review of 'Big Bang' by Simon Singh, New Scientist, 4 December, p51.

Singh, S. 2004, 'How a big idea is born', New Scientist, 4 December, p23.

Singer, E. 2004, 'Life force', New Scientist, 4 December, p46-49.

Knight, W. 2004, 'Be your own god', New Scientist, 4 December, p51.

Editorial, 1998, 'And God created Darwin', New Scientist, 18 April, p3.

McLynn, F. 1995, Famous Trials, cases that made history, Vineyard Books.
(The State of Tennessee v. John T. Scopes, p 148-151.)
(The High Priest Caiaphas v. Jesus of Nazareth p12-15)
(The Holy Office v. Galileo Galilei p68-73)

Creationism: articles about it by selected authors, 2000, New Scientist, 22 April, p32-48.

Kline, M. 1982, 'Mathematics: The Loss of Certainty', Oxford University Press.

Wilber, K.,Engler J., Brown, P.B., with chapters by Chirban, J., Epstein, M., Lieff, J., forward by Horowitz, M.D. 1986, '*Transformations of Consciousness, Conventional and Contemplative Perspectives on Development*', New Science Library, Shambhala, Boston & London.

Davies, P.C.W. & Brown, J.R., 1986, 'The Ghost in the Atom: a discussion of the mysteries of quantum physics', Cambridge University Press.

Bell, J.S. 1987, '*Speakable and unspeakable in quantum mechanics: collected papers in quantum philosophy*', Cambridge University Press.

McCrone, J. 1994, '*Psychic Power: What are the Odds?*', New Scientist, 26 November, p34-38.

Baggot, J. 1995, '*Down with the Danish priesthood*', review of book 'Quantum Mechanics: Historical Contingency and the Copenhagen Hegemony' by James T. Cushing, New Scientist, 28 January, p41.

Newton, I, '*Principia: Volume II The system of the World*', translated Motte, A., 1729, revised Cajori, F., University of California Press, Berkeley and Los Angeles.

Stewart, I. 1994, '*Two's integrable, three's chaos*', report on the work of Zhihong Xia in celestial mechanics, New Scientist, 15 October, p16.

Crown, C. 1998, '*Constant Chaos: was the speed of light different in the early universe*', New Scientist, 28 March, p12.

Krebs, D. & Blackman, R. 1988, '*Psychology: A First Encounter*', Harcourt Brace Jovanovich. (Plutchik's Theory of Emotion, p336-338.)

Brooks, M. 1988, '*Crazy Logic*', New Scientist, 2 May p38-41.

Davidson, C. 1997, '*Creatures from Primordial Silicon*', New Scientist, 15 November p30-34.

Buchanan, M. 2004, '*Mind games*', New Scientist, 4 December p32-35.

Moran, S. 1999, '*The Secret World of Cults*', Quadrillon Publishing Ltd.

Mihill, C. 1995, '*Fifth of world's people live in poverty*', article on W.H.O. report, The Guardian, Tuesday May 2.

Goleman, D. 1988, '*The Meditative Mind: The Varieties of Meditive Experience*', Crucible.

A French 13th Century Mystic, '*A Mirror for Simple Souls*', translated, edited, adapted Crawford, C., 1981, Gill and Macmillan.

Bohm, D. 1980, '*Wholeness and the Implicate Order*', Routledge & Kegan Paul.

Anderson, A., Holmes, R., Else, E. 1996, '*Zombies, Dolphins and Blindsight*', New Scientist, 4 May, p20-27.

Cohen, P. 1996, '*Sugaring the Pill*', New Scientist, 27 January, p26-29.

Pascal, B. '*The Mind on Fire*', edited by James Houston, 1991, Hodder and Stoughton.

Penn-Lewis, J. with Roberts, E., 1987, '*War on the Saints*', Diasozo Trust.

Wertheim, M. 1995, '*God in the Lab*', New Scientist, 23/30 December p 40-42.

Morris, H.M. 1964, '*The Twilight of Evolution*', Grand Rapids: Baker.

Blackmore, S. 1994, '*Alien Abduction*', New Scientist, 19 November p 29-31.

Collins, P. 2000, '*The field workers*', New Scientist, 5 February p 36-39.

Editorial, 1995, '*The courage to ask hard questions*', New Scientist, 14 October p3.

Lockyer, H. 1973, '*All the Messianic Prophecies of the Bible*', Zondervan Publishing House.

Volume 2 *(unless referred to earlier):*

Holmes, R. 2004, '*Ancient genes rise from the dead*', New Scientist, 4 December p6-7.

Morris, H.M. Twentieth printing 1996, first published 1974, 1985, 'Scientific Creationism', Master Books.

Cumbey, C. 1983, 'The Hidden Dangers of the Rainbow', Huntington House Inc.

Day, M. 1998, '*Mostly in the Mind: Antidepressants may be little better than placebos*', New Scientist, 11 July p13.

Day, M. 1997, '*Death of a dream?: The spectre of addiction could burst the Prozac bubble*', New Scientist, 6 December p14.

Campbell, C. 1998, '*Good Health*', article on Obsessive Compulsive Disorders, Daily Mail, January 6 p32-33.

Milne, D. 1998, '*Doctors on the Edge*' : alcohol and drug addiction among the medical profession is a growing concern. The Big Issue in the North, 194, 26 January, p6-7.

Battersby, S. 2005, '*Are we nearly there yet?*': The hunt for a theory of everything is turning into a road trip from hell. New Scientist, 30 April, p30-34.

Chown, M. 2005, '*End of the beginning*': Is it time to admit that the idea of a big bang just doesn't stack up? New Scientist, 2 July, p30-35.

Polkinghorne, J. 1995, '*I am the Alpha and the Omega Point*', review of book 'The Physics of Immortality: Modern Cosmology, God, and the Resurrection of the Dead' by Frank Tipler, New Scientist, 4 February, p40-41.

Schilling, G. 2004, '*Pop go the universes*', review of book 'Big Bang' by Simon Singh, New Scientist, 4 December p51.

Blackmore, S. 1994, '*Alien Abduction*', New Scientist, 19 November p29-31.

Collins, P. 2000, '*The Field Workers*', New Scientist, 5 February p36-39.

Concar, D. 1995, '*Happiness is a magnet*', New Scientist, 5 August p24-29.

Anderson, A, Holmes, R, Else, E. 1996, '*Zombies, Dolphins and Blindsight*', report on Tucson conference: 'Towards a Science of Consciousness' New Scientist, 5 May p20-26.

Motluck, A. 1997, '*Touched by the word of God*', New Scientist, 8 November p7.

Owen, R. 2000, '*Faithful await revelation of Fatima secret*', The Times, Friday, May 12, p16.

Volume 3 *(unless referred to earlier):*

Baker, O. 2002, '*Law of the Jungle*': Forget all about ingenious adaptations and well tailored lifestyles. What makes a successful species is good luck', New Scientist, February 2002 p28-31.

Johnson, P. 1997, '*Testing Darwinism*', an easy to understand guide. Inter-Varsity Press.

Deuteronomy 32, 17-18
1 Corinthians 10, 20-21
Romans 8, 38-39
Genesis 15, 13-14
Genesis 22, 1-2
Genesis 22, 9-12
Hebrews 11, 17-19
Genesis 22, 15-18
Deuteronomy 30, 17-20
Psalm 40, 4
Psalm 66, 8-12
Exodus 7, 10-13
Exodus 10, 16-20
Exodus 11, 1-2
Exodus 12, 36
Exodus 12, 2-3, 6-7, 12-13, 29, 31
Exodus 13, 17-18
Exodus 14, 1-4
Exodus 14, 9-12
Exodus 14, 31
Exodus 16, 2-3
Exodus 16, 4, 11-15, 31
Exodus 19, 5-6
Exodus 20, 4-6
Exodus 23, 25-26
Exodus 23, 31-32
Exodus 32, 8-9
Exodus 33, 2-3
Micah 5, 2
Genesis 22, 7-8
Hebrews 1, 3
Hebrews 2, 16-18
Isaiah 53, 4-7
Psalm 106, 37
1 Corinthians 11, 25
Luke 18, 31-33
John 19, 10-11
Jeremiah 31, 31-34
Romans 3, 20
Galatians 3, 21-24
Colossians 2, 13-15
Hebrews 9, 15
Romans 3, 22-23
John 14, 6
Hebrews 11, 1
James 2, 14, 26
Galatians 3, 6-9
Isaiah 59, 20
Galatians 3, 10-14
Romans 11, 11, 15-18, 25, 28-29, 31
Mark 9, 47-48
Romans 6, 23
Luke 15, 7
Matthew 10, 28
Matthew 28, 18-19
1 Corinthians 15, 22-28
Revelation 5, 1-5
Matthew 25, 41, 46
Luke 20, 9-16
1 Timothy 1, 15-16
1 Corinthians 1, 20-23
Romans 10, 12-15
John 16, 7-13 (NRSV)
Acts 2, 2-4
Joel 2, 28-32
1 Corinthians 12, 3
1 Corinthians 12, 13
Ephesians 2, 1-3
1 Corinthians 12, 8-11
1 Corinthians 12, 18-19
Acts 4, 13
2 Corinthians 10, 5
Galatians 5, 17-21
2 Peter 2, 19-22
Isaiah 51, 5-6
Matthew 24, 29
Luke 10, 17-21
1 Corinthians 1, 17
1 Corinthians 2, 4-5

Chapter 8

Psalm 18, 30
Proverbs 8, 1-9
Isaiah 5, 16 & 18·20
Psalm 136, 2
Psalm 31, 5
Job 34, 10
Psalm 7, 11
Jeremiah 32, 27
Proverbs 3, 11
Hosea 6, 6
Lamentations 3, 33
Proverbs 68, 20
Isaiah 46, 11
Isaiah 46, 10
Isaiah 51, 6
Psalm 111, 7-9
Psalm 106, 3
Psalm 9, 4
Isaiah 35, 4-6
Isaiah 13, 9-14
Psalm 89, 14
Psalm 97, 2-3
Deuteronomy 6, 14-15
2 Kings 22, 17
Psalm 11, 7
Proverbs 28, 5
John 10 , 33-39
1 John 5, 3
Matthew 7, 6-14
Matthew 5, 18-20
Luke 1, 77
2 Corinthians 10, 3-5
Psalm 97, 7
Psalm 82
Isaiah 14, 12-21
Genesis 6, 1-4
2 Timothy 4, 4
Psalm 4, 3
Isaiah 45, 5-7
1 Chronicles 16, 25-27
Galatians 4, 9
Acts 26, 9-18
Genesis 17, 13-14
Jeremiah 9, 25-26
Jeremiah 31, 31 & 33
Romans 2, 29
Galatians 5, 3-6
Colossians 2, 13-18
1 Peter 3, 22
Proverbs 16, 6
Matthew 22, 37-40
Matthew 5, 44
1 Peter 4, 8
John 8, 47
2 Kings 17, 16-20
Psalm 97, 2
Romans 8, 38 to 9, 9
1 Timothy 1, 5-9
Romans 2, 17-24
Isaiah 9, 2
Isaiah 52, 5-10 & 13-15
Isaiah 10, 20-22
Isaiah 29, 22-24
Isaiah 1, 15-20
Deuteronomy 30, 1-6
Isaiah 9, 6
Isaiah 8, 11-17
Romans , 30-33
Psalm 73, 1-6 & 9
1 Samuel 15, 23 & 16, 14-16
Isaiah 28, 11-13
Ephesians 3, 6-11
2 Timothy 4, 3-4
1 Timothy 4, 1-7
Mark 8, 29
Mattthew 26, 52-56
Matthew 21, 18-22
Acts 17, 22-32

Chapter 9

1 John 3, 4-5
Matthew 13, 36-43
Psalm 11

Job 28, 12, 23–24 & 28
Galatians 5, 22–23
Romans 9, 25–26
Luke 21, 12–28
Wisdom 2, 11–12 NRSV
2 Thessalonians 2, 8–12
2 Peter 3, 3–6
1 Corinthians 1, 25
Romans 1, 25
Romans 1, 21
John 16, 13
Job 28, 20–22
Psalm 2
Isaiah 57, 20–21
Psalm 93, 3
Revelation 13, 1–5
Wisdom 14, 27–31 NRSV
Colossians 2, 13–14
Isaiah 43, 25–28
1 Peter 3, 17
Revelation 2, 10–11
Luke 23, 28–43
1 John , 16–18
Matthew 10, 34–36 & 40–42
Proverbs 5, 3–5
Ephesians 6, 17–18
Revelation 2, 12–13
Revealation 13, 14–15
Psalm 64, 3–8
Zechariah 1, 11–15 & 3, 1–4
Luke 16, 13–15
Revelation 13, 11 & 15–17, & 14, 9–11
1 John 2, 1–6
Romans 4, 4–8
Proverbs 17, 26
Matthew 12, 7
Isaiah 53, 4
Isaiah 53, 9–10
Wisdom 1, 12–13 NRSV
Isaiah 40, 25–26
Isaiah 40, 2
Matthew 5, 44 & 48
Matthew 5, 17–18
Psalm 135, 8–10
Numbers 15, 32–36
Proverbs 1, 20–33
Isaiah 28, 15
Matthew 12, 26–32
Mark 6, 1–6
Matthew 9, 28–31
Mark 9, 38–41
John 15, 7–10
2 Corinthians 11, 13–15
James 5, 14–16
Matthew 9, 12–13
John 9, 1–4 & 6–7
Matthew 10, 1
1 Corinthians 1, 27–29
Luke 13, 10–16
Acts 14, 8–10
Hebrews 11, 1 & 3
Jeremiah 7, 4 & 9–10
1 Kings 21, 19 & 21 & 24–28
Isaiah 30, 1 & 9–15

Chapter 10

Psalm 75, 5–7
Matthew 11, 5
1 Kings 19, 11–13
Mark 4, 37–39
1 Corinthians 3, 9–16
Matthew 7, 11–12
Psalm 24, 3–6
1 John 4, 1–3
2 John 9
James 4, 4–7
Romans 10, 9–10
Wisdom 1, 3–5 NRSV
Psalm 103, 18
Matthew 7, 21–23
Colossians 2, 8 & 18–19
1 Corinthians 14, 32–40
Acts 9, 15

Chapter 11

Isaiah 14, 1–7
Isaiah 12
John 4, 6–14 & 22–26
John 7, 37–39
1 Corinthians 12, 12–13
Romans 12, 4–6
Revelation 22, 1–3
Revelation 21, 1
Revelation 21, 4
Isaiah 55, 1–11
Psalm 63, 1
Psalm 69, 2–3
Genesis 3, 7–9
John 16, 8
Luke 22, 25–26
Romans 6, 20–23
Acts 18, 9–17
Genesis 3, 22
Psalm 25, 7
Jeremiah 10, 23–24
Psalm 146, 8
2 Peter 2, 19
Romans 5, 7
Luke 7, 28
Mark 2, 17
Matthew 25, 31–41
Genesis 4, 7
Psalm 25, 10
Psalm 40, 1–3
Psalm 25, 14
Psalm 50, 2–17, 23
John 20, 22-23
Jeremiah 29, 8–9
Romans 8, 28–30
1 Corinthians 7, 17–23
1 Peter 2, 18 & 3, 1–2
Romans 12, 14–21
1 Thessalonians 5, 8
Romans 13, 1–7
1 Samuel 8, 6–9 & 19–20
Romans 8, 31–36
Psalm 34, 21
Matthew 22, 15 & 17–22
Exodus 1, 17–22
Daniel 3, 16–18
Genesis 12, 3
1 Chronicles 21, 1 & 5–7
1 Chronicles 21, 11–17
John 15, 22–25
Matthew 11, 6 (NRSV)
Luke 13, 1–9
Isaiah 24, 1–6
Isaiah 11, 1–4
Proverbs 13, 24
John 14, 6-10
Deuteronomy 18, 17–22
Revelation 19, 11–21
Revelation 6, 1–10
John 10, 14–18
Psalm 12, 1–2
Romans 5, 1–2
Luke 18, 1–8
Proverbs 14, 25–35
Matthew 4, 4
Romans 14, 1–4 & 7–10 & 13–17
1 Corinthians 9, 19–23
Mark 7, 18–23
Isaiah 7, 9 & 14
Isaiah 58, 1–3, 6, 9–10, 13–14

Chapter 12

Deuteronomy 16, 20
Psalm 125, 3
Proverbs 28, 16
Matthew 12, 20 or Isaiah 42, 3
Psalm 73, 9–10
2 Samuel 23, 1–2
2 Peter 1, 20–21
Daniel 12, 9–10
Matthew 5, 3–10
Psalm 145, 17, 20
Psalm 103, 1–13, 17–18
Romans 3, 29–30

Chapter 13

www.ingramcontent.com/pod-product-compliance
Lightning Source LLC
LaVergne TN
LVHW020710110826
845149LV00012B/2189